Crushed But Not Destroyed

By Sharon Longenecker

Certain names of the persons and institutions connected with the medical and legal professions have been changed to protect their right to privacy.

ISBN #0-9614244-0-0

For information contact:
Sun Ray Publishing Co.
27885 S. E. Sun Ray Drive
Boring, Oregon   97009

Dedication

. . . To the countless friends, relatives and casual acquaintances who encouraged me to write this book.

. . . To my husband Dave who insisted, when I faltered, that our story had to be told in the hope that others might be helped by our experiences.

. . . And especially to our three children – Steve, Lisa and Jan – who nearly lost both parents as a result of this accident. It was they who spent their formative years without strength, guidance and support that their parents would have wished for them. It is a tribute to them that they raised themselves as well as they did.

This is particularly dedicated to them as to why I stopped being "Mom" for a while.

I don't believe God **caused** this interruption in our lives or **willed** it to happen, but I do give credit to His later intervention and it is to His glory that we endured.

I

It looked like it was going to be another dreary February day as I glanced out the window and watched the rain blowing in sheets across the driveway in front of the large picture windows of our living room. On a clear day we had a beautiful view of Mount Hood, but today the mountains and hills were shrouded in gray clouds.

Any moment I was expecting my husband, Dave, to come driving down the long driveway to our home, nestled on a hillside with rolling pastureland spread out before it. Dave and I had spent many months building our home and we were proud of our small farm which consisted of six acres and various assemblages of livestock. Our three children – Steve, who was ten; Lisa, nine; and Jan, nearly seven – were all in school, and I was looking forward to a quiet afternoon in front of a crackling fire.

Dave worked the midnight shift for Wonderbread Bakery in Portland. He liked working the night shift because there was never enough hours in the day to get everything done that he had planned. The more daylight hours, the better. But above all, he loved the thrill of steering an eighteen-wheeler down the open highway and across the coastal mountain range to the bread depot in Tillamook.

I glanced out the window and saw that the rain had stopped. I looked at the clock on the wall – 12:15. Dave should have been home at 10:30 a.m., but it wasn't unusual for him to be this late if he had a break-down or flat tire. Only on an exceptionally good day could I expect him home at 10:30.

In the eleven years of our marriage I had worried a lot about him, but I had learned not to let it take over my life. I knew Dave was an excellent driver and truck driving was his life. What I had to accept was the fact that I was a habitual worrier and yet, ironically enough, I wasn't worried about Dave on this particular day.

Each day when Dave arrived at the bakery he would call home and ask me to put lunch on. This had become routine for us. It took him a half-hour to get home and that always gave me plenty of time to have lunch waiting for him on the table when he drove in. By this time, however, I was getting hungry – too hungry to wait for him to be home at one o'clock. I made myself a sandwich and sat down to eat it.

I had just finished eating when the phone rang. I picked up the receiver, expecting to hear Dave's voice, but instead it was a woman's voice, asking "Is this Mrs. Longenecker?" I acknowledged that I was the person she was calling, and then she continued, "This is Valley General Hospital. Your husband has been in an accident. Would you like

1

to talk to the doctor?"

I had always lived in fear of a call such as this, but I was too startled by it now to allow the information to sink in. "Yes, of course," I said. Then the doctor came on the line.

"Mrs. Longenecker, your husband is in good condition except for a head injury. We have called in two of the best specialists." His voice was calm and reassuring as he explained that I should come to the hospital, but then he added, "Don't come alone – have someone bring you." I thanked him and hung up.

I was very concerned about Dave, but uppermost in my mind was finding someone to take me to the hospital. Dave's parents lived a short distance from us on the hillside, and I could see their house from our front window, but as I looked out now, I could also see that their car was not in the carport. I had no idea where they might be, and I didn't have time to dwell on it. I was confused and intent upon getting to the hospital myself.

I hung onto the words "good condition" and felt comforted that the doctor had merely called me from the hospital rather than sending someone out. Dave's condition must not be *too* serious, I kept telling myself, for on television they always inform people in person, don't they? I remembered seeing police officers arriving at the home of someone who had been seriously injured in a car accident. As these thoughts went through my mind, I dialed my sister, Bonita. She didn't answer.

With Dave working the night shift, our friends were limited to other couples whose lives were similarly topsy-turvy. It was difficult to foster relationships with other couples when Dave had to go to bed just the moment they arrived home from work. Most of our friends worked at the bakery or were wives of those who did. My entire life revolved around Dave. Rarely did I meet with friends for lunch or coffee. We lived a mile from Boring, a town with a population of a few hundred people. To see anyone, I had to drive to their homes or have them drive to mine. But what I wanted most was to spend my days with Dave when he was home from work, and we both enjoyed family life and spending time with our children.

So who could drive me to the hospital? Were there any friends or relatives who weren't at work at that time of the day? Before I could settle on anyone in particular, I thought of our minister, Marden Wickman, and his wife, Ruth. They would want to know about Dave. They had moved to Gresham, a nearby town, five years before, at the same time that we moved to Boring. They had been instrumental in helping Dave and me establish a stronger foundation for our faith. It was then that we had begun attending Powell Valley Covenant Church and all our children had attended kindergarten there. I dialed their telephone number.

2

I felt a wonderful sense of relief when I heard Ruth's voice; she was a connection to all that was safe and good. I explained to her about the accident and how the doctor told me not to come alone. Ruth said, "Marden has just come home for lunch. He'll be right down to take you in."

I felt a twinge of guilt for bothering Pastor Wickman. Wasn't the doctor being a little too protective of me? But he probably thought I was an overly sensitive wife, I thought. When it came to Dave I was willing to tackle almost anything, but I realized the doctor didn't know me. In my twenty-eight years of living, I knew about death and unhappiness. I had learned to deal with a lot over the years and I had developed a stronger faith in God because of it.

My father was a hopeless alcoholic from as early back as I can remember. My mother raised my two sisters and myself although she had only a high school education. At first she supported us by working in the berry fields near our home in Troutdale. Many times Yvonne and Bonita, eleven and eight respectively, were left home to care for me, since I was still an infant. A few years later Mama found work at a vegetable shed near the train depot, a short walk from our house. The work was still hard, but it wasn't the back-breaking toil of the berry fields – and she had a roof over her head to protect her from the Oregon rains and the hot summer sun.

Mama was small in stature and as I watched her go to work each day the large butcher knife she carried looked as big as a machete. She chopped carrots and celery, which were then packaged and sent out on the train. An aroma of carrots always seemed to be emanating from her clothing, as if she had been drenched with carrot juice.

I grew to admire the strength that helped Mama persevere no matter how difficult things became. "God will take care of us," she would say, with a firm belief that nothing was too big to conquer if we had faith.

We lived in a ramshackle house, but it was spotless. Mama would work all day, come home and cook dinner, and still have energy left over to make me a dress on her old treadle sewing-machine. Dishes were done after each meal and it was inexcusable to leave even a cup in the sink. My sisters and I had our chores, too. Saturdays were designated "housecleaning days" and none of us could find a good enough excuse to escape.

Even though my father was an alcoholic, I felt especially close to him. In the 1940's in a small town such as Troutdale, I was allowed to be in places that a child wouldn't be permitted today. I can remember sitting on a bar stool next to my father in the neighborhood tavern. Beautiful dolls were standing in the windows and on the shelves behind the counter. They were dressed in brilliant-colored taffeta, satin, and velvet gowns, with their hair in long, cascading ringlets. Each doll could be

3

won by betting dimes on a punchboard.

Daddy knew how much I loved those dolls and he would hand the bartender enough money to make the purchase. Some of the dolls were alike in costumes or hair styles, but Daddy obtained one of each kind for me. They were much too delicate to be played with, so they ended up on a shelf in my bedroom, added to my small collection of stuffed animals.

Being so young, I never questioned how much Daddy spent on the dolls or on anything else he bought for me. Years later I realized that if he hadn't spent it on trinkets for me, he would have spent it on whiskey. Perhaps Mama felt the same way, because she never mentioned that *she* would have wished the money to be spent on food.

Daddy's drinking binges began to envelop him more and more and our days together diminished until they were nonexistent. I have unhappy memories of nights when Mama ranted and raved at Daddy while he sat in stony silence. I remember pressing a pillow against my ears, wishing Mama would just leave him alone. She continued to nag, however, and he continued to drink. It ended only with Daddy's death at the age of forty-six. I was eleven years old.

We never had much money while Daddy was alive and we didn't have any more after his death. We were still poor. My girlfriend's parents were buying their second car, and we didn't have even one car. Mama didn't drive, so we walked or took the bus wherever we had to go. My friends had automatic washers and dryers, and it was through these things that I could see how different we were. We had a washing machine called a "spin-dryer", one step from a wringer washer.

When I was nine we had moved to Gresham into another ramshackle house and by the time I was ten both of my sisters were married and were starting families of their own. Mama had progressed from working in the Flav-R-Pac Cannery in Gresham to clerking in the stationery department of Meier and Frank, a department store in Portland.

I was devastated by my father's death. I pressed myself further into church activities. Mama and I joined the First Baptist Church in Gresham and we were both active members.

I was a quiet child, spending most of my after-school hours alone. I was what you might call a "latchkey child." Mama didn't think it wise for me to have friends over while she was still at work, nor could she afford to pay someone to take care of me. But I didn't mind being alone and I soon learned to entertain myself with books. With my imagination I could transfer myself into another world by reading WUTHERING HEIGHTS or JANE EYRE, and on weekends I could do the same thing with a trip to the movie theater.

I loved high school and enjoyed my four years at Gresham High School. When I was a junior I got a job working behind the soda fountain at Rexall Drug Store. During my senior year I became a typist for KGRO Radio Station. Winter months were the hardest since I had to walk to and from work, but I loved both of my jobs and each day I looked forward to going. Still, my problem with transportation to school functions diminished. I was old enough to date now, and if I had a date, I had a ride.

I met Dave on a blind date which I'd agreed to as a favor to his sister, Carol. She was one of my close friends at school and her brother had just come home from four years in the Air Force, three of which were spent in Europe. He was trying to fit back into a community that had changed slightly during his absence.

I admit, it wasn't love at first sight for me when I met Dave. But it didn't take him long to win me over.

Dave was a perfect gentleman. He helped me with my coat, and rushed around the car to open the door for me. On this first date we had planned a late dinner at the Oyster Bar Restaurant in Portland. It was a rainy December evening, and as we prepared to cross the street to the restaurant, I saw a puddle near the curb. I was preparing to jump it when I felt Dave gently lift me over and put me down on the dry pavement. The evening turned out a success. He had stolen my heart.

Dave and I were married a little more than six months after we met. From that moment on he came first in everything I did. Being with him every moment wouldn't have been too much for me, and though Dave wasn't used to having a wife with him every minute, we began to work on how we could spend time together.

We were alike in personality, but different in hobbies. I was happiest with a book in my hands, while Dave loved racing across open fields on a motorcycle. For the first decade of our marriage I tried to adapt to his lifestyle. I would have done anything for him.

I had always been shy and reserved, avoiding any kind of confrontations, and hoping only to make people like me. Consider, for example, my lavender wedding.

Before the wedding a member of the wedding party brought a swatch of fabric over for her dress. I had not expressed my color scheme and she, being bridesmaid, had chosen material to make a lavender dress. Not wanting to hurt her feelings, I meekly accepted lavendar as my wedding color. The wedding would last thirty minutes at the most, I thought, and it seemed to be a small concession to make. Though blue would have been my chosen color, I quickly forgot about it in the flurry of the rest of the wedding preparations.

Gifts began to arrive. On the day of the wedding, I found myself drowning in a lavender sea. People apparently had asked about my color scheme, for the majority of gifts were lavender. There were lavender towels for the kitchen and lavender towels for the bath, there were

5

lavender sheets and blankets for the bedroom, and there was one lavender throw rug that ended up in the hall. I had nothing against lavender, but I didn't really want to decorate our first home in that color. Still, before long I got used to lavender splashed throughout our apartment from kitchen to bedroom. I was, at any rate, centering on the new baby that would be entering our lives.

Dave adored our three children, who were born in our first four years after our wedding. For a long time my days were taken up with washing diapers and putting formula into bottles, but I could always count on Dave to help out. He came home every day eager to spend the afternoon with the children. I never needed a babysitter when I went shopping, for Dave had the children with him anyway, whether it was in the backyard working or at the lumberyard buying building material.

I learned more about cooking from Dave than I had from my mother. We shared the housework, too, although there was no formal division of chores. If the refrigerator needed defrosting, Dave tackled the job when he got home that morning. If the kitchen floor needed to be waxed, he would do it while I was on a shopping trip. In many ways Dave was more efficient than I. He could handle the chores in less time than I could – and he exerted less effort.

On Dave's night off, he often cooked dinner. The children loved this change in chefs and I learned to relinquish my spatula willingly. I had discovered that I really didn't like to cook, anyway. At least not as much as Dave did.

Once, when Steve was an infant, I had just placed him down for a nap when the doorbell rang. Irritated at the thought of a salesman standing on the porch trying to sell his wares, and afraid that Steve might reawaken, I rushed to the door. I stood looking down at three little boys about the age of nine or ten. "Can your husband come out and play?" one boy asked.

Stunned, I paused a moment, then said, "Ah, just a minute. I'll see." I went to the garage where Dave was working on his pickup and told him he had visitors. I was surprised to see Dave spend the rest of the afternoon with the boys after he had worked all night the night before.

The following days and months the boys became regular visitors. They watched Dave work in the garage and spent hours in quiet conversation. One day I overheard them tell Dave about a creek nearby that was teaming with crawdads. Their eyes grew big when Dave told them that crawdads were good to eat. They promised to bring him some the following day.

I glanced out the window the next afternoon to see the boys walking up the driveway with a large bucket. They smiled and placed the bucket at Dave's feet. I retreated to the living room and Dave and the boys went into the kitchen to put a kettle of water on to boil. While Dave cooked crawdads, the boys sat wide-eyed at the kitchen table.

We moved twice after meeting those boys, but they always seemed to find us. Even several miles didn't prevent them from riding their bikes over to spend an hour or two with Dave while he worked on one of our cars.

Not only was Dave efficient around the house, but he could fix nearly anything in it. To save money, we bought all our appliances at the local auction. I didn't worry about any of them, for Dave repaired them all with very little difficulty.

Without any formal mechanical training, he took two engines that didn't run and built, for his pickup, one that did. We never hired a repairman for anything; Dave kept our home in good running order right down to the TV set. I remembered what it had been like growing up with nobody around who could repair things. Whenever something broke, Mama usually asked a relative to fix it for nothing, or we did without. Now that part of my life had changed. No more did I have to ask people for things as I had before my marriage. I got my driver's license and even had my own car.

No matter how busy he was, Dave always took the time to stop and help someone in distress. Over the years of driving a truck he took a man to get gas for his disabled car on the freeway, delivered two young people to college after their car caught fire, and took a woman to a phone to call a friend after she became stranded on the freeway a hundred miles from home. And I couldn't count the many tires he changed for other people over the years.

Although Dave was a quiet man, he thrived on activity. Over the years he took up boating, bowling, water and snow-skiing, and motor-cycle riding. A friend once described him as "poetry in motion on that cycle." Dave worked hard to be good at everything he tried.

After we moved to our small farm we bought horses and Dave began raising registered Tennessee Walking horses. He enrolled in the Tennessee Walking Horse Association and was elected vice-president of the organization the following year.

I couldn't completely share his enthusiasm for the horses and the shows we entered them in. Although I helped him raise them and shared in displaying them at the shows, I hated riding them. I liked them only from the vantage point of having my feet firmly planted on the ground.

Dave was fearless of the most troublesome horse. In contrast, I was terrified of everything. Dave was confident and strong-willed; I had no self-esteem and an insurmountable inferiority complex. Both my parents had low self-esteem and it came to me almost as an inheritance. When I married Dave, I burrowed into his life and I nearly ceased to exist. I spent the following years living through him and his experiences. Mine were so insignificant in contrast that they didn't seem to matter – at least to me they didn't.

Dave had a great protective quality about him. He had energy enough, it seemed, to take care of the whole world. My sister Bonita's two sons visited often. When her oldest son got his driver's license, Dave took him to the mountains where there was snow and taught him to drive on the slick roads.

I thought of Dave as indestructible, I guess, since he was the protector of us all. He was needed by so many people.

Dave went hunting with a friend one autumn. After four days he came home with nothing and looking discouraged. He had applied for a doe tag that year and received it. He described his experience, "I got within shooting distance of a doe, but when I looked into her big, brown eyes, I couldn't pull the trigger." Not only was Dave strong, but sensitive, too.

An ancient barn located on Dave's parents' property housed several birds, two owls and a pigeon, that had been injured by passing cars. Dave would scoop up such little victims, bring them home to recuperate, and release them when they were able to fly again.

Dave loved driving a truck, but the idea of becoming a pilot became a compulsion. A friend, Larry Adams, had just begun flying for United Air Lines and the desire struck Dave, too. He enrolled at Skyways in Troutdale and began instruction for his private pilot's license. He sandwiched in his flying hours between fixing fences in the pasture and shoveling out the barn.

When the children and I heard the roar of an airplane engine we would run out onto the sundeck and watch as Dave "waved his wings" at us. He spent hours over the house practicing his maneuvers as we watched. Twice I went on long-distance trips with him, but I learned that flying wasn't for me. I was terrified. During the last flight, a particularly frightening trip because of severe turbulence, I made the decision to stay at home with the children lest they become orphans. By 1972 Dave had acquired both his private pilot's license and his commercial license.

While I was waiting for Pastor Wickman to pick me up, I called a friend of my sister's. I left a message for Bonita that I would be going directly to the hospital and asked her friend to keep trying to reach Bonita for me.

Although I was anxious to get to the hospital, I still wasn't overly worried about Dave. He was strong, six feet tall, and weighed 205 pounds. I didn't think anything could hurt Dave. He could load an entire truck with hundred pound sacks of flour and never get winded. And, too, he was the one who rescued other people. It was just unthinkable that something would happen to him.

I didn't give the children a thought. I assumed Dave and I would be

8

back home from the hospital before they were even home from school. They were independent children and would be all right for a little while even if Dave and I returned a little late.

Over and over again those words flashed back at me: "good condition except for a head injury." Perhaps he has cuts and scratches on his face, I thought; maybe even a slight concussion. If they won't let me take him home today, I decided, they certainly will by tomorrow.

I pulled my coat from the closet and glanced in the mirror at my face. I was appalled at the sight of the curlers still in my hair. I had rolled up my hair that morning and forgotten them. But my hair was much too wet to take them out, so I applied a dash of lipstick, thrust my arms into my coat, and was out the door as Pastor Wickman pulled his car into the driveway. There was no time to be concerned with how my hair looked.

Much later the accident was pieced together for me by two witnesses, the police report, the attending physician's report, and the nurses in the Intensive Care Unit. I learned the gruesome details on different occasions spaced out over a three-year period, but never was the information easy to accept.

Dave was ten minutes from home and one-quarter mile from the freeway exit when he entered a sharp curve to the right. Approaching in the opposite direction was a 75-year-old man who was driving in the inside lane.

As the man turned his car into the extreme right lane, the car lurched as if it had struck a rock or a hole in the pavement. The car then veered to the right. The man feared it would leave the roadway as he entered the curve of the freeway and he attempted to correct it by turning the wheels to the left. This pointed him directly into the path of the on-coming cars.

He frantically tried to bring his car under control, but the steering wheel had locked. He pushed against the power brake, but it, too, did not respond. The car slid across the grassy median, hit an overpass abutment, catapulted into the air and landed upside down in the path of Dave's car as it exited the concrete bridge.

There was no way Dave could have avoided the collision. The railing on the bridge prevented him from seeing the other car until the moment of impact.

A tow-truck driver and a man driving a van just ahead of Dave observed the accident and stopped to give aid. The tow-truck driver radioed on his CB for an ambulance. They then extricated the other driver from his car, but Dave was so badly injured that they chose to leave him in his car until the ambulance arrived.

Dave had bent the steering wheel in half when he apparently braced for impact. I'm assuming that he saw the other car at the split second that they collided. It would have looked to Dave as if the other car was falling out of the sky. The right side of Dave's face was crushed, and a depressed skull fracture penetrated the right frontal lobe of his brain as if he had been looking to the left in the direction from which the car came. He slumped over, unconscious, onto the passenger's seat.

The time of the accident was listed as 11:27 a.m. on the medical report. For some unknown reason Dave had neglected to call me that morning to ask me to put on lunch.

Within minutes the ambulance was there and both Dave and the other man were taken to Valley General Hospital where their injuries were evaluated. There was only one neurosurgeon on staff at this hospital, and he happened to be in surgery at the time Dave was brought in. This seemed miraculous, for he was also on staff at two other hospitals in the area. The emergency room physician called in a plastic surgeon and then asked Dr. Emery, the neurosurgeon, to assess Dave's injuries.

Dr. Emery left this patient in the operating room, checked Dave over, left orders for the emergency room personnel, and then went back to surgery again. Later that afternoon he would return to the surgical suite with Dave as his patient.

II

Pastor Wickman and I were both silent on the ride to the hospital. The farmhouses and pastures were familiar scenes along the side of the roadway, but my eyes saw nothing. I could have been instantaneously taken to another time and place without me even being aware of it. I gazed out the window and prayed that Pastor Wickman would drive a little faster.

The words kept flashing back to me – "good condition, good condition." It had a reassuring affect, until the last of the sentence resurfaced without warning. I remembered the doctor had told me not to come alone, and then I began to wonder. If Dave was *not* seriously injured, why did the doctor tell me not to come alone? I braced myself as a sudden wave of nausea overtook me. I regreted that sandwich I had eaten less than an hour before. Now I was praying, "Please God, make us get there quickly, and don't let me get sick!" The ten-minute drive seemed to take forever.

When we finally arrived at the hospital parking lot, I followed Pastor Wickman as he led the way through the hospital entrance and into the foyer. A sign directed us to the Emergency Room, a short distance down the hall.

I was a few steps behind Pastor Wickman as we entered the hospital. I glanced toward the counter of the admitting office where two policemen were standing facing the clerk at the desk. I slowed as I heard one of the officers say, "The westbound car crossed over the median and struck the eastbound vehicle." Frantically I tried to remember which direction Dave was driving. I was irritated with myself for being poor at directions, but suddenly I remembered: Dave's would have been the eastbound vehicle. I quickened my steps as relief surged through me. *Thank God, it wasn't Dave's fault!* I knew Dave would be relieved at that, too, since his driving record was so important to him.

I quickened my step as I looked ahead and saw Pastor Wickman standing halfway down the hall talking to a nurse at the entrance of the Emergency Room. The moment I reached him, he motioned for me to follow him around the corner to another part of of the hospital. I half-ran trying to keep up with his long stride, and at the same time felt gratitude that Pastor Wickman was with me as we rounded the corner of another unfamiliar corridor. We were then at the Intensive Care Unit.

Much of that day is still a foggy memory, but I do remember Pastor Wickman telling me that Dave was being kept in ICU for the time being and that they were discussing the possibility of surgery. I didn't know what kind of surgery, except that the doctor had said Dave had a head injury. I don't recall signing any consent forms, although I suppose I must have done so.

I felt empty. It was all so unreal, as if it couldn't really be true. I was certain this had to be a nightmare, and in the morning I would wake up and everything would be back to normal

Pastor Wickman was a buffer between me and the hospital staff. All of the information was filtered through him and none of the nurses approached me for anything. In some ways I wanted to know what was going on, but in other ways, I wanted to be protected from it.

This very same hospital had been bathed in a glow of happiness at the births of our three children, but now I felt the lingering nausea begin to mix with despair. I sat down in a chair near a cluster of other chairs and a sofa that lined the narrow hall, but in another moment I found myself standing once again. I paced slowly down the hall, lifing each foot with great effort as I stiffly managed another step and then back to the chair again where I sat down once more. The minutes began to turn to hours.

Nurses in their white uniforms swished past, giving a slight glance in my direction before they turned the corner and were out of sight. Their faces seemed to say that they knew who I was.

· I felt cut off from my familiar world, but the alien environment began to soften as the news spread. My sister, Bonita, arrived about the same time as Dave's parents, Ken and Hilda, and one of Dave's three sisters, Sally. Bonita had been contacted by the friend whom I had called, and then Bonita, in turn, discovered that Ken and Hilda were at Sally's home. Carol (another one of Dave's sister) arrived, too.

Bill Folk came. He was one of Dave's closest friends from work and a relief driver at the bakery. Dave had taught Bill to drive the eighteen-wheelers and had kept encouraging him although the prospects of an opening for a truck driver at the bakery were slim. I knew now that Bill would be taking over Dave's position.

We all sat down and waited. No one said a word. As each moment passed the fear and nausea only became more intense and the suffocating odor of medicine and cleaning solutions permeated the air. I had to get outside for a few moments to get the stiffness out of my legs and fresh air back into my lungs.

Dave's sister Carol and I walked down the sidewalk next to the small hospital. For the first time since I entered the hospital I began to talk, and Carol graciously listened. "Dave was a good husband," I said, "and he was a wonderful father. There was no one better." It was during this walk that I began to face the fact that Dave might die, and the children and I would be left alone. I didn't like it, and I certainly didn't want it to happen, but it looked as if I was helpless to prevent it. The most important person in my life might be breathing his last breath in the

Intensive Care Unit and there wasn't a thing I could do.

The air was crisp and cool and throughout our walk no rain fell. In a short time we returned back to the corridor outside ICU. As I neared the group of friends and relatives I noticed a nurse step out of ICU. A second later I realized she was walking directly toward me.

I felt panic hit me with a surge as my knees began to buckle. My heart pounded in terror of what she might tell me. The nurse stopped in front of me, "Would you like to see him before he goes into surgery?" It was such a simple question, but it began to unleash all the torment that had built up inside me the past few hours. I had never made decisions without Dave. Throughout our life together I had needed him to guide me through every situation, and now perhaps one of the most important decisions of my life was to be made and I didn't have him to ask.

"I don't know," I answered. "What should I do?"

"It's your decision," she answered. A sob clutched at my throat and I felt tears burn my eyes as they began to pour over. I reached out for the wall, leaned against it for support, and wept.

The tears eventually drained me. The next thing I knew I was sitting beside Dave's mom and her arms were around me, but I didn't have the slightest notion how I got there. I glanced around for my purse and pulled out a tissue to wipe my nose. I had never lost control like that before and I felt a slight bit of embarrassment.

Remembering the rollers in my hair, I removed them and tucked them into the knitted hat I wore to the hospital. After running a comb through the curls, I began to get myself composed.

Dave's father and Pastor Wickman went into ICU and a moment later they had returned. Dave's father was visibly shaken as tears welled in his eyes and he moved slowly and with great effort toward a chair. Pastor Wickman came toward me and said, "I don't recommend that you go in." I nodded, but said nothing. Somehow I knew I shoudn't go in; I felt it deep inside and I didn't need anyone to tell me. It was reassuring, however, to have Pastor Wickman confirm my feelings.

Pastor Wickman prayed as we all sat in silence with heads bowed. When he finished I asked him, "Can you get me a Bible?" I watched Pastor Wickman walk away toward the front office of the hospital as I realized I hadn't spoken to God myself.

I had always been shy, and this was a private prayer for just God and myself as I sent up my silent thoughts, "Dear Lord, please accept my prayers for Dave if he can't pray for himself. I am placing him in Your hands. You know how much the children and I need him and I am asking you to send him back to us healthy and strong. But, if he is so badly injured that he can't recover, Dave would not want to live. In that event, I am asking only that Your will be done. Amen."

I knew I would have to trust as I had never trusted before. This would

13

be a tremendous testing of my faith. I could have pleaded for Dave to be returned to us, but I couldn't bear Dave's recovery to be solely for my own selfish needs. It had to be for other reasons – either that he would fully recover, or whatever the Lord's will would be.

As a Christian I was secure in the knowledge that Dave would go to heaven the moment he died. Dave had accepted the Lord as his personal Saviour and I knew Jesus was with him at this very moment. With those thoughts, I didn't fear death for him, but instead felt anguish for the children and myself at being left behind.

A widow? I wondered if I could face being a widow. The word seemed cold and ugly. Somehow I felt that Dave, intelligent and capable, could live without me, but I wasn't so sure I could make it without him.

The one certain thing I knew was I didn't want to see him fighting for his life as a final memory of him. I knew he would understand this. I couldn't be of any help to him if I went into ICU and broke down into a flood of tears. That couldn't possibly be good for him, I decided, and I couldn't bear to watch him suffer.

Then something strange happened. I felt a surge of peace flow through me, and a protective shield seemed to drop down and completely surround me. I felt as if the Lord had enfolded me in a covering that I could reach out of and others could reach into for giving comfort; but no one could get past it to hurt me. I felt and understood that Dave would be taken care of on earth or in heaven and he was now in the hands of the Lord. We were both being cared for in a way I could not understand, but the comforting feeling was intense.

My watch said 3:30 p.m.

Pastor Wickman placed a Bible in my hands and I turned the pages in search of scripture. I watched for a verse to pop out at me, but instead I saw disjointed words. Even the sentences meant nothing. My mind couldn't make sense out of any of it. Consequently, I rested on the inner peace that had consumed me a few moments before.

Pastor Wickman spoke to a nurse and then he announced to us all, "They are waiting for his blood pressure to stabilize before they take him into surgery." We again took this information in silence, and I clutched the Bible tightly in my hands.

At five o'clock a nurse came out of ICU and said Dave was now in surgery.

Though I felt at peace, I had conflicting thoughts. The human element came through anyway, and I continued to pace the halls occasionally. I didn't want Dave to die, but another part of me said I had to face up to whatever happened. I walked gently as if a sudden step or movement might cause a detrimental change in Dave's condition. I was so lost in my own thoughts that the hospital could have fallen down around me and I don't believe I would have noticed a thing.

14

When Pastor Wickman said the children had been taken to my aunt's and uncle's home for the night, I realized I hadn't even thought of the children since I left home. All I had been able to think about was Dave. Now that Pastor Wickman brought them to my attention, I was grateful that Bill and Peggy would be taking over their care until I could think more clearly.

After one of Pastor Wickman's prayers, he said, "Christians often have to endure more than other people, although I don't know why." I realized I didn't understand it at all. Dave could certainly do more good alive than he could dead, and I wondered for what possible purpose this accident could serve.

Dave and I were certainly no strangers to problems. Steve, our son, was born with a minor form of club-foot. He had to wear casts for five weeks. They extended from his toes to his hips, and they were applied just after he had learned to walk during the hottest part of the summer. The doctor made the casts in a sitting position so Steve couldn't walk on them. "I don't want them broken down," the doctor had said. I think I suffered throughout the ordeal more than Steve. He was a very happy baby both before and after that episode in his life.

The day that Steve's casts were applied, Dave was laid off from his truck driving job at Marckx Bakery in Gresham because of a merger with United Grocers. We successfully struggled through it all, but I felt I made it only because Dave was in control.

I remembered my early years in church. Nothing is too difficult for God to accomplish, I had heard over and over from the pulpit as I sat in the church pew each Sunday morning. Our beloved minister explained how a good person could reap his reward from God and live a life free of sorrow. The instruction was to be a good Christian by following the Golden Rule and putting everyone else first. This was taught as the only way to obtain God's wonderful gifts. I even heard you could get struck down by lightning if you didn't obey God. It was frightening.

However, I saw terrible things happen to people in our town, people in whom I thought God would take great delight. A car crash killed a father in one family, a disease took a child from another. Three children were left orphans when cancer took the life of their mother; a year later their father died of the same illness.

Other church families were untouched by tragedy and went from year to year free of any misfortune. Some people prospered financially and their wealth continued to grow.

The explanation for everything was always, "It's God's will." Somehow I couldn't accept this reasoning. Why didn't God paralyze all four limbs of a criminal rather than allowing an innocent child to be paralyzed in a needless accident? If God was teaching orphans a lesson by taking away their parents, why didn't He do it to everyone and teach all people the same lesson? I didn't believe God would do those things: cause earthquakes or human suffering just to teach lessons. Those who died would never benefit from the experiences and those left behind don't necessarily learn from the disaster. Some become cynical and bitter. Others reap rewards from the disaster that befalls someone else. All the pieces didn't fit the puzzle, I realized. Good people are not always given lives of blessings, nor are bad people perpetually punished.

I couldn't blame God for all the problems in the world any more than I blamed Him for Dave's accident. God didn't receive the blame for Eve eating the apple, nor should He receive blame for mankind's sinful nature or a weakness in the earth's surface.

I looked up to see my mother walking toward me and my uncle Bill right behind her. We embraced and they sat down with us. Many of my mother's brothers and sisters lived in the area and as soon as the news reached them, they came to the hospital. Mama was the oldest of fourteen children.

Dave's older sister, Sue, lived with her family in Springfield, Oregon, and she came later in the week. But even now there was a large group in the hall keeping a silent vigil for Dave. After a greeting each person would sink into a chair and add his or her presence to the others already there. At family gatherings we had always been a noisy group, with endless chatter and constant laughter, but now everyone was strangely silent. I counted fifteen people waiting for news of Dave. Several weeks later a nurse told me she had never seen so many people waiting for one patient to come out of surgery.

At seven o'clock I looked up and saw a friend from church walking toward me. Sharon Meier and I had become acquainted only a few months before and our conversations were limited to discussing church business over the phone. There was a glow radiating from her as she walked toward me. Her hair is blond and she had on a red dress; she looked just like what I thought an angel would look like. Sharon took my hand and sat down beside me. I was surrounded by so many people, but Sharon was different. Her touch gave me an added assurance. It seemed as if the Lord had placed everyone in my life at the precise moment that I needed them, not too soon and not too late. Pastor Wickman suggested Sharon and I have a cup of coffee with him in the hospital cafeteria.

The tables were all empty when we entered the little coffee shop. We sat down at the first table by the door. Sharon told us about the man who was driving the van in front of Dave. She said he was a friend who was coming to her house to fix her stove. He was quite shaken when he got there, explaining that he had been delayed because of a car accident. He had noticed Dave's jacket with the Wonderbread label, and when a short time later someone called Sharon from church and told her about Dave, she realized that this had to have been the same accident.

Sharon told me about a fatal car accident in her family. She said her sister-in-law had been killed. The more Sharon said the more I realized she understood a little of what I was experiencing. Pastor Wickman, too, had suffered through several surgeries. Their eyes didn't show pity, but a warm compassion. I felt them trying to share with me the burden that weighed me down.

Sharon continued to be a source of strength and inspiration over the month's of Dave's hospitalization. She laughed with me when I needed to laugh and she gave me scripture when I felt despair. Not a day passed that she didn't either call or come to the hospital.

Dave was in the surgical suite, but we continued our vigil in the hall where we had begun. A nurse suggested wo go to a room down the hall where we could have privacy, but no one moved. I wanted to be near ICU to hear quickly of Dave's condition, rather than be stuck off in a room where they might have to hunt for me. The nurse walked away and no one mentioned it again.

Now another nurse came running down the hall to tell us that the switchboard was jammed. "Would someone come and handle the calls?" Still no one spoke. I was surprised that so many people were concerned about Dave. I didn't think we knew that many people, and I was surprised at how quickly the news had spread.

As the nurse stood there looking at each one of us, I said, "Would you please tell them that there's no news yet?" Without hesitation the nurse accepted my suggestion and returned to her station. I was puzzled that she followed my instructions since I had never given orders to anyone before except the children. Now I did it out of reflex rather than knowledge of what I was doing.

Most of my relatives who could come to the hospital had already arrived, but now I noticed one last couple walking toward me. My uncle greeted me with outstretched arms and I felt tears sting my eyes once again. He embraced me just as his wife walked up behind him. She said, "Oh, come now. It can't be that bad!" I quickly pulled away from him and gathered my composure. I didn't want to lose control and I had relaxed my guard too quickly. I wanted to shout back at her that yes, it certainly was *that* bad, but I kept silent.

It was 10:30 when I looked up to see a doctor standing at the end of the hall. He had appeared silently like an apparition. He was still dressed in his surgical greens and I learned later that this was the neurosurgeon, Dr. Emery. Up to that point I hadn't seen anyone but nurses.

The doctor spoke very slowly and matter-of-factly as he explained, "This is very, very serious. I removed the crushed bone fragments

17

and repaired the brain by scraping away the damaged tissue. There may be a change in personality. It will be seven to ten days before we'll know if an infection develops in the sinus cavity." Still no one said anything. We all just sat in the hall as if no one knew what to do first.

The doctor turned and walked away as quietly as he had come.

Pastor Wickman rose and went back into ICU where Dave was lying in recovery. He returned to say, "He looks better now. He's asleep, but you can go in and see him now if you want to."

I shook my head. Every muscle in my body ached; I had never been so tired in all my life. I was still terrified at the thought of seeing Dave; of what he would look like. My imagination could only conjure up horrible visions of what terrible injuries Dave had received to have necessitated brain surgery. Dave wouldn't even know I was there and anyway, I thought, he knows I'm with him even if I'm not in the room. I needed rest. If I saw him, the memory might keep me awake all night. But if I went home now and slept I would be refreshed for tomorrow. Then I could see him when I was in better shape. I knew I had to keep up my strength for him and for the children. "I think I'd better go home," I answered.

Everyone stood when I did. Bonita offered to drive me home and Mama offered to spend the night. She said she would take the day off from work tomorrow. I accepted both offers.

As we climbed into the car for the trip home, I continued to wonder if this day would prove to have been just a bad dream and if tomorrow I would wake up to find Dave asleep beside me.

We learned that the man who caused the accident had suffered a concussion and a broken leg but was expected to have a full and complete recovery.

The drive home was much like the one coming in with Pastor Wickman. No one said a word, or at least nothing that I heard. I heard nothing and saw nothing; my senses seemed dulled by the horror of the day. That is, until we reached home.

As the car careened off the main highway onto our long drive, I was stunned to see the house sitting as a sparkling gem on the hillside in the darkness of the night. My voice broke through the silence, "Well, look at that. It looks like every single light in the house is on." I knew the children had done it when they came home to pick up their clothes, but I wondered why they felt it necessary to leave all the lights on. It didn't matter, but it wasn't like them to leave the house in that manner. Of course, none of us felt normal tonight.

Mama and I got out of the car, told Bonita good-bye, and she turned the car around to leave. Mama and I walked to the front door. I turned the knob. It was locked. I tried the door leading into the living-room from the deck, but it, too, was locked. I watched as Bonita's car disappeared in the blackness of the main highway. I looked at Mama, and shrugged, "I think I left my bedroom window open this morning. We'll have to go around to the back of the house and I'll climb up the ladder."

Our black Labrador retriever, Cinders, guarded the house with a vengeance, and we rarely locked the doors. No one could get within walking distance of the house with the black monster guarding the driveway. Now we were locked out.

I dragged the ladder around to the back of the house after checking two other doors that might be unlocked. No such luck. I propped the ladder up against the house.

The ladder was short by about a foot, but if I stood on the last step it would be possible to get through the window. I asked Mama to hold the ladder while I climbed.

The soil was soft and muddy and the ladder sank into the sodden ground. As I climbed I could feel the ladder digging deeper with each step, but I managed to feel my way to the window. The many days I helped Dave roofing the house had given me courage that I didn't know I had. Of course, I felt I had no choice. I *had* to get into the house.

I pried the screen off and let it drop to the ground. I held my breath as I pulled against the windowglass, hoping that I had not closed it tight that morning. This was our only hope of getting into the house.

I felt the window move. I pulled it wide open, and raised myself up and over the side of the windowsill. Than I dropped carefully into the room. But not carefully enough, I learned, for I had forgotten about the muddy ground until I saw the streaks down the wall. Ignoring the mud, I went downstairs to let Mama in. Then we went from room to room, turning off the lights.

Next we called some out-of-state relatives. Even through the telephone lines I could hear a profound shock and sadness as I explained to my sister, Yvonne, about the accident. Yvonne and her husband, Chuck, were "outdoor" people like Dave. They loved boating, horses – all the things Dave loved. One time Yvonne said, "Our husbands are exactly alike."

Now Yvonne asked, "How does he look?"

"I don't know. I haven't seen him yet."

Yvonne gasped as she said, "You have to get in to see him as soon as possible. He needs all the strength you can give him." I didn't hear any more of what she said as I suddenly had a horrifying thought. I had never considered that Dave needed *my* strength; now if he died, it would be my fault. The last sentence I remember Yvonne saying was, "You have to be strong for him." That was exactly what I intended to do – but it would have to wait until tomorrow. I had to get some rest tonight.

I was fortunate to have the ability to sleep. Especially when depressed, I could sleep. At a time like this, I looked forward to sleeping as a panacea that would take me away from the present problems and drop me into a dream world of escape. However, that night I dropped into a fitful sleep, hearing sounds I had never heard before. I had spent many nights alone in that big bed with Dave gone to work, but for the first time I noticed the alarm clock emitting an annoying hum and the house creaking and groaning - completely unfamiliar sounds. Even so, eventually I drifted off.

I awoke the following morning with a wrenching in the pit of my stomach. For a split second I had forgotten about the accident until I felt the knot in my throat – a reminder that something was dreadfully wrong. The waves of nausea started again and I realized the nightmare had followed me into the second day.

I was grateful for Mama's silence. I was not in the mood to carry on a conversation, so we kept to the bits and pieces of sentences that were essential, and she quietly moved through the house as if any noise would awaken someone – when in fact she and I were entirely alone.

Mama offered to cook some breakfast, but I let out a groan of protest that my stomach couldn't keep anything down. Mama replaced the skillet without making anything for herself.

The need to get to the hospital was uppermost in my mind, and when Mama said she was ready to go we headed for the car. I remembered the missing housekey as I groped through my purse for the car key which would be attached to the same keyring. The moment I wondered if perhaps the key was in the ignition, I saw the keychain flashing at me through the car window.

I remembered the harrowing climb through the bedroom window, the deep exhaustion I felt as I hauled the ladder around to the back of the house, the mud on the wall, and the needlessness of it all. It would have been so simple to remove the key from the ignition and unlock the front door. Dave would have thought of that, I was certain, or at least he would have taken the time to check the car before going to such extremes as I did. Why did I manage always to take the hardest route?

I pulled the keys out of the ignition, held them up in the air, and said, "Here's the housekey." Mama smiled. We climbed into the car for the trip to the hospital.

III

The hall outside the Intensive Care Unit was quiet and empty. However, a crowd of people would have been invisible to me. I was too overcome with the urgency of seeing Dave to be observant of what was going on around me. Mama said she would wait out in the hall for me.

We approached the door of ICU. I knocked gently and stepped back. A sign was posted on the door; no one was to be admitted without authorization from the nurses inside, nor was anyone allowed who was not immediate family.

My heart was racing and my legs felt like rubber. I felt as if I would faint, and now I regretted knocking so quickly. The desire to see Dave had made me forget my fears of yesterday, but now they came rushing back at me in a torrent. I knew I had to be strong for Dave, but suddenly I couldn't move. *This can't be unusual for a patient's family,* I told myself. *When the nurse comes to the door, I'll just tell her I'm not ready yet. . . she'll understand. If I just have a few more minutes, I'll be strong once again.*

The door opened and a nurse peeked out. I gave her my name, but before I could say another word her hand was on my arm and I was suddenly whisked into the Intensive Care Unit. I didn't know I had moved until I came to a standstill and my legs were miraculously holding me up.

There were four glass cubicles with the nurses' station located in the middle. Each patient had a private room, but because of the glass enclosure, the nurses could see directly into each room from the main desk. The vital signs of each person were being monitored by instruments that recorded and relayed the data to the desk.

As I stood next to the entrance of ICU the nurse guided me into the last enclosure adjacent to the door from which I had just entered. As I was steered gently through this doorway, I was puzzled. This couldn't be Dave lying on that bed. This man was a total stranger.

His face was horribly swollen – possibly twice normal size – and his head was swathed in bandages down to his eyebrows. His eyelids were blackened and swollen tightly shut. I would never have recognized him on my own. I approached his bed cautiously with the nurse still by my side. Everything seemed to be happening so fast now. I still couldn't believe this was Dave.

When I reached the foot of the bed, the man began to cough – hard, rasping, body-wrenching coughs. I jumped back as blood spurted from a hole in his throat and splattered forcefully against the walls and onto the ceiling. Just as suddenly the nurse stepped forward and put her arm around my shoulders, "This is good; he can cough it out by himself." The gentleness of her voice helped me relax as the spasm subsided and

21

he breathed easily once again.

I looked for something recognizable about this man who the nurse said was my husband. Then my eyes fell on his left hand. His wedding ring flashed at me. Those fingers were Dave's, I finally realized; that hand, strong and masculine, most certainly was Dave's hand. I walked over, took his hand in mine, and held it tightly.

His hand was warm and I felt the words well up inside me, *He's alive! Thank God, he's still alive!* I wanted to shout, but the constricture of my throat prevented any sounds from escaping. I had been so afraid that he would die before I could get back to the hospital, but it seemed now that God had given me another chance.

I stood by Dave's side as one of the two ICU nurses took a tissue and cleaned the mucous from around the tracheotomy tube in his throat. Her nametag said "Pam." The nurse who ushered me through the doorway was Joan, her nametag said. Neither of the nurses bothered about the blood on the walls and ceiling, but gave all their attention to Dave.

The only covering on Dave was a small hand towel over the genital area. No blankets or sheets. The room felt cool, but he felt so warm that I was encouraged. Ironically, the strength that I planned to give Dave was being given to me by him. Each breath he took was another moment alive and I thanked God for that extra time. Yesterday I had been so sure he was going to die, but with the calm and confident movements of the nurses, I felt reassured.

The nurses talked to him as if he understood everything, although it was questionable how much he did understand. They said his name as they worked round him, "David, I'm going to take your blood pressure now." Their hands were gentle and their voices were kind.

Dave looked horrible, but at the same time *wonderful!* I still felt the presence of the protective shield surrounding me, but now I felt something new – hope.

Pam and Joan explained Dave's injuries. The right side of his face had been crushed and the shattered bone had been removed from his forehead. This allowed the brain to swell without restriction. Joan said there would be plastic surgery done in a few weeks or so to reconstruct his right cheek. The thought that they were planning surgery to be done gave me further hope. If he wasn't expected to live, they wouldn't be considering more surgery, would they? I could see that his jaws were broken. When he yawned his teeth dropped down out of alignment, looking like false teeth that had not been glued in. The left cheekbone was "floating", Joan said. The anticipated surgery would secure all these broken facial bones in place.

Pam said he had an open palate from further injury to his mouth. When they tried to give him water, it came up out his nose rather than going into his stomach. Until this opening healed, she said, they wouldn't able to give him any more fluids by mouth.

22

I was astonished by all they were telling me, but was grateful to know everything about Dave's condition. I realized I felt less fear in knowing than I had felt in the ignorance I had lived through the previous day.

Another astonishing fact was that Dave's face had neither a cut nor a bruise except for the swollen, black and blue eyelids – a condition which could have been caused by the surgery. Joan pointed to bruises on his knees and said he had another bruise on his buttocks that could have been caused from the car seat pinching him. The bruises were superficial; the scars that he would retain were those made by the surgeon.

An incision had been made across the top of his head from ear to ear, creating a flap so that the skin could be pulled down and the surgeon could remove the crushed bone from his forehead. The bony structure beneath his eyebrow and across the bridge of his nose were also removed – in all, about 3 inches in diameter. His head had been shaved – even his sideburns – and then securely wrapped with a turban of gauze.

The tracheotomy tube prevented Dave from making any sounds. If he were to speak, the hole in his throat would have to be covered, but there was no sign of his even trying, at this point.

I wondered if he was in pain, but both Pam and Joan said he was not. They said his brain was swollen and a person doesn't feel pain under that condition. It seemed as if that incision *must* be painful, but if they said he wasn't in pain, I had to believe them.

Dave was quiet as he lay there, but he was not motionless. In a continuous, somewhat rhythmic movement, he kept pulling his left leg up and down, up and down. This was constant throughout the days and nights that followed. No one understood what caused him to do it; it puzzled even the doctors. When I described it to Dave's friend, Bill Folk, he said is sounded like Dave was double-clutching. This term meant nothing to me, but Bill said he would do it while driving his truck. The nurses felt this was as good an answer as any.

Most of the time Dave's left hand was kept restrained to prevent him from tampering with any of the necessary apparatus that was attached to him. He was quick to grab at anything that caused him discomfort or annoyed him.

Peculiarly, Dave did not move either his right leg or right arm. It's the left side of the brain that controls that right side of the body; but the injury to Dave's brain had been on the right side and if any paralysis developed it would be on the left side - which was, on the contrary, quite mobile. The doctors were also puzzled at his right-side immobility. Time was the only thing that would shed any light on this problem.

The nurses said he was "semicomatose." He could not communicate with us, but he would respond to simple commands.

The small, glass-enclosed cubicle bustled with activity. Nurses quietly scurried about and the machines processed the vital information. A catheter drained Dave's bladder; his blood pressure was regularly monitored at 15-minute intervals; a glucose solution dripped through an intravenous needle; a plastic hose connected to a machine emitted a fine mist into his tracheotomy tube; and finally, a rectal thermometer allowed the nurses immediate knowledge of his body temperature at all times. I had felt relieved at the warmth of his body, but I learned that in fact that was caused by the head injury. The area of Dave's brain that controlled body temperature had ceased to function, and this caused his temperature to soar; therefore, they placed an ice blanket beneath him to bring his erratic temperature under control. The machine the blanket was attached to was regularly filled with ice cubes and ice water was then forced through the tubing. The freezing ice blanket caused him to shiver and the nurses injected him with a medication to halt this reaction. Shivering, they said, counteracted the work of the ice blanket.

If his temperature rose above 99°, one of the nurses would also throw open the window and door connecting directly outside, and the frigid February air would rush in. I wasn't sure who was going to freeze to death first, Dave or me. I sometimes wondered if icicles were hanging from my nose, and my feet felt as if they were encased in ice blocks. Dave stayed warm throughout, however.

Though Dave coughed hard and often, it was not good enough. Periodically, he had to be suctioned free of the mucous that accumulated in his lungs. The nurses were adept at this procedure and although it was uncomfortable, it was quickly finished and Dave was allowed to rest undisturbed for a few moments. The nurses were gentle with him as they went through their many regularly-needed procedures.

I stood holding Dave's hand and watching as the nurses worked. I remembered the five minute limit posted on the sign at the door. It had said each visitor would be allowed to stay only five minutes each hour. However, neither Joan nor Pam asked or suggested that I leave. When both of the nurses left the cubicle, I slipped into the chair at the foot of Dave's bed. For over a month this was where I could be found from nine in the morning until nine at night.

I remembered to bring Dave's Bible with me that morning. It was a gift from an Air Force buddy while they were stationed in France. Dave treasured it, and now I kept it nearby. When I held it, I felt in direct contact with God and closer to Dave. Throughout the following weeks I kept it within reach at all times, with the hope that it would ward away evil.

When Dr. Emery arrived, I jumped to my feet. He was a frightening figure of a man, well over six feet tall, dark-haired, and dressed in a black suit with black shoes. Terror gripped me as he nodded in my direction, said, "Howdy," and walked past me to Dave's bedside. He checked the dressing covering Dave's head, and then removed a safety pin from his

24

pocket. Starting at the sole of Dave's foot he poked him with the open pin up the right side of his body. I stood silently next to my chair wondering what Dr. Emery was doing. The thing that puzzled me the most was that Dave didn't even flinch throughout the examination.

Much later I learned that Dr. Emery was looking for reflexes. Dave was paralyzed on the right side, and this was contrary to his injury to the right side of his brain. Each day Dr. Emergy continued inflicting the safety pin torture, and each day Dave showed no response to it.

Dr. Emergy then put the safety pin back in his pocket, looked intently at Dave for a few seconds, while I continued standing nearby in fright. "Well, okay," he said and then left the room.

Dr. Emery possessed an aura of supreme control and power over life and death. Even the nurses admitted apprehension when he did his rounds and I overheard one say, "I'm sure glad Dr. Emery doesn't come in while I'm on duty!" It was at that moment that I realized my fear was perhaps not unfounded.

The doctor was a man of few words, it seemed. The only time he had spoken in any length was the night after the surgery. His face, throughout the following weeks, never betrayed what he was thinking; and each day he showed very little expression as he entered Dave's cubicle. I became speechless the moment I saw Dr. Emery and just the sound of his voice when he entered the unit threw me into a fit of terror.

Fortunately I had a good rapport with the nurses and occasionally I quizzed them. As from the first moment I saw Dave, they continued to give me hope and encouragement. Everything he did they would describe as "good" or "he responds very well."

Joan told me that Dr. Emery would eventually put a plate in Dave's forehead where he had removed the bone fragments. This wasn't unusual, she said. There are a lot of World War II soldiers walking around with plates positioned over a brain injury, Pam added. Dave had to have one to protect his brain that was now exposed except for the skin covering it.

Suddenly I remembered I had left Mama out in the hall. Pam said they were going to give Dave a bath so she asked me to leave for a little while. I went out into the hall where I found Mama sitting with Bonita where we had kept our vigil the day before.

A man approached me. He introduced himself as the driver of the van that had been ahead of Dave. He asked about Dave. I told him what little I knew about Dave's condition, and that it was very serious.

The man explained how the accident occurred and how Dave didn't have a chance to avoid it. He added, "I could see directly into that car as it came sliding across the freeway. It almost hit me, too. I could see the guy was really tugging on the steering wheel. It looked as if his steering went out."

He said he tried to give Dave first aid, but apologized for being rather rusty at it. I thanked him and told him I was certain whatever he did was exactly right. I was grateful there were people like him who cared enough to stop and at least made an effort to help Dave. For all the times Dave stopped along the highway and helped others, he had the favor repaid.

Bonita pulled a book from her purse that she said was a gift to me from her neighbor, Grace Walters. Across the cover was printed the words HOT LINE TO HEAVEN by Francis Gardner Hunter. I realized if there was any time I needed a hot line to heaven, it was now. I gratefully took the book.

This was the beginning of my search for books of a spiritual nature, and for books with information about others who had survived a personal injury such as an assault to the brain. That month one women's magazine carried an excerpt from a book about a brain-injured child who eventually recovered from her injuries. A friend told me about a Vietman vet and his struggle to recover from a devastating head injury caused by a helicopter blade. I read voraciously, never getting my fill.

I quizzed friends and relatives who knew others who had been severely injured in an accident. I didn't care what the injury was, just how long it took them to get well. I clung to the success stories, and those that had less favorable outcomes I pushed aside. I struggled to retain my hope for Dave's recovery and I didn't want to think about anything less than a perfect restoration.

Each afternoon I left the hospital as school was letting out, went home to take care of the children when they got off the bus, gave them a snack, and planned for their evening care. During those times, and also weekends, I depended on friends and relatives to take care of them. Bonita kept them nearly every weekend, from Friday afternoon until Sunday night. Weekdays they were scattered around the community to so many homes that I have forgotten them all.

The children, unfortunately, came second after Dave. I had to give Dave all the strength I could, and I thought if we sacrificed as much as we could now Dave would get well faster and everything would be back to normal. Each evening the children went without complaint to stay with a friend or relative.

When I arrived home every afternoon I found the mailbox filled with cards and letters. We got mail not only from friends and relatives, but from total strangers, too. Or perhaps there *were* no more strangers, now. We all drew together from the tragedy.

Flowers were not allowed in ICU; the cards took their place. Bonita gave me a tote bag and each greeting that came in the mail was added to the collection of messages that I carried with me wherever I went. I didn't let them or Dave's Bible out of my sight as I kept vigil at Dave's bedside. I was like a dog lying beside his injured master and refusing to budge. No one prevented me from this ritual and my motherly instinct only surfaced in the evening when I retrieved my children from a babysitter and took them home to bed. Even at home, however, I found my mind going back to Dave, lying in a coma on that hospital bed.

Taking the children home each night forced me to rest and have a change from the hospital scene. I hated being separated from Dave for even one moment, but I knew it was best for all of us if I didn't allow myself to become over tired or strained from too much time at the hospital. Still, the moment I left his room, I feared he would die while I was gone. I didn't want him to die alone. And besides, my strength was supposed to be keeping him alive, my sister Yvonne had said. I lived in terror of the phone ringing during the night and telling me it was all over.

Depression coupled with the tiring hours of being in the hospital brought exhaustion down around me. I dropped into bed each night, feeling every ounce of energy drained from my mind and body. I was grateful for being able to sleep so easily now, but over the following years I learned it was difficult to live a normal life when depression continued to make me take to my bed.

Even the release of tears didn't help. I remembered the tears I had shed after my father died. They neither lessened the mourning period nor did they change the situation. Now I continued to remind myself – tears will not change anything! However, sometimes on the weekends when the children were with Bonita, the tears become stronger than my will to prevent them, and I would give in and allow them to flow.

Although I had no appetite and my mouth felt as if it was stuffed with cotton, I forced myself to eat. I fed the children breakfast before they left for school each morning, but I couldn't handle the thought of food until I got to the hospital and satisfied myself that Dave was still alive. Then I went to the coffee shop and bought an egg salad sandwich. I had never liked eggs in a sandwich before, but now I found they slipped down my throat easier than anything else on the hospital menu. Each morning while Dave was having his bath, I would spend the time trying to wash a sandwich down with a cup of Sanka coffee.

One afternoon when the children and I walked into the house after we had arrived home simultaneously, we saw the kitchen table laden with food, from casseroles to home-baked cookies. Suddenly, with this grand spread of food in front of me, my appetite reappeared. The children and I ate ravenously. The children were starved after a day in school, and I was just plain hungry. The egg salad sandwich was forgotten.

I learned that everything had been brought over by the mothers from Lisa's Camp Fire Girl Group. I never found out how they got past our dog Cinders.

I called one of the mothers a few days later and thanked them for being so kind. She said, "You'll never know how many people you have touched. All the husbands and wives in this community have been taking one another for granted. Now they appreciate each other more." As I hung up the phone a rush of emotion overwhelmed me. But it was not what you might expect.

Even I had seen a change in some couples who came to the hospital, those who had spent a lot of time bickering in the past. Now they were affectionate to one another. All at once I realized, selfishly, that I didn't want to be used as a tool to bring other people back together – losing my own husband in the process. "Please, God, don't use us," I pleaded. The cloud of despair that hung over my head was more readily visible than the protective shell that the Lord had dropped over me that first day.

It just wasn't fair! Dave was a good, kind man, and I didn't believe any of us deserved this.

IV

It was now February 27. Five days had passed on our countdown of the seven-to-ten day danger period. Dave was no better, but neither had he become any worse.

The coffee shop had become a meeting place for all of us. Whenever anyone came to the hospital, they would ask for me in ICU and then we would retreat to the little cafeteria for a cup of coffee.

A few relatives had stopped in on their way home from church that morning and we were gathered around a table, aimlessly chatting. I looked up just as Bill Folk came striding in, a slight smile on his lips. "They took him off the critical list today!"

"What?" I said, somewhat dazed. "I didn't even know he was on it." Then Bill told me how he called in every day to find out Dave's condition and each morning he was told he was critical. Today, however, they said he was "serious." We were all overjoyed at this news; it had to be a sign of improvement. I was still a bit disheartened that no one had actually told me Dave was in such grave condition. Then I realized it was just as well. I probably would have brooded over it, and now Dave was actually improving.

I remembered seeing a cartoon in a magazine in which a man who had been hospitalized called the front desk each morning to inquire about his own condition. How true, I thought, for we had learned nothing from Dr. Emery since that first night after surgery. And he wasn't becoming any more informative as the days progressed.

I could never have considered actually stopping the man in the hospital corridor and asking him point-blank about Dave. *What if he tells me something I'm not prepared to hear? Perhaps he doesn't know himself how Dave is doing . . . perhaps that's the reason he hasn't given me any further information. After all, he said it would be seven to ten days before we knew anything definite. I just have to wait and be patient. Besides, I have to stay strong spiritually . . . God is the only One who knows all of the answers.*

Everyone was living by that ten-day time frame. All our friends and relatives were counting, not just the doctors and nurses. Written across the bottom of one of the letters from our friend, Connie Adams, was a notation, "Today is the seventh day."

Dave had always handled the driving during bad weather. I simply refrained from getting behind the wheel whenever I thought the roads were hazardous. In plain language, I was a coward.

Now, with Dave in the hospital, I had no choice. If I wanted to be with him, I had to drive – no matter what the weather. I thanked God that there were no major snowstorms and added thanks for my little Volkswagen with the engine in the back which gave it better traction on slickened streets.

The previous spring I had gotten caught in a hailstorm about a half-mile from home. Halfway up the steep hill a short distance from our house, I was forced to take refuge by driving our American-made station-wagon into someone's driveway. Four cars were stranded near the top of the hill and another car just in front of me began to fishtail and slid toward a ditch. A friend from church lived a couple of houses up the road. I pulled the car into the driveway and ran up the road to my friend's house. Just as I knocked on the door I saw Dave coming down the hill in his Volkswagen Bug looking for me. I climbed into the Volkswagen and he gave me a shove. With his truck-driving expertise, he drove my car home and we both arrived just shortly before a head-on collision occurred at the top of the hill.

Now I no longer had Dave to retrieve me from slick hillsides. While he lay unconscious in that hospital bed, it was all up to me.

Sharon Meier asked me to attend a study group at church. The function of the class was to study the book FASCINATING WOMANHOOD by Helen B. Adelin. I don't know what I planned to get out of the class, or why I attended it, but the class was scheduled during the time Dave got his morning bath, and since I was kicked out of ICU during that time I thought an hour away from the hospital would be good for me.

The chairs were arranged in a circle in the Fireside room at Powell Valley Church. Sharon and I sat down with the other women to listen to the speaker who advised proper ways to rejuvenate a marriage or be a good wife. As she discussed various chapters of the book, I felt a lump fill my throat. If I hadn't been so near tears, I would have laughed. *What am I doing here? My husband's in a coma and doesn't even know I exist. He doesn't know the difference between me and his nurses.* I was relieved when the class ended and Sharon took me back to the hospital. At Dave's bedside I made the decision not to attend again.

Although Mama returned to work a couple of days after the accident, she and Bonita came over each weekend to clean my house and bring groceries. They never asked what needed to be done. I was surprised to learn that they were the elves who turned my messy house into an orderly home.

I tried to pay Bonita for the food she brought, but she refused to take money. A check was useless; she wouldn't cash it. And if I secretly placed money in her purse, I would find it in *my* purse the next time we met.

Our get-togethers at the coffee shop went from lighthearted banter to serious business according to who was there. I had a mountain of business to attend to and it was this group of friends and relatives who helped me sift through the necessary chores. Most of it I had to attend to myself, but they helped advise me of priorities. I was determined to keep our business affairs as orderly as possible, not just for myself, but for Dave, too. I didn't want him to wake up and wonder why I had let everything plunge into calamity. I would do everything as I felt he would want it done, so no problems would arise from my lack of organization. I felt I owed it to Dave.

There were things I did without any reason other than that the thought simply entered my mind. On the second night after the accident, I thought of the State Veteran's Administration who held the mortgage on our home. Deciding they should be informed about the accident, but with no idea there would be any benefits to receive, I sat down and wrote them a letter.

Not long after, I came home to find a state official from the Veteran's Administration parked in my driveway. Our trusty watchdog kept him at bay until I arrived to pick up the children after school. The gentleman informed me that the VA were willing to allow a moratorium on our house payments for six months if Dave's condition met with their approval for such action.

I checked with the hospital about a letter for the VA explaining Dave's injuries and his expected recovery. The letter was immediately written and a few days later I was informed that the moritorium had taken effect. That was one burden off my mind since Dave was now considered unemployed.

There was a fir tree beside our home that had been doing double duty as a power pole. When we built our house, we had been negligent in pushing dirt too close to the trunk of the tree. Before we knew what was happening, the tree had dangerously deteriorated. I lived in fear of a sudden windstorm that might cause the tree to topple. Would I awaken to find the children and myself wrapped in fir boughs? Or would I, perhaps, *not* awaken–?

I remembered a neighbor telling me how the power company had trimmed some of their trees free of charge because they were endangering the power lines. I decided to see if they would do the same for me, so I placed a call to the electric company.

The following day when I arrived home, I found that the tree had been topped, branches chopped up, and a pile of wood cut for winter. The man in charge said the tree was sturdy enough to be left for a power pole with the wires still attached to it. It would last many more years, he said. I thanked him for their prompt response and knew I would sleep much better during storms from now on.

As the man hopped into his truck he asked, "How's your husband?" I wanted to say, who in the world are you, but I didn't. I explained what little I knew even yet about Dave's condition, and he was then on his way.

I learned a few days later that the man lived a couple of miles away and was a friend of Dave's parents. The world just kept growing smaller and smaller.

Conversations in the coffee shop led me to other priorities. Because of a TV commercial she had seen, Dave's sister, Sally, suggested contacting the Social Security office. If your husband is disabled for over a year, she told me, you can receive a disability income. Actually checks can be received in the seventh month of disability, but if the person returns to work before the year is out, the money must be repaid.

I called the Social Security office. Much to my relief, all the necessary information was taken by phone and all transactions were handled through the mail. All of the office staff was especially kind and willing to make things as easy as they could for me.

Because Dave was a veteran, someone suggested that he might be entitled to disability benefits through the government. We learned he wasn't eligible, however, because he was in the service between wars. He missed both the Korean and the Vietnam war.

I checked with the Teamsters about a disability pension, but he was ineligible for that also. Dave had to have worked for fifteen years to receive a pension, and he had accumulated only eleven. All of the pension funds that had been paid in for him were lost to us.

I called Workman's Compensation, but Dave was not entitled to any benefits there because he had clocked out at work and had been on his way home when the accident occurred.

However, when I called the credit union for a savings withdrawal, the secretary informed me of the disability clause connected to our car payments. Although we had made only two payments, our Volkswagen stationwagon would be paid off. I was thrilled with this information, but I thought of what Dave would have said: "Wish we had bought a Thunderbird!"

On that second day after the accident, I was sitting in the coffee shop with Dave's parents when our insurance agent walked up.

Mr. Truman had been Ken and Hilda's (Dave's parents) insurance agent for many years. He greeted the three of us with tears in his eyes as he told us how sorry he was to hear about Dave's accident. He sat down with us and explained what insurance would be coming to us.

Dave's car would be paid off. We later learned it had a value of $250 which the insurance company paid immediately. Mr. Truman said this was a "no-fault" state and if I wasn't planning to get an attorney, he had some "no fault" papers for me to sign. Dave's parents were against taking any kind of legal action, but I realized I hadn't even given it a thought. I was so wrapped up with what was going on with Dave, that I had forgotten that legal technicalities might develop.

Mr. Truman said, "I can't advise you, but I do think it would be wise if you obtained an attorney. The Teamsters have two excellent ones. Perhaps you should call them and get the names." I thanked Mr. Truman and told him I would not be signing the no-fault papers, but instead would be getting an attorney.

I went to the hospital telephone and looked up the Teamster's office in the directory. When the secretary of Dave's local answered I explained about the accident. I had no reason to believe he wouldn't give me good advice since this man was the one who worked with Dave and the other truck drivers on increased benefits in their contracts. Dave had always said he could do anything; he had a way with employers.

The secretary responded, "You can't afford an attorney and you probably won't need one."

I thought he must have misunderstood what I said about Dave. "But Dave's in a coma," I replied.

"You can't afford one, and you probably won't need one," he said firmly.

Perhaps he's right, I thought. Since's Dave's parents didn't want an attorney and this man said I couldn't afford one, I decided to abide by their wishes. I agreed to settle no-fault.

A few days later Mr. Truman came back to the hospital. He said the other man had $10,000 insurance of which Dave and I would receive $9,000 immediately. The other $1,000 would come in installments as I needed it, for work to be done around my house, such as lawnmowing.

I had no information at that point what Dave's hospitalization was going to amount to and I was depending on these professionals – insurance agent, Teamsters secretary, and any other office worker that answered the phone when I called – to provide the knowledge I didn't have. All I could do was trust all these strangers. The only thing I knew for certain now was that we were going to receive $9,000. *Dave had better get well awfully quick,* I thought.

A week had passed and I was sitting at the foot of Dave's bed going through passages of scripture when a man entered the cubicle with Joan. "Sharon, this is the doctor who's going to check David's eyes." I greeted him and after he said a quick hello, he pulled out a small flashlight from his coat pocket. As he leaned over Dave shining the light in his eyes he said, "Oh, this is a much better response than before."

That was a surprise to me, "You've been here before?"

"Yes. Just after he was admitted and there was very little response. This is good to see."

"It's good to hear," I answered. As far as I knew, this visit was a minor technicality; checking Dave's eyes was routine since Dave's condition had been so grave when he was admitted. Without another word the doctor left the unit.

I sat back down in my chair and my eyes drifted back to what I had been reading when the doctor entered the room. Dave's temperature had risen and Pam had opened both the window and door that led into the breezeway. It was rightly named; the wind was whipping down between the two hospital wings and into Dave's room. Even with my coat wrapped around me, I was freezing. I didn't see how Dave could stay so warm.

I noticed a flurry of nurses out of the corner of my eye as they readied the adjacent cubicle. I got up and walked to the door and watched Pam and Joan making certain everything was prepared for the next patient to be admitted. "What's going on?" I asked.

"We just got a call that a nine-year-old girl is being admitted in a coma," she answered.

My heart jumped into my throat as I thought, *Lisa! Lisa is nine!* My cousin Linda was spending the day with the children. Just before I left that morning they had been talking about having a picnic in the treehouse in our backyard. *Maybe Lisa fell out! If this terrible tragedy could happen to Dave, what could prevent it from happening again?* I paced the floor of Dave's cubicle – two steps forward and two steps back again. I was frantic, waiting for them to admit the little girl that I thought could be my daughter.

I saw the outside door opening. I stopped in my tracks as I watched a gurney being pushed inside. Pam and Joan helped the emergency nurses bring it inside. I caught of glimpse of a blond head, and breathed a sigh of relief. Lisa's hair is brown. Thank God, it wasn't Lisa, I said under my breath. Then I saw the child, clad only in a pair of panties and surrounded by wadded, wet sheets. My heart went out to this little girl and her family and I felt guilty for being grateful that she wasn't mine. Some parent was within the walls of this hospital in as much fear for this child as I was for my husband, and I was overcome with empathy.

The nurses called the little girl Julie. As the hours progressed I over-heard discussions about her. The nurses talked about her at the nurses' station. "Dr. Emery thinks she has meningitis," I heard through the thin walls. "But Dr. Marlow thinks it's hepatitis," another nurse said. I knew nothing about either illness.

Dr. Emery had said Dave might get an infection in his sinus cavity – he had to be protected from that, I knew. I remembered hearing the word viral associated with hepatitis – viral hepatitis. Then I realized a virus could cause an infection. What if a nurse could transmit Julie's virus to Dave's sinus cavity?

I hated approaching anyone about a problem as if I were a know-it-all. The truth was, I didn't know how to confront people about *anything*. I realized Julie had to be in the Intensive Care Unit since she was in very serious condition, However, they owed us protection from any danger-ous germs, I argued with myself. Dave certainly couldn't protect himself, so if anyone did anything it would have to be me.

I struggled with the problem all that day. The children were spending the weekend with Bonita so I stayed at the hospital until evening. I pondered about the problem over a cup of coffee in the coffee shop. It was dinner time for the night nurses, and I watched them file into the room and take their places in line for their trays.

I saw one of the intensive care nurses come in and I waited until she got a table and sat down with her dinner tray. I decided it was now or never. I got up and walked over to her.

"I overheard some nurses saying Julie might have hepatitis. The reason I ask is because of my concern about Dave getting an infection in his sinus cavity. Is she contagious?"

"Oh, no," she answered. "If Julie were contagious, she would have been put in isolation. There's no need to be concerned about David. We'll take very good care of him." I was so glad to hear that, I could have kissed her. I thanked her and went back to my table. For the first time since early afternoon, I allowed myself to relax. Through the next few weeks Julie's mother and father added to my vigil. It was comforting to look through the glass partition and watch her mother knitting at Julie's bedside. We spoke very few words, but there was a closeness between us that was inevitable.

The stress was almost unbearable, however. The peaks and valleys always seemed to catch me unprepared. Just at the moment when I thought everything was coming along better, Dave's condition would take a downward turn.

V

"Dave, you are in Valley General Hospital. You've been in a car accident, but you're getting better. Today is Friday, March 3, and you're improving every day. The accident was not your fault . . . another man caused it and he has already been discharged from the hospital. The children and I are fine. We miss you and want you to get well quickly and come home." I repeated those words to Dave every day. Since I didn't know how much he understood, I repeated them several times a day just in case he might be more lucid at one time than another.

Although I didn't know if he was getting well, I told him anything that was encouraging to both him and me. I had to keep my own spirits up and it was just as important for me to believe that he was getting well as I thought it was for Dave – if he could hear me.

Memories were hardest to deal with. As I stood at Dave's side, holding his hand, I would see flashes in my mind of how he used to be. I could see him riding across the pasture on his palomino horse; sometimes, walking toward the barn in his Levi jeans and cowboy boots. I couldn't stop these memories except by forcing myself to think of something else. Even then a reminder would come back to me when I least expected it.

On my way home to get the children from school one afternoon, I stopped at the market to pick up milk and a few other groceries. As I began writing the check to pay for my purchase, I remembered how it used to be, how on marketing day on his way home from work, Dave would drive through Gresham and check the parking lots of all the stores where he knew I did my shopping. When he found my car, he parked beside me, came into the store and carried my bags to the car. Then he followed me home so he could carry the bags into the house. How he had spoiled me! I wasn't sure if he would ever be able to carry my groceries again.

If he could only talk to me. If I could only know if he knew me. I felt so envious of all the couples who came to the hospital. There was a special closeness between everyone I saw, people who had realized because of Dave's accident how quickly a life can be snuffed out. They had another chance to build attachments. My chance might have ended ten days ago.

The swelling of Dave's face had subsided and he looked more like the Dave I remembered. He could open his eyes, but he had a glazed look as if he were looking but not seeing. He continued to move his left leg back and forth, and his left arm had to be restrained when no one was with him. There was still no response from his right arm and leg. Dr. Emery poked him every day with the safety pin, but he lay as if he didn't feel a thing. The mist flowed into his trach, the ice water rushed through the blanket beneath him, and the IV dripped a sugar-water solution into the vein in his left arm. The ten dys we had been counting down had ended but Dave showed no significant signs of coming out of the coma. I had hoped for some dramatic recovery by this time; still, I refused to get discouraged.

While Dave was getting his morning bath, I went into the coffee shop where I was met by Ken and Hilda, Dave's parents. They came in every morning, too, but we arrived in our separate cars. Ken surprised me with a statement, "I want you to get your relatives out to move the cattle." I sat down at a nearby table, and Ken and Hilda sat down with me. I didn't respond to Ken about the cattle, and nothing more was said. However, every morning he began greeting me at the hospital with that same sentence. And every morning I said nothing.

Ken and Hilda had no livestock, and Dave had worked out an agreement with them to use their barn and pasture during the winter months. I didn't know if Ken was rescinding this agreement, but since so many things were in limbo now until Dave got well, I didn't think the cattle were important enough to be concerned with. It was too soon for the grass to begin growing again, and it was easier to toss the hay out of the loft right into the pasture. If they were moved to another pasture the feed would have to be carried out of the barn and across a driveway.

Dave had always taken care of business transactions with his parents, and I had always avoided confrontations of any kind with anyone. But the accident had promoted me. I was the person in charge now, whether or not I was sure of what I was doing.

A few days later Ken and Hilda met me in the coffee shop again. Ken said, "You'll have to get your family out to put rye on the pasture." Rye on the pasture–? This took me completely off guard. I not only had very little responsibility for the cattle or their feed, I was even afraid of them, so I rarely had given them any direct care at all. Moreover, I was a "city" girl who loved staying indoors and I knew next to nothing about the technical aspects of raising livestock. But I did take care of the budget and I knew what expenditures went out for feed and other necessary items, and I remembered one thing: Dave never bought rye to put on the pasture. So I told Ken, "I don't remember Dave every putting rye on the pasture, and I don't believe it's an expense I can afford right now."

Ken's face reddened. "Anybody who knows anything about farming knows you *have* to put rye on the pasture!"

Fortunately Hilda cut in and I didn't have to say anything more. "She doesn't know anything about farming!" The conversation was over.

But the following day Ken started in on the cattle again, and every day after that he continued greeting me with that demand, "I want you to get your family out to move the cattle." My family was doing so much for me, things I never asked them to do – clean my house, babysit my children, buy groceries – I couldn't ask them to move cattle when I felt so strongly that it was wasted effort. All I could do was hope Ken would eventually tire of the subject and forget about it. However, he didn't. This was apparently his way of dealing with his sorrow, but at the same time I wondered if he were somehow blaming me for the accident. Was he taking it out on me?

I went back to ICU to see if Pam and Joan would let me back in again. When I got there Joan said Dr. Emery had just left. Dave was not improving as he had hoped, and brain tests were scheduled for Monday morning if he didn't show some sign of improvement over the weekend.

Pam said the brain tests were considered dangerous to someone in Dave's condition, and they would be done only if they were absolutely necessary. I sat down in the chair as Pam worked with some instruments at the head of Dave's bed. I felt so helpless. There wasn't a thing I could do for Dave except spend my days holding his hand.

Pam released his hand from the cloth strip that was tying it to the rail. The nurses also allowed me to untie his hand from the rail when I was standing next to him. We were all trusting him more and more each day. He never bothered any of the tubes that were attached to him.

I took out some paper and a pen to write a note to a friend when I heard Pam gasp. I glanced up to see her leap onto the bed, straddling Dave. His thumb was under the strip of cloth that was holding his trach in place. There were two strips of cloth, one tied to each side of the trach and then they were tied together in a knot at the nape of his neck. As Dave moved his thumb the trach lifted up slightly. Pam grabbed his hand, "David! Let go! David, let go!" Usually he responded well to commands, but this time he kept his thumb wedged under the cloth strip. Pam gripped his hand tightly, trying to pull his thumb out.

I jumped to my feet, but there wasn't a thing I could do to help. In fact, I was frozen in my tracks. That trach was vital for Dave's breathing. He might die without it. Through clenched teeth Pam kept at him, "*Let go, David! Let go!*"

After what seemed like an eternity, he relaxed his thumb and Pam pulled it out from under the cloth strip. Then she straightened his arm down and tied it to the rail once again. We both let out a sigh of relief. As Pam continued her duties, I sat back down in my chair once again to finish my letter. I realized Dave was not going to be trusted as much anymore. I certainly knew I would think twice before I released his hand from the rail again. Under my breath I said, "Dave, why did you have to do that?"

I spent the weekend sick with worry. Anxiety was always present but it varied in degree. The tightness in the pit of my stomach just became stronger when problems arose. Dave's present condition was serious enough, and now I had the added burden of worrying about what damage the brain tests might do. Perhaps he could become worse, I thought. But then how could he get worse?

Evenings were especially hard. In eleven years of marriage Dave and I had only been separated for a period of four days. That was when he went hunting. The rest of the time I could depend on him being home all afternoon and evening. He didn't leave for work until midnight.

Just before the accident Dave and I bought a stereo. Our first and only tape was by The Carpenters, "Rainy Days and Mondays." Although we had many records, that tape meant the most to me. Each evening I fell into the habit of loading the tape into the stereo and letting it play over and over until I relaxed enough to go to sleep.

The children watched TV in the evenings, but I found it impossible to concentrate on any programs. My mind kept going back to Dave. Music was all I could handle.

Driving home at night, I would see the lights of the houses along the road. I thought about these "normal" families – families who didn't have a husband or father in the Intensive Care Unit fighting for his life. I thought about close friends and relatives who came to visit at the hospital. They all went home, closed their doors behind them, and their lives were back to normal again. They could free themselves from the reminder of Dave in the hospital by just leaving and putting themselves back into a normal routine. I couldn't forget for a moment. When I walked in the door of my home, Dave's absence was heartbreaking. I missed him so much. The only thing I could do to ease the pain was to play the tape "Rainy Days and Mondays". A verse in one of the songs says, "Where will I find another you?"

Saturday afternoon Bill and Louise Folk came in to see how Dave was doing. Bill never missed a day coming to the hospital and Louise always came with him on the weekends. I told them about the anticipated brain tests and the danger.

One of Dave's sisters and her husband came in to the coffee shop, along with Ken and Hilda. We pulled two tables together so we could all sit within talking distance of one another. I sat at one end of the table near Bill and Louise.

I don't remember what we talked about until I heard Dave's brother-in-law say something about how the accident didn't have to have happened. "If David had taken another road home," he said, "he would not have been in that accident." This was an upsetting subject and I didn't want to add to it. Hindsight was wonderful – if it only worked.

I whispered to Bill, "Do you know why Dave takes the freeway?"

"Yes," Bill answered. "So he won't have to stop at so many traffic lights. All truckers stay away from the roads with the most lights; I know I do, and so does Dave." I nodded in agreement. At least Bill understood, and that was all that mattered even if he was only one person.

Then I heard Dave's sister say, "I can't wait until David wakes up and I can tell him I saw him with no clothes on." For me, that sentence was the last straw. Humor was fine, but not at Dave's expense. I couldn't see anything humorous about his condition. Above all, he had no control over any of it. I wasn't so certain Dave would be amused if he knew what was going on; Dave was a very private person.

I decided to go back to ICU where people (that is, nurses) understood the gravity of Dave's condition. I stood up. "I'm going back to ICU." I was surprised to see everyone else stand, too. As I walked out of the coffee shop Dave's family and Bill and Louise walked with me.

I stopped at the door leading into ICU. Dave's family came in every day, but they stayed for the allotted five minutes and then went home after a visit with relatives in the coffee shop. Just as I started to tell them all good-bye, Hilda turned to me and said, "I know exactly what you are going through."

My reaction was automatic. All I could think of was the conversation in the coffee shop. "If David had taken another road . . ." and "I can't wait until David wakes up . . ." And now Hilda was claiming that she *knew* what I was going through.

"No, you don't!" I snapped back at her. "Not until your husband has been in a coma for eleven days will you know what I'm going through!" They looked at me – Ken, Hilda, Dave's sister and her husband – and then they turned and rushed out of the hospital.

After I told Bill and Louise good-bye and closed the door of Intensive Care behind me, I spent the rest of the afternoon wondering about my outburst. It wasn't like me at all.

I thought about Dave. His condition was serious, he was not responding as the doctor had hoped, and now brain tests were planned for Monday. There was a sign on the door leading into ICU that only direct family members were to be admitted. This *must* be for the protection of critically ill patients. However, the nurses were not holding to the rules. It felt like Grand Central Station in there sometimes.

When I went home to get the children after school one day, Joan handed me a note on my return. "This is from an old Army buddy," she said. I looked at the name on the slip of paper. "Somehow he slipped in here with another patient's family," Joan added.

Another day my aunt Phyllis and uncle Vonnie knocked on the door of ICU and asked for me. The nurse said, "Yes, she's here. Come in." I was startled to see them walk toward me as I sat reading at the foot of Dave's bed. I jumped to my feet.

"Let's go to the coffee shop," I whispered. "I'm surprised they let you in."

"So were we," Phyllis whispered back.

Now as I spent the rest of Saturday afternoon thinking over these incidents, I wondered why the rules were posted on the door if the nurses didn't have to follow them. I realized they were bending the rules by allowing me to stay so long with Dave, and Julie's mother stayed long hours with her, too. That seemed entirely different. If strangers could walk in with another patient's family, how many people were wandering in just to satisfy their curiosity?

When I went home that night, I continued thinking about the curiosity seekers who might be drifting in and out of Dave's room. Dave couldn't protect himself, so I had to do it for him. I decided to call the nurse at the hospital. After the episode with Julie, I learned that asking usually turns out for the best. In this situation, however, that assumption turned out to be wrong.

When the nurse answered the phone, I explained what had happened that afternoon. I told her how I had snapped at Dave's mom and what had precipitated it. I added, "It really seems like Grand Central Station in there, but perhaps I'm just being over-emotional. Do you think so?"

"I think you should call Dr. Emery right now and tell him everything you have told me," she answered. I hung up the phone. *Since the nurse told me to call Dr. Emery she must think my feelings are correct.* I looked up Dr. Emery's number and placed the call.

"Dr. Emery is not on-call this weekend," the operator said. "Dr. Marlow is. Would you like to have him call you?"

"No, thank you," I answered. "It's not important." It was important, but not enough to get a strange doctor involved in it. I decided to wait until Monday morning and then present the situation to Dr. Emery in person.

The following morning, Sunday, I awoke to sunshine. Because of Dave's condition, I thought it should have been cloudy and rainy. I showered and dressed, put on my make-up and combed my hair. I could get to the hospital faster on weekends since I didn't have to worry about getting the children off to school, or handle the never-ending business transactions that I usually did by phone. In January I had had my ears pierced and now I was having a problem with irritation from the telephone receiver. How could my ear heal completely with the telephone receiver pressing against it so much of every day?

For the first two hours each morning I was on the phone talking to friends or business offices. The moment I set the receiver back in its cradle, the phone would ring again. In order to get to the hospital as early as I wanted to each day, I had to leave quickly so I wouldn't get detained by another call. Everyone was calling to find out how Dave was doing.

As I entered the front door of the hospital, I saw Hilda sitting in the foyer. Ken was standing a few feet away from her. They always went directly to ICU each morning and then on to the coffee shop; they had never waited in here before. I panicked. "What are you doing here?"

Hilda said, "We're waiting for the girls. You, Dad, and I are the only ones allowed to see David."

"Why?"

"I don't know," she replied.

Perhaps my fears had come true, I thought. I worried about Dave dying after I left the hospital, and the doctor admitted he was not improving. Perhaps his condition had deteriorated further during the night! Without another word, I rushed to ICU.

Joan answered my knock, and I squeezed through the narrow opening in my hurry to get inside before Joan had the door completely opened.

"What's wrong? Who stopped visitors?"

"We did," Joan said matter-of-factly.

"Why?" I glanced at Dave. He looked the same as he had yesterday.

"The night nurse left a message that you called. We stopped the visitors this morning. After all, this is just a circus to the sisters." I was so relieved that Dave's condition hadn't worsened, I gave no more thought to Joan's statement. At least the nurses were going to be more careful who they let in, and I didn't care who they stopped just as long as Dave was taken care of.

However, Dave's family were very cool toward me for the rest of the day, and I knew they were angry. Here was another situation in which I needed Dave to help me. I wasn't so sure their anger was justified, however. The children weren't allowed in to see their father and they were more closely related than Dave's sisters. I thought if I could explain the situation to someone who would listen to me, they would understand.

I had a good relationship with Dave's grandmother, so the next morning I stopped by to see her. She had not been in to see Dave, and I thought I could explain how serious his condition was. She could then explain it to the rest of the family. The nurses were only following hospital policy, and they weren't before. It was all for Dave's protection.

I realized I was mistaken as soon as I tried to begin my explanation. She flew into a rage before I could say a word. "How dare you take him away from his family!" I didn't know I was taking him away from anyone. I knew a conversation was senseless now, she wouldn't be able to listen calmly. I went back to the hospital.

Dave was getting his bath when I arrived so I sat down on the sofa in the hall. Dr. Manning, our family physician, came around the corner. "How are you?"

"Terrible!"

He stopped in his tracks and sat down beside me.

"What's the matter?" he asked.

I explained what had happened. "They're blaming it all on me," I said. I knew I had stirred up a hornet's nest, and I had to find a way to stop it. Since my marriage I had always felt inferior to his family, wondering if they liked me, and many times I felt discouraged at trying to fit in, trying to become a part of them. It seemed to be wasted effort.

Now I wished I could run away and hide, leave Dave to his parents and his three sisters. I couldn't do that, though. I loved him too much.

Dr. Manning said, "I just left a meeting with Dr. Emery. I want you to go into ICU and have him paged right now. Explain everything to him." He gave a slight wave as he walked away. He turned at the corner and said, "You're not all bad." Then chuckled as he disappeared from sight.

Pam paged Dr. Emery, and then I returned to my usual place on the sofa in the hall just outside ICU. I'd been reading books about other injured people, other families confronted with disasters, but not one of them mentioned family problems. It seemed inevitable that families would have them when strain bore down, but none of the books told me how to handle them. The fine art of communication had never been a part of my education either. I regretted having to involve Dr. Emery.

When Dr. Emery sat down on the sofa beside me, I explained the entire situation. "But what about the sign on the door?" he inquired.

"The nurses are not following it," I answered. "They let anyone in who knocks."

"Humm." He paused. "I'll write a notation on the chart that the sisters can come in, but only for five minutes each hour." I thanked him and we walked back to ICU together. This was the day Dave was supposed to have the brain tests.

Dr. Emery checked Dave over, went to the nurses' station and read through the chart. Pam came into Dave's cubicle a few minutes later, "Dr. Emery just left," she said. "He's decided not to order the brain tests. David is showing improvement." Pam explained that he was responding better to stimuli.

Although Dave appeared much the same to me as he did the day before, I was thankful Dr. Emery could see some change.

Much later I wondered if the response he showed was when he tried to pull out his trach.

Pam suggested bringing in a radio. She read about coma patients being stimulated with radios and the results seemed to be positive. Dave's sister, Carol, brought one in the next day and we turned the station dial to KRDR, a local station that played country music.

Although Dave loved country music, he never listened to this particular station. I chose it because of the local commercials. If he understood anything at all, it would be a comfort to him to know that he was close to home.

The radio blatted away constantly, both day and night, breaking into the agonizing silence of ICU.

44

When I didn't have any friends visiting at the hospital during lunch, I could be found sitting with a group of nurses. More than once I even had lunch with Dr. Emery. This was such a small hospital that I just became an unpaid part of the staff.

One afternoon Carol and I were sitting with Pam during lunch. Pam began telling a story about a friend of hers who had suffered a head injury similar to Dave's. However, his injury resulted in amnesia. His present fiancee had become a stranger and he went back to dating a girl he had broken up with a couple of years before. His memory of the two years immediately past had been wiped out entirely.

Pam was apparently trying to prepare me for the possibility of this happening to Dave. Then Carol said, "Wouldn't that be funny if he didn't remember you?"

–Funny?! I remained silent, but I vowed to never allow anyone to put any such discouraging thoughts in my mind. After all, God was in charge and He wouldn't allow that to happen unless that was His will. And why would *that* be God's will? A loving God wouldn't do that.

Just after the nursing shift changed one afternoon, I overheard two nurses talking. "I hope his wife knows how to handle the checkbook," one said.

I walked out of Dave's cubicle and asked, "What are you talking about?" The nurse who had just spoken glanced at me and said, "We just admitted a patient who had a tumor removed from his brain. He won't care if he sits on a hot stove or not. He and his wife are changing roles, and she will have to take care of everything from now on." I was stunned. The nurses returned to their work and I went back to Dave's cubicle. I sat down and thought about this unfortunate situation. What a terrible shock that must be for that woman, I thought, feeling glad that it hadn't happened to me. I could certainly never change roles with Dave. Dave was the stronger of the two of us in every way. I couldn't imagine how I would handle such a thing.

Every day when I came into Dave's cubicle I was faced with the sight of his shoes sitting on a shelf next to a large black plastic bag that was closed with a twist-tie. I wondered what was in the bag, but I didn't ask about it.

Someone had given me a small envelope that contained Dave's personal effects from his pocket. I took it home and put the entire envelope in his bureau drawer in the bedroom. I couldn't bring myself to look at the contents, but I did withdraw the three dollars he had in his wallet. I shoved the wallet back in the envelope and tucked it into the side of the drawer.

Now I heard Joan say, "Why don't you take David's clothes home with you today? They need to be laundered." When I left to get the children that afternoon, I took the large black bag with me, along with Dave's shoes.

I arrived before the children's bus so I went to the laundry room to sort through his things. I pulled out his wool jacket first. It was covered with streaks of a reddish-colored stain. It didn't look much like blood. I knew Dave would need the jacket when he went back to work, but it was wool, and I was concerned that it might shrink during cleaning. Blood might be troublesome to remove, too.

I pulled out his shirt and dropped it into the cold water that I was already running into the machine. It would need to be soaked. Next came the pants. Nothing could have prepared me for them. Not with *any* preparation. Both legs were slit up one side. I gasped and my eyes filled with tears as my imagination conjured up images of Dave in the emergency room – nurses cutting off his pants, a doctor making a hole in his throat so he could breathe. Why hadn't Joan given this chore to someone else? In fact, she could have thrown the entire contents of the bag away and it would have been easier on me.

I shoved the pants back into the bag and took them to the garbage can, threw them in, and slammed down the lid. Then I put the jacket in the car for a stop at the cleaners on the trip back to the hospital. Through tears I heard myself saying, "Why, why why? Why, Lord, did this happen to Dave?"

All at once I felt self-pity take over, and I realized the Lord didn't feel as close as he had been. Then I felt an evil presence sitting on the passenger's seat. Although I could only see Satan in my imagination, I was certain he was close by. He seemed to be saying, "Ha, ha. I've got her now." I could almost hear a chuckle.

I forced myself to stop feeling sorry for myself and I focused in on the Lord. I knew in my heart that God hadn't caused Dave's accident and I was certainly not going to start blaming him for something He didn't cause. In an instant Satan had vanished, never to return again.

However, new problems were always just around the corner.

VI

Two weeks had lapsed and I could finally see some of the improvement that the nurses had been talking about, although they seemed skeptical when I told them he was responding to me. Now when I talked to him he squeezed my hand or pressed my hand with his thumb. In the past he would do it on command, but never on his own. Now he did it the moment I picked up his hand and began talking to him. I didn't really care if anyone believed me, because I knew for certain he was responding.

But once again I wasn't prepared for the shock that greeted me when I arrived at the hospital that morning. Dave was scheduled for surgery to repair his fractured jaws and cheekbone. Dr. Barrett, the plastic surgeon, had explained that he would be operating on Dave. "It will only take about three hours," he had said.

Dr. Barrett had a friendly face, reddish hair and freckles. I didn't feel the least bit afraid of him. Dr. Barrett had planned to take Dave into surgery at eight that morning, and since I couldn't possibly get the children off to school by that time, I dawdled a bit. I didn't want to spend the entire morning at the hospital waiting for him to come out of surgery when I had so many things to do at home. I made necessary phone calls, took care of some household chores, and then drove leisurely into town. Even yet Dave might still be under the effects of the anesthesia, I thought.

It was about ten o'clock when I knocked on the door to ICU. Joan let me in, and said there was a problem. I saw Dave lying in his bed with the somber Dr. Emery hovering over him. I had never seen Dr. Emery smile and had often wondered about this, but now a chill ran down my back. He was not only not smiling, but he seemed to be frowning. Dr. Emery saw me as I entered the room. He came around the side of the bed.

"I understand David is a veteran," he said.

"Yes," I answered and backed agaist the wall as Dr. Emery walked nearer. How can this be happening, I thought. Things kept going wrong.

Dr. Emery continued, "His kidneys are malfunctioning. We are preparing to have him admitted to the Veterans Hospital to be placed on a kidney dialysis machine." Later I learned that Valley General did not have a dialysis machine and this was Dave's only hope – to be transferred. Although his medical care would be free of charge at the Veterans Hospital, I was sick at this turn of events. I wasn't concerned one whit about the cost of Dave's care. I would sell our home if I had to to help him recover. I just didn't want to take him away from Dr. Emery. I felt certain that it was because of Dr. Emery's good care that Dave had even

47

survived to this point.

It was obvious that the surgery was cancelled. After Dr. Emery left, I approached Dave's bed.

Pam explained how Dave's knees gave them an indication that there was something wrong. When the kidneys fail, uremic poisoning develops and a weak spot on the body is often the exit point. In Dave's case it was his knees. Pam pointed to the fluid weeping from the bruises. Pam and Joan continued with their duties, but now in a subdued spirit. They seemed to share my despair.

The day dragged slowly by, but no news arrived that the VA hospital had accepted Dave's admittance. I considered what this transfer would do to my regular visits. Dave was being transferred to a hospital that was a 45-minute drive from our home. With three children to care for, I couldn't possibly make the trip twice a day as I was now doing. I had to be home when the children arrived from school each day so that I could take them to a babysitter. This would no longer be possible.

The drive would be another problem. The weather in March was often unpredictable and there might be days I would not be able to drive there at all. The hospital was located on a hill and the possibility of icy roads impeding my travel was a new fear I would have to face. I didn't like to drive, but especially disliked traveling on rain-slickened roadways and even more at night. There would be no more late evenings with Dave.

I hated the thought of Dave being taken out of Dr. Emery's care. He had enabled Dave to reach this point. What if the other doctor were not as good a neurologist? But we had no other choice. Dave had to be placed on a dialysis machine.

Later that afternoon I asked one of the nurses what was holding up the transfer, since the need for dialysis had seemed so urgent that morning. She said the government offices were slowed down for the weekend and since this was Friday, an unusual amount of red tape had to be cut. I continued my wait by Dave's side.

By nine that night I was becoming more tired and increasingly nervous at the continued delay. Kidney failure was something that I considered urgent and I was getting more and more frightened. I approached another nurse. "If there is a problem because of a shortage of beds, I will buy one for him," I said. I had heard that they were trying to find him a bed at the hospital, and naively I thought it was as simple as being overcrowded with just the need for one extra bed.

"If it was just a bed they needed, we would roll him in in the one he's in now. But if anyone can get him in, Dr. Emery can," she said.

I felt a little comfort in her confidence in the doctor. I wondered if Dr. Emery's lack of friendliness was due to his uncertainty of Dave's expected recovery. Perhaps he is so glum because he doesn't know if Dave will survive. Perhaps he also feels helpless, I thought.

I told the nurse I was going home, but asked her to call me when they chose to make the move. I wanted to accompany Dave in the ambulance so he wouldn't be alone. The children were at Bonita's and I didn't have to worry about them being cared for.

Fright made me exhausted. After spending the entire day at the hospital, I was so tired that I dropped into bed that night as if I had been drugged. I was not the kind of person who needed sleeping pills very often. I could wear myself out just by worrying.

When I awoke it was daylight. I looked at the clock – 7 a.m. The phone had not rung all night long. That meant Dave had not been transferred yet and it was over twenty-four hours since his kidneys began to fail. I jumped out of bed and ran into the bathroom to wash my face, and put on some make-up. As I pulled a pants suit from the bedroom closet, I realized how little it mattered what I wore from day to day. No one saw me without my coat buttoned up the front, an afghan wrapped around my legs and feet. Every night I looked forward to crawling back into bed, turning the electric blanket on high, and trying to get warm once again. I was always so cold, but I had to stay with Dave. I combed my hair, fluffed it up a bit, and was ready to make the trip to the hospital.

When I arrived Joan said they had not received authorization for Dave's admittance, but Dr. Emery had ordered further tests – a liver scan to see if there was damage to the abdominal area that had previously gone undetected.

Dr. Emery arrived, somber as usual. He said the results of the liver scan would be returned tomorrow and he would let me know at that time what further information had been obtained.

I felt sorry for my mother. She was a highly energetic person who suddenly slipped into low gear at the time of the accident. She was reliving memories of the death of her younger sister, who died in a car accident in 1945. She had received a head injury similar to Dave's; however, in those days surgery wasn't even considered. My aunt suffered intensely for three days before she died. She left behind her husband and two-year-old daughter.

My mother was worried enough without my adding to those worries by losing control. There seemed to be a common look on everybody's face when they greeted me each day at the hospital – fear in their eyes and actions of quiet desperation. All any of us could do was sit and wait.

On Sunday morning I happened to be in the coffee shop with Bill and Louise when Pam came in. "Dr. Emery has just arrived," she said. I excused myself and followed her back to ICU.

Dr. Emery was at the nurses' station going over Dave's chart when I arrived. "I haven't seen the results of the tests yet," he said. "I'm going down to radiology right now and I'll be right back." I watched as this tall, dark man walked toward the door and then disappeared out of the

Intensive Care Unit. Pam and Joan were kept busy with their patients.

I paced the hall in front of the cubicles in my usual reaction to panic. I was terrified of what Dr. Emery might find, but at the same time I was anxious to hear whatever news he had. I watched Pam and Joan for a minute or two while they went through their usual morning routine – until my terror reached its peak. There were two doors into ICU, one at each end of the hall. The moment I turned my back and began pacing in one direction, I wondered if Dr. Emery would come in the opposite door at the far end of the hall. I turned around quickly and began pacing in the opposite direction. Then I thought of the door behind me again. Either way I walked I had a door to my back and I couldn't bear the suspense of having him walk up behind me. I decided to step out into the hall and do my pacing out there. I knew which direction Dr. Emery would be coming from now. There was only one direction he could exit radiology and I would have plenty of time to prepare myself for the bad news as I watched him walk toward me.

I didn't have enough composure to read my Bible, hence I depended on memorized verses, one of which was the 23rd Psalm. Then as I began the Lord's prayer, "Our Father who art in heaven . . ." I saw Dr. Emery come out of the radiology department. I stopped my pacing and reached out for the wall. I decided that when he reached me and told me the bad news, I would already be pressed against the wall. This way I could slither down the wall when I fainted and he wouldn't have to catch me.

Though the hall was not very long, it seemed to take him an incredibly long time to reach me, as if he were moving in slow motion. This man, it seemed to me, had power over life and death. This dark shadow of a doctor – not dressed in white as doctors are expected to be, but in a black suit – held Dave's life in his hands.

Dr. Emery stopped a few feet in front of me. My heart was pounding so hard I could hear it. Dr. Emery said, "I can't find a thing wrong with him." And then he smiled. I couldn't believe it. Dr. Emery was actually smiling. He was telling me that Dave was okay. A feeling of rejoicing surged through me. I could have kicked my heels in the air. Instead I said a silent, "Thank you, God," and then I thanked Dr. Emery. Dr. Emery went back into ICU and I returned to the coffee shop to tell Bill and Louise the wonderful news.

Somehow I had forgotten all about the urgency of getting Dave on a dialysis machine. All I could think of was Dr. Emery could find nothing wrong with him. That was the news I was waiting to hear.

Later that afternoon Pam and Joan explained that a nephrologist had been called in to examine Dave Monday morning. At the present time the transfer to the Veterans Hospital had been cancelled.

The following morning I learned what had happened to Dave. When the brain suffers a severe trauma, most fluids are stopped to decrease the swelling of the brain tissues. This lack of fluid was sending Dave's kidneys into failure out of protest. A tube had been placed into his nose by the nephrologist. This allowed them to pump fluids directly into Dave's stomach and the nurses received orders to give him eight ounces of fluid every two hours. Almost immediately he began to show signs of improvement and the weeping from his knees ceased. Not being able to get Dave into the Veterans Hospital had been a blessing in disguise.

A few days of calm were followed by another setback. Even though the nurses were scrupulous in the maintenance of Dave's trach, he came down with a Staph. infection. I wondered if it had been transmitted by one of his visitors since the germs could have been brought in from outside the unit. That was also something I would never know for sure since a Staph. infection was impossible to track down. It thrived in a hospital setting and pounced on unsuspecting victims.

Joan met me at the entrance of ICU. I gripped my tote bag a little tighter when I saw the door to Dave's cubicle had been pulled closed. Joan said he was in isolation and anyone entering the room would have to gown up. Anything taken into the room would be disposed of in a receptacle at the door.

I had been bringing an afghan every day to wrap around my legs, but I only owned the one and I didn't want to throw it away. Moreover, Dave's grandmother had crocheted it for us. I thought of Dave's precious Bible and how dependent I was on it. Dave would be furious if I allowed it to be destroyed, this cherished reminder of his friend in the service. Besides, I thought, destroying a Bible must be blasphemous.

The cards and letters would also have to stay outside while I went in since there was nothing I could bring myself to take in and allow to be destroyed later. I just had to learn to depend on my memory for the time it took for Dave to recover from this infection.

I removed my coat as Joan handed me a gown to place over my clothes. A mask covered my nose and mouth and surgical gloves went over my hands. I saw my reflection in the glass partition. If Dave recognized me before, he certainly wouldn't now! I looked just like all the other masked people who tended to him.

The extra time it took the nurses to help me get into my isolation garments caused me to use my time wisely. I left only when I couldn't endure the cold any longer, and returned when the nurses weren't busy with other patients. Three days later the infection had been arrested.

Throughout the past three weeks of Dave's hospitalization, I was required to send in an insurance form – one for each and every week. Those first weeks I signed my name with the notation that I was Dave's wife. The forms were accepted without question since the hospital listed his condition as comatose.

Suddenly the forms began coming back with the demand, "Insured's signature required." I attached a note, "Patient is in coma and can't sign," and signed it once again with my signature. Since there was, after all, no way to get Dave to sign the form, I thought they would have to accept the forms with my name.

The previous three forms had gone through as signed, but now the insurance company refused to authorize payment without Dave's signature no matter if he was in a coma or not. This was the beginning of my experience with the bureaucratic red tape that no business seems to be free from whether it is an insurance company or the federal government. I wondered how I was supposed to accomplish getting Dave to sign the forms. Even if he could hold a pen, he was right-handed and his right arm was paralyzed. But I had to get the forms signed to pay the hospital and the only way was to have Dave's signature on the insurance forms.

I went home that evening, dug out some old cancelled checks that Dave had written, sat down at the dining room table, and began practicing his signature. I felt like a criminal, but I realized I had no other choice. With the medical costs running $1500 a week minimum, it was imperative that we have insurance. Besides, the insurance company didn't say they wanted Dave to sign the forms, they said only that they wanted his signature. Well, I was going to give it to them.

I turned in a signed form the following morning and it went through without question. The following week I forged Dave's name once again and the form also was processed. For the rest of the hospitalization, I forged my husband's name.

However, for some unknown reason the lesson was not learned well enough. As long as Dave couldn't sign his name, I had a problem.

Our tax refund check arrived. I never considered there would be a problem cashing it since Dave was obviously in no condition to sign the check. However, my brother-in-law checked with the Internal Revenue Department in Portland to find out how I should go about cashing it. He was told to get a letter from the doctor about Dave's condition, take it to the bank, and the money would be deposited in our joint checking account.

Since Dr. Barrett, the plastic surgeon, was less frightening than Dr. Emery, I asked him to write me a letter stating Dave was in a coma. After I obtained the letter, I signed my name to the back of the check, and went to the bank to cash it.

The teller read the letter, looked at me strangely, stepped back a few feet, and said, "I can't cash this! It will have to be sent back to Utah to be reissued." The teller said the government office in Utah would mail me a new check, then she looked past me to the next person in line and said, "Next." I stepped aside and left the bank $300 poorer.

I waited for the check, but instead received a card telling me they would let me know within six weeks what they were going to do about the matter. I was shocked. That was our money and we needed it! I had no idea how much of the medical expenses the insurance would cover, and I wanted at least what we were entitled to.

I called the Portland Internal Revenue office and explained the situation to the gentleman who answered the phone. He chuckled. "There isn't a thing we can do until June or July," he said. The only thing I can advise you is to contact your congressman or senator." Then he added, "If you had withheld that amount from your taxes, you'd probably be in jail by now." He chuckled again.

After I hung up the phone, I sat down and wrote a letter to Oregon Senator Mark Hatfield. I explained in detail what had happened and asked him for help in obtaining the money.

Within two weeks I had a reply from Senator Hatfield and a check in my hand from Utah that had been reissued in my name. I was surprised at the prompt results, and relieved that there was another problem I no longer had to worry about.

It seemed as if I had enough complications in my life with Dave lying in a coma, but stumbling blocks were being put in my way by businesses as fast as they could manage it. And it didn't stop. Over the following years every company I had to do business with, people who were supposed to be in business to help me, caused me gigantic headaches.

VII

The past few days had been relatively quiet with no unusual happenings and no great changes in Dave's condition. I longed to see him again as he had been before, vigorous and active. I could see him in my mind going toward the barn in his cowboy boots, with that swagger to his walk. But he still showed no awareness of my daily arrivals and departures. Some evenings one of his sisters would sit with him as I was leaving to pick up the children. Dave was seemingly oblivious to this changing of the guard.

It was Sunday, March 19, when I neared the doorway to Dave's cubicle. I saw the nurses had turned him onto his right side. Every two hours he had to be turned. His back was to the door, and his left hand was unrestrained. Even before I entered the room, it seemed he sensed my presence. He turned slightly, looked directly at me, and reached out his left arm in my direction. My heart skipped a beat. He was looking at me for the first time in nearly a month!

I walked over to him, and took his hand. He drew my hand up to his chin, and held it against his chest, pressing the back of my hand with his thumb. Then as quickly as he had awakened, he drifted off to sleep again. I stood with my hand still in his and called his name, but he was unresponsive.

But I knew now that he hadn't forgotten me. There was no amnesia to worry about, and I was certain he would recover.

When I was certain Dave had drifted back into the coma, I went to the nurses' station to tell Pam and Joan that he had recognized me. They both smiled, but another patient made a sound and their attention was drawn to her. I was disappointed in their reaction, but so overwhelmed with my own happiness that I chose to ignore anyone who didn't feel as exuberant as I.

Pam and Joan understood Dave's injuries through their medical experience and they were not living on blind faith as I was. They lived on facts and case histories of other patients like Dave. For instance, the man who had the tumor removed from his brain. "He won't care if he sits on a hot stove," the nurse had said. She might as well have said it about Dave, but in my inexperience I assumed they all expected Dave to have a full recovery, except for a possible change in personality. With the Lord on our side, I expected that to be a minor problem.

To me there was death and there was life. If Dave did not die, I was certain he would resume the life he once lived. Pam and Joan on the other hand, knew that brain damage can show many forms. It was possible that he did remember me, but there was the greater possibility that this was just an isolated incident. Even greater was the chance that other portions of his mind might have been impaired. No one knew if he would remember how to read, how to do simple arithmetic, or to do any of the things that most people take for granted. He was a husband and a father, but no one knew if he would recover enough to resume those roles once again.

Occasionally a nurse would be excited by some incident, however. Just as I arrived home from the hospital one night, the night nurse called me on the phone. She said Dave had moved his right leg on command and looked directly at her when she was taking his blood pressure. She said, "I just thought you would want to know." I thanked her for taking the time to call, and because of her, I went to sleep that night with a lifted spirit.

Dave drifted in and out of consciousness for the next two days. He would wake up for a moment and then slip back into the coma for another 24 hours or more, and then wake up for another moment or two again.

One of the nurses said, "I was taking David's blood pressure when I felt something brush against my leg. I looked down to see David running his hand up my leg." We both laughed. Before the accident, I would have been jealous and angry to hear of Dave's doing such a thing. Now I was glad to hear anything that confirmed Dave's recovery was progressing and all I could say was, "At least we know there is still life in him." I didn't care who he reacted to as long as he showed a reaction to something.

I received a legal paper in the mail from the hospital with the word LIEN written across the top in bold print. They were putting a lien on the insurance money, and/or Dave, it said. It emphatically stated that it was not against our home or furniture, but I couldn't understand how a lien could be put on a person. According to the hospital business office, we owed them nearly $10,000 – and Dave was still in Intensive Care with no anticipated date of discharge. They didn't need to put a lien on Dave, they already had possession of his body.

Someone told me not to worry. "I know someone who had a heart attack and the entire hospital bill was paid by insurance except for two dollars."

I read a story in the Teamster paper about a family whose daughter had died of cancer. When she died the entire hospital bill was paid by the same insurance company that handled our coverage. None of this information could stop me from fretting, however, so I decided to check with the business office at the hospital. They would know if I should be concerned.

The woman at the desk said, "Don't worry, Teamsters cover very well." She laughed when I told her I couldn't help but worry, since I owed the hospital so much money. As I left the hospital I tried to convince myself to forget about the hospital bill. If the hospital wasn't worried, why should I worry?

I saw an elderly man and woman leaving the hospital one afternoon. The man said he had been hospitalized for a heart attack a few months previously. They couldn't afford to pay the hospital bill so they were on their way to put their home up for sale. Since they lived on social security, they had no other source of income.

I had already made the decision to sell our home, if and when that need arose. I felt sorry for that couple, however, who were losing everything they owned. At least when Dave got well we could start over. After all, we were young and energetic.

The next afternoon when I arrived home to pick up the children after school, I retrieved the mail from the box. In it was a memo from the insurance company. They wanted to know whether the accident was a one or two-car wreck.

Immediately I went into the house and called them on the phone. "What will this do to our insurance if I tell you?"

"Not a thing," the insurance clerk said. "We just have to have it for our files. It's just a technicality."

"Can I tell you verbally, or do you have to have it in writing?" I asked.

"We prefer to have it in writing," she answered.

I hung up and wrote a quick note that this was a two-car accident. Two months later I learned that because it was a two-car accident we would not be eligible for major medical insurance, despite the woman's telling me it would do nothing to our insurance coverage. Tucked away inside the policy brochure was a paragraph labeled "Third-party Liability." In the event someone else was responsible for the accident, it said, major medical coverage would not be available.

When I returned to the hospital that afternoon Mr. Truman, our insurance agent for the car, arrived. He brought the no-fault papers for me to sign. We went to the coffee shop where he spread the forms out on the table.

I wanted to get the papers taken care of so the hospital would start receiving the portion of the $10,000 they were entitled to. At that time I didn't know that we wouldn't be receiving major medical. I wouldn't find that out for two more months. I signed the papers and Mr. Truman left.

Mama called me that night, "I just called Ken and Hilda about hiring an attorney, but they still don't want to get one."

"Yes, I know," I responded.

"But what if Dave wakes up and he's crippled and he wonders why somebody didn't do something?" That suddenly jolted me wide awake. I hadn't thought about it in that light. She was right, I realized. I was working so hard trying to keep everything together for Dave and I never considered the obvious. We had three small children to raise and right at that point the future was in a fog. Since I was Dave's wife it was up to me to make the final decision on anything. Even though I listened to friends and relatives for advice, I couldn't possibly know all the legalities of the situation I was in.

I told Mama, "Tomorrow I will get an attorney."

Two days after Dave reached out for me, he emerged from the coma again. He was lying on his right side with his back to the door once again just like he was on Sunday morning when I arrived. This time I was talking to him, telling him where he was, that he had been in an accident, and how we all missed him.

Just then Ken and Hilda walked in. As they entered the cubicle I said, "Oh, Dave. Here's your mom and dad." Dave turned his head and looked directly at them.

Ken said, "Hi, Dave." After they stared at one another for a moment, Dave closed his eyes and drifted off to sleep again, back into his coma.

That afternoon I sat down in a chair across the desk from Mr. Dyer, the attorney. I explained the accident, Dave's condition, and that I had just signed no-fault insurance papers. Surprise registered on his face as I told him I had been advised not to get an attorney.

"How have you been handling things?"

"I just do what has to be done," I responded.

Mr. Dyer explained how an attorney could take over many of the responsibilities and leave me free of the day-to-day worry. There were many things, he said, that I shouldn't have to be concerned with.

I remembered my federal tax refund check and the problem getting it cashed. I was carrying the state tax refund check in my purse at that very moment, and didn't have the slightest notion how I was going to get it deposited into our checking account. I didn't want another check returned. I explained the problem to Mr. Dyer.

Mr. Dyer suggested I sign Dave's name and deposit the check. "If anyone says anything just tell them you didn't know it was illegal." I was reminded of all the insurance forms I had forged Dave's name on and I realized this was no different. I just had to stop thinking I was a criminal. After all Dave was my husband and I wasn't taking anything from him, but only obtaining what was rightfully ours.

Mr. Dyer said he would contact Mr. Truman and try to retrieve the no-fault paper I signed. He then would be in touch with me when he had further information.

On my way back to the hospital I drove to the drive-in window of the bank. I calmly wrote Dave's name across the back of the check and jotted mine in just below it. I was pleased with how well I could make his signature. It looked just as if he had written it.

As I stopped at the window, my hands began to shake. I held my breath while the teller glanced over the check, printed out the deposit slip, and handed it to me with a smile. I tried not to look like the crook I felt I was when I reached for the paper. "Thank you," I said, struggling to keep my voice from shaking.

As I drove out onto the street, I realized our money was safe in our checking account, and at last the tremors of fear subsided.

On Tuesday, March 22, exactly one month after the accident, the plastic surgery was done on Dave's face. Dr. Barrett followed the gurney as Dave was wheeled back into ICU after surgery. He explained the surgery to me, "If we took an X-ray of David's face, it would be full of tiny wires that we used to rebuild his shattered right cheekbone. The left cheekbone was wired into place and his jaws were secured and anchored with a complete set of braces." Dave could no longer open his mouth since the upper and lower braces were wired together.

Dr. Barrett pointed to two incisions. There was one incision at the edge of each eyebrow and each incision was an inch in length. Dr. Barrett said the entire operation had been done through those two tiny incisions and inside Dave's mouth. In time, the incisions would fade and be barely noticeable, he said. It seemed incredible that so much damage could be repaired and leave Dave with so few scars. Both doctors left incisions that would either be well hidden in the hairline or small enough to fade away.

The feeding tube in Dave's nose had been removed and now a tube had been inserted through a small incision in Dave's neck. Dr. Barrett said this would be less irritating to Dave. All nourishment would continue to be pumped directly into his stomach bypassing his mouth completely.

I relaxed a bit with the knowledge that Dave had survived another assault to his body, the facial surgery. Before the accident he had been in excellent health both mentally and physically. This was in his favor as he struggled to recover.

Although Dave was the initial victim of this accident, others became victims from the resulting strain. As the weeks passed none of us escaped the continued pain and sorrow. My concern then went from Dave to the children and how to ease their unhappy situation.

VIII

Dave's temperature had stabilized and no longer did we have to endure the frigid temperatures. The ice machine was wheeled out and the ice blanket was removed. Sheepskin was placed under Dave to prevent bedsores. But in spite of the sheepskin, Dave still got sores on his lower back.

Pam placed Bandaids on the two sores, but the moment Dave's hand was untied from the railing he would reach around and rip off the tape. The tape seemed to bother him the most. Considering everything going on around him and to him, I probably should have worried about his lack of reaction to definite irritations. For instance the little vacuum hose that suctioned secretions from his lungs. Sometimes this caused him to gag when the nurse stuck it down his trachea. And then there was the safety pin that Dr. Emery stuck into the sole of his foot and ran pokingly up his side. Dave reacted to none of this. Even I got used to the many kinds of torment that Dave was subjected to every day. I knew they were all necessary, but I didn't know why. I kept telling myself that the doctors and nurses knew what they were doing and I shouldn't bother them by unnecessary questions. They were keeping Dave alive and I trusted them.

My sister Yvonne drove up from California for a few days. She and Mama called Dr. Emery's office to find out exactly what Dave's condition was. Dr. Emery's secretary wouldn't let them talk to him. She said, "Dr. Emery has told everything he knows. He just doesn't know any more."

The frustration of it all was unbearable, but no one could do anything about it – even the doctor was helpless.

I told Mama, "I wish the accident had happened to me rather than Dave. He could have coped so much better than I."

She responded, "I wish it had happened to me instead of to either of you."

I knew Dave would want me to keep life normal for the children, as normal as possible. That was another reason I brought them home to sleep in their own beds each night.

The children would turn on the TV and watch "The Brady Bunch" or whatever children's programs happened to be on at that hour. After staring at the picture for a few moments I would get up in frustration and put "Rainy Days and Mondays" on the stereo and retreat to the kitchen.

One night shortly after we arrived home, Lisa turned on the TV and she and Jan planted themselves on the floor in front of it. Steve sat down in the rocking chair near the kitchen door. I started the water running in the sink and began loading the dishwasher. Steve turned his

61

chair toward me and said, "My friend Tim says his dad told him that Dad's brains are scrambled." I turned in shock.

"Oh, no," I said in astonishment. How thoughtless some people were to say such things. It hurt me just as much as it did Steve to hear those words. "Tim's father has never even been to the hospital. He can't possibly know anything about Dad. I certainly haven't talked to him." I wiped my hands on a dishtowel as I walked closer to Steve, "I see Dad every day and he really is getting better. His brains were *not* scrambled."

Tears filled Steve's eyes as he asked, "Why did that man have to hit Dad?" I looked at him as I pondered an answer to his question.

"I don't know. I just don't know." Suddenly Steve's attention was drawn to the TV. The girls were laughing about an incident on the program they were watching. Steve jumped up from the rocking chair and plopped down in front of the TV. I was thankful to be given this reprieve. I was at a loss to answer Steve's questions.

Over the years I heard answers to why people suffer. Some people suffered, they said, because they sinned. But then I heard someone say Christian people suffer to be tested and tried.

I remembered my aunt saying, "Someone asked me if Dave was a Christian. I told her of course he is." I felt certain that that wasn't an isolated incident. It hurt the children and it hurt me to have people talking about us behind our backs. Some of the things they said were insensitive and painful to hear. Aquaintances were curious and some didn't stop to think before they spoke.

Steve was not taking it all easily, by any means. Twice previously he had locked himself in the bathroom after we arrived home. The second time I called our family doctor, Dr. Manning. He had been a physician for many years and I assumed he would have some wisdom I didn't have in helping Steve. I had all I could do to keep my own spirits up, and I hoped someone else would advise me with the children's questions. However, I was disappointed with Dr. Manning as he said, "Tell Steve his dad has the *very* best doctors." I already knew that; I wanted to hear something else.

Dr. Manning always answered my questions as if he knew everything about anything. Now he wasn't at all informative, what he said meant nothing to me, and I didn't want to tell Steve something so flimsy. I felt that Dr. Manning didn't expect Dave to recover, that he thought he was hanging by a thread. It seemed as if I was the only person who expected Dave to survive, and that was on blind faith.

I knew going to the hospital every day helped me by being near Dave. So far no one gave me any definite reasons why they might expect Dave to survive, neither could anyone boost Steve's hopes. I decided to take Steve to the hospital whenever I could. When the girls went to Bonita's I kept Steve with me. Although Steve couldn't see Dave – the sign on the door prevented anyone under 12 from entering – perhaps being nearby would help. My feelings about this turned out to be right.

Steve spent the entire weekend with me at the hospital. We went home at night. Bill Folk took him out for a coke and comic book. When they returned, Steve had a smile on his face and the pressure that had been building up in him began to lessen before my eyes. We had so many visitors each day at the hospital that I could leave Steve with them in the coffee shop when I was with Dave. I spent more time with Steve and less with Dave than I had previously, but it seemed to be helping Steve, just to be at the hospital and with the many friends who dropped by each day.

On Sunday, March 26, nearly five weeks after the accident, while I was visiting with Bill and Louise Folk in the coffee shop, Dave was transferred out of ICU to a private room. When I returned to his cubicle I found the door to ICU standing wide open and his bed empty. There were no other patients in ICU and I couldn't see any nurses anywhere. Panic struck again.

I had no idea where they would take him, but I started running toward north wing. No one had informed me of the impending transfer and all I could think of was that disaster had struck again. I came skidding to a stop when I almost ran into Pam as she was walking out from behind the counter at the nurses' station. She pointed to the room at the end of the hall and said, "He's in 105," and then she asked, "Do you want to stop visitors?" I hesitated, remembering the disaster that had occurred when visitors were stopped a few weeks earlier. Then Pam went on to explain, "An aunt has already been in to see him." I was surprised since I had seen only Bill and Louise so far that day. I couldn't imagine who this "aunt" was. "If he was my husband, I would," Pam added.

I decided it wasn't fair to Dave to allow curiosity-seekers in, but those who were visiting with Dave's best interests in mind would be allowed in as soon as they contacted me.

Dave was now being put in hospital gowns, but a gown didn't provide much covering, nor did the sheet that the nurses were putting on his bed. He continued to move his left leg back and forth and the sheet always went astray within a few minutes of his being covered.

To prevent blood clots from forming due to his immobility, he was now wearing elastic knee-high socks. This was only something new for him to work against. He wore the socks day and night, and all day long he rubbed against his right leg with his left foot until he worked the sock down to his ankle. I spent my days in frustration trying to keep the sock on his right leg up, and he spent his days trying to get it down.

After that phone call from the night nurse telling me that Dave had moved his right leg on command, he never did it again, nor did he move his arm or hand.

The room had two beds, but no one was ever admitted to occupy the other bed. During the afternoons I became so tired that occasionally I considered lying down on it, but I feared that I would be charged with the use of two beds or perhaps even scolded by a nurse for having the audacity of lying on clean linens. I discarded the notion. I never did anything if I thought it might be against the rules.

The morning following his discharge from ICU was quiet. Dave drifted off to sleep after kissing me good morning, and I sat down to write a letter.

I was startled by a choking sound. I looked up to see a dark brown fluid gush from Dave's trach with such force that it shot across the floor, up the wall, and hit the ceiling. It was so violent that he didn't even have time to catch his breath. I ran out the door to get a nurse.

There was no one at the nurses' station. I ran down the hall, looking into one room after another until I found a nurse at the opposite end of the wing. She ran back with me to Dave's room. He was still vomiting when we returned, and the nurse tried to calm him. "Relax, David! David, relax!" She kept saying it over and over. Then another nurse came in and I decided it was time for me to step out into the hall.

Two doors down the hall was a solarium with a sofa and a few chairs grouped around a television. A few people were sitting there watching a quiz show. I saw a chair behind the TV and I walked over and sat down. Then I remembered my Bible and tote bag. I had forgotten to bring them out of Dave's room when I left. I was much too terrified to go back in as I heard the nurse's voice filtering down the hall, "Relax, David! David, relax!"

Momentarily my connection to God seemed to have been cut off. *If only I had remembered to bring my Bible.* Then a voice came through to me from the TV. The game show host said, "Who said, 'This is my beloved Son in whom I am well pleased'?" It was as if a voice from God was telling me that He was with me even without my Bible.

The nurse's voice continued carrying over the noises in the solarium. I had to get away from the sound. I hurried down the hall, past Dave's room, toward the Intensive Care Unit. Anywhere was better than sitting in the solarium listening to the nurse yell at Dave.

As I neared the hall toward west wing, I decided to wander down the unfamiliar hall. I had found that walking helped during immense pressure, and distractions by strange sights and sounds could relieve the emotional drain in times of crisis. I could only pray that God would let Dave know I was with him. As I rounded the corner, I almost walked into Dr. Emery. I looked up in surprise.

"How's he doing?" Dr. Emery asked.

"Something terrible has happened," I answered. Dr. Emery didn't ask me to elaborate as he headed for north wing. I followed.

I watched Dr. Emery enter Dave's room and then I slowly walked nearer. Although I didn't want to be too close in case of another terrifying scene, the suspense was drawing me back. I wanted to run away, but at the same time I wanted to be reassured that Dave was okay.

I looked toward the solarium door just as Bonita and my aunt Phyllis walked in. Everyone seemed to arrive at the precise moment disaster struck. The three of us sat down in the hall within view of Dave's room and we waited.

I watched as they wheeled the ice machine back in. I knew his temperature was back up again and a few minutes later Dr. Emery emerged from the room and said it had risen to 105°. "We're going to take urine cultures to see if he has a urinary tract infection," he said. "The results will be back in a couple of days."

Two hours later Dave's temperature was down to 101°. By evening the ice blanket had brought his temperature back to normal. Frigid temperatures were once again the norm in Dave's room. Dave and I shivered through the next two days. I should say I shivered. Dave was given shots to prevent him from shivering.

When the culture results were returned, they were negative. Dr. Emery said he didn't know what caused the vomiting episode since it wasn't due to a urinary tract infection.

The surgery done on Dave's jaws and cheekbones had been done exactly one week ago. Could this have been the result of the operation? What he had vomited looked like old blood, but no one mentioned this possibility. As usual, I didn't ask.

I felt rather guilty when the cleaning lady came in, looked at the ceiling and said, "This whole room is going to have to be repainted." I wondered if she thought that about Dave's cubicle in ICU. Both rooms had blood spots on the walls from ceiling to floor. I hated to cause people extra work, and I would have preferred to live a quiet life and never be noticed by anyone.

The nurses on north wing cared for Dave with a Florence Nightingale attitude. Although none of the nurses could compare with Pam and Joan, I couldn't have asked for better. Dave would have been a severe strain on any hospital staff, but this hospital withstood the rigors.

The night nurse said she loved caring for Dave because he didn't complain. Debbie's husband was in Vietnam and her loneliness was spent caring for Dave. She and I visited while she did her nursing duties and we included Dave in our conversations as if he followed it right along. We had no way of knowing if he did or didn't.

The radio was still running day and night, but now when I came in each morning I found the station turned to "beautiful music." I learned one of the nurses was turning the dial when she came on duty each morning. I admired her taste in music since it was the same as mine, but I wasn't playing the radio for her or for me. I was playing it for Dave, and *he* favored country. I changed the station when she left the room.

Another nurse walked in and said, "I just love working in David's room because I love country music." But when a couple from church stopped in, the wife walked over to the radio and changed it to a religious station. I acted as if I hadn't known of its existence; the moment they left the room, I changed it back to KRDR for Dave. The commercials were most important to Dave, I thought, since they were all local. None of the other stations could give him the comfort this local station would. I had to keep the radio tuned to that station even if there might be others that people thought were better. And, I didn't have the courage to tell all those station-changers, "Hands off!"

One morning I arrived to find bits of toilet tissue sticking on Dave's freshly shaved face. The nurses in ICU had been so efficient at shaving him that I hadn't even thought about the daily process. I could see there was going to be a bit of a problem now and I couldn't tolerate arriving each morning to find him slashed to ribbons. I asked permission to shave him myself. After all I was in no hurry and could take the entire day if need be.

After I received permission I asked our friend Bill Folk how to do it. Dave had a heavy beard and I knew there was a technique to shaving it. Electric shavers were inadequate – they made Dave's face look as if it had been covered with mud. I brought in Dave's shaving gear the next morning.

With Bill's instructions I became proficient with the razor and did not inflict a single wound on him. Each day I got better and faster until the procedure took less time than just getting all the utensils together.

Ken was still complaining about getting my relatives out to move the cattle. Every morning he greeted me with this suggestion.

One day when I was shaving Dave, Ken and Hilda walked into the room. Ken said, "I wouldn't let her near my throat with a razor, Dave."

I glanced up and gave a curt smile. I had to agree, however; it might be dangerous to allow me near Ken's neck with a razor.

Dave's awareness grew as the days went by. He seemed to know when I arrived each morning or else he was waiting for me to come. No matter how quietly I approached, he opened his eyes as I neared the bed. Now when I kissed him good morning, he would reach up with his left arm and embrace me.

But he still showed no signs of talking and I could only make a guess as to what went through his mind. It was as if he was responding only to instinct. I was thrilled with the response, however. He showed no response to anyone else who entered his room.

Mr. Dyer, the attorney, called and asked me to come to his office. When I arrived he informed me that there had been a computer error. He had managed to retrieve the no-fault form that I signed and it was then learned that instead of $10,000, we would be receiving $25,000. I don't know if that information would have passed on to me if I had not hired an attorney, but the thought ran through my mind that rather than not being able to afford an attorney, perhaps – I could not afford to be without one.

On April 5, Bonita came to the hospital to have lunch with me. We drove over to Dea's Drive-in Restaurant for a hamburger and fries. It had been a stormy morning and now as we ate our lunches, I looked out the window to see tall fir trees bending against the wind.

Wind frightens me, and when Bonita dropped me back at the hospital, I looked forward to the quiet of Dave's room.

As I tried to distract myself with a book, I could hear the wind whistling around the solarium room door as the door slammed and banged against its hinges. I looked up at the ceiling when I heard the roof creaking and groaning. It sounded as if the boards were being pulled out, nails and all. I got up and walked to the hall. Just then Bill Folk walked into the solarium from outside. Happy to see a familiar face, I walked toward him.

"Did you hear about the school blowing down?" he asked.

"What school?" I envisioned my children buried in the debris of their wrecked schoolhouse; but it was, Bill told me, a school in Vancouver, Washington.

A short time later a nurse told me a tornado had just gone through Portland and touched down in Vancouver, blowing over a school, shopping center, and bowling alley. The hospital began preparing for patients that might possibly be brought to Valley General. I could hear the ambulance calls as the nurses sat next to the dispatching radio.

The world was coming apart around me. I had to get home and make sure my children were safe and secure. For the first time since the accident, I spent the evening at home with the children and left Dave in the care of his nurse.

IX

I had always been taught to pay favors back, but now I learned that it isn't always possible. When I was a child we didn't have much money, but my mother and I tried to repay others by babysitting for those who had children. All I could think of during these days was the amount of babysitting chores I would have had to do to repay all the wonderful friends and relatives.

My aunt Phyllis and Bill Folk appeared at the door within a few minutes of each other. Bill handed me a couple of cards that he said were from the employees at the bakery. Just then a nurse appeared, intent on changing Dave's bed, so Phyllis, Bill, and I walked out into the hall. We sat down on some chairs in a quiet area outside Dave's room and I opened one of the envelopes that Bill had given me. Both of them were thick and of equal weight.

The first one was a multi-paged humorous card. I flipped slowly through the pages, reading the names of Dave's friends inscribed throughout the card. I didn't know most of the people, but their names were familiar from conversations I had had with Dave before the accident. I knew Dave would especially enjoy this card full of witty jokes. I hoped to be able to share it with him sometime soon. I always read all the cards to Dave though he never showed any response, but this card would mean most to him since it was from his co-workers. I placed it back in the envelope.

I pulled the next card from its envelope, fully expecting another multi-paged card, but instead the contents floated down into my lap in ten- and twenty-dollar bills. Tears welled up in my eyes and a lump caught in my throat as I tried to thank Bill, but the words wouldn't come out. Phyllis put her arm around me, and I managed a squeeky, "Thank you." So many people had been so kind, a kindness that was incomprehensible.

After Bill left, Phyllis and I talked for a while. "I'll never be able to pay you all back," I said tearfully.

Phyllis answered, "We don't do it to be paid back, we do it because we love you."

Never before in my life had I been on the receiving end of so much. Accepting so much from so many, whether it was from strangers or dear friends, was hard, but it did show how many wonderful people there were in this world. Even years later I learned of strangers who had included us in their prayers, people who lived in other states and had heard of us through friends.

Easter was on its way. I saw a notice tacked on the wall "Children under the age of 12 will be allowed to visit patients on Easter Sunday."

What a surprise! – but did it mean all patients or just those who were in better condition than Dave? I decided to be brave and approach Dr. Emery when he made rounds that afternoon. I hoped he would allow the children in to see Dave. Steve especially would be happy to see his Dad once again.

Hospital visiting rules had always seemed so strict. Though I was fourteen when one of my nephews was born, I was not allowed in to see him when the family visited my sister. Children under sixteen were not allowed to visit the maternity ward.

When our three children were born, even fathers were not allowed to visit except one hour in the evening from seven until eight. After Steve was born, Dave said a nurse stood in the hall with her arms outstretched until the clock struck seven. Then she put down her arms and allowed the fathers to come into the ward. He said he could see directly into the room and there didn't appear to be any reason why they couldn't enter. The nurse had her rules and she wasn't about to let anyone break them.

I never wanted to risk causing any problems here at the hospital or to make any enemies out of the nurses. I wanted to be liked by everyone and I never tried to overstep my bounds. Rules were meant to be kept, I thought, not to be broken.

I was talking with a friend in the solarium when Dr. Emery slipped in and out of Dave's room. Before I could get to the nurses' station, he had disappeared. I said to the nurse, "I thought Dr. Emery was here. I wanted to talk to him."

"He is here," she answered. "Follow me." The nurse turned toward ICU and I half-ran behind her down the hall. "I'll be right back," she said as she opened the door and entered the unit. I stood in the hall and waited. I was tempted to go inside with her since I had spent so many weeks in ICU myself, but I did as I was told and waited in the hall.

A minute or so later the nurse walked out with Dr. Emery right behind her. He was smiling as he closed the door behind him and the nurse walked back to her station. Dr. Emery smiled only one time and that was just after he received the results of the liver scan. This wasn't like him and I wondered what was so funny. I pushed the thought out of my mind because of my concern with the children.

The next day a nurse told me what happened. Most of the nurses were afraid of Dr. Emery. His unsmiling, commanding appearance and easy anger intimidated not only me, but others as well, I learned. The head nurse of north wing was not one of those, however. She came into ICU while Dr. Emery was with a patient. She told him I wanted to see him. He said, "I'm busy now. I'm changing a dressing." She snapped at him, "That poor girl comes here every day and all she wants is one kind word from you." With that the nurse left ICU and Dr. Emery came out to see me.

I asked Dr. Emery, "Can the children come in to see Dave on Easter?" "Who's stopping them?" he asked. I wasn't used to getting answers with a question and I was speechless. I realized I had never asked for them to be admitted before.

"Well, I guess I am."

"If it's okay with the head nurse, it's okay with me," he answered. He went back into ICU and left me standing in the hall wondering what had happened. The nurse who had just rushed down the hall with me to ICU was the nurse who would have to okay it. I walked back to the nurses' station to see that the shift had just changed and the afternoon nurses had just taken over. I realized I hadn't mentioned the sign admitting children on Easter Sunday and I wondered if Dr. Emery even knew it existed. The way he answered me, it was as if I was asking for special treatment for my children. All I wanted to know was if my children were included with those who would be admitted.

I walked over to the nurses' station. The nurse in charge at night was a man. I didn't know him as well as the day nurse, but I chose to ask him anyway.

"Is it all right if my children come in on Easter to see their father?"

He looked at me with a puzzled expression and furrowed brows. "Do you think that's wise?" It seemed as if I was getting nothing but questions to my questions, I thought.

"Well, they'll have to see him sometime," I said. It seemed like one little sign was getting me caught up in more and more turmoil. All I wanted was a simple answer to my question. The nurse said no more, but went back to the chart he was reading. I walked back to Dave's room. At least he didn't say no, I thought.

One of Dave's friends came in with Bill Folk one afternoon. Dave's family was there and a few friends filled the room. I had some errands to run and since there were so many visitors, I decided to go to the store. As I leaned down to pick up my purse, I heard a thud. I turned around to see everyone rush toward the door.

Later Bill told me that the friend had come willingly to the hospital with him even though he had a fear of medical facilities. He walked up to Dave and said, "Hi, ya, Dave. How are you doing?" With the bone removed from Dave's forehead, the skin above his right eye pulsated from the movement of the brain just beneath. The hole in his throat was covered with a plastic cover with a hose connected to a machine which pumped moisture into his lungs. A urinary catheter was attached to a bag which was hooked to a rail at the foot of the bed. And above all, Dave had lost an incredible amount of weight. He hadn't had any food except for a type of baby formula for over a month. They had only just recently started the formula and for three weeks after the accident he

71

didn't even have water. For the past couple of weeks they had increased his water intake, but he wasn't getting enough calories to keep a mosquito alive.

After one look, Bill said, this young man began to back out of the room. Out in the hall, Bill said, he leaned up against the wall – and then fell flat on his face in a faint. By the time I got through the group of people by the door all I could see was a circle of white. Throughout Dave's hospitalization I never saw so many nurses in one place at one time except at the coffee shop during lunch.

But somehow I wasn't concerned about the children's reaction to seeing Dave. They *had* to see him eventually. I didn't see how it could be any worse now than it would be then. The children had heard descriptions of Dave over and over. It wouldn't be as if they had heard nothing and were taken in without warning. Perhaps I was extremely naive, but I did feel a sense of relief when I first saw Dave and was able to touch him. One of Dave's sisters had been fearful of seeing him. I offered to go in with her and after the visit, her fear was gone. Fear of the unknown can sometimes be the greatest obstacle. Well, if the children showed any sign of not wanting to visit, I would allow them to stay outside his room. Otherwise we were all going to visit on Easter.

The visit was nearly as I expected. Steve held tightly to Dave's hand, and Dave clung right back. The three children were lined up at Dave's bedside with Steve closest and Lisa, who was nine, in the middle. Jan, who had just turned seven, was standing at the end. I noticed Dave glancing at Lisa periodically, but still holding on to Steve's hand. Lisa was apprehensive as she gazed around the room, trying not to look at her father too much, it seemed. Jan, too, kept her eyes more on me than Dave, but they all three stood quietly at Dave's bedside. Suddenly Dave reached out for Lisa's hand which she had just placed on the rail of the bed. She jumped slightly and looked alarmed for a moment.

Dave's attention drew back to Steve as he reached out to Steve once again. I think this must have been a relief to Lisa. Her eyes had been darting back and forth as if she didn't know what to do about the stranger who had just grabbed her hand. Both Lisa and Jan showed less interest in their father than Steve did. Jan shifted from one foot to the other and I knew it was time that they should leave. I didn't want to push them to being with Dave more than they were prepared for. It was plain that they were weary and bored.

Though I was pleased with Steve's reaction to Dave, I wasn't disappointed in the girls. Seeing a father like this would be a shock to anyone, and I knew they would get used to him eventually. So I showed the girls the solarium and the television, and they amused themselves for the rest of the evening, occasionally checking for me in Dave's room. That first evening the hospital was a frightening place to be. Over the following weeks, the children grew more relaxed and they did get used to Dave's appearance.

Throughout the evening Steve continued to cling to Dave, and Dave kissed Steve's hand now and then. Until that night Dave had showed very little response to anyone other than me. Now his eyes were intent upon Steve's every move. Later while we were on our way home Steve said, "Dad kissed my hand ten times." There was an easier, happier quality in Steve's voice and I knew I had been right to bring the children in.

I presumed the rule banning the children under 12 would be in force the following days, but I decided to ignore it. Steve was much happier. He needed his father. Never mind rules.

From that point on I had decided not to take the children to babysitters in the evening except on an occasional basis. Instead, I took them back to the hospital with me, where they could do their homework in the solarium or watch TV. They were free to see Dave whenever they liked.

I chose not to ask anyone if they could be admitted. My plan was to bring them in until someone demanded they be kept out. In any case I would have gotten them in one more day than if I had not brought them at all.

Throughout the following days no one ever mentioned that the children should not be admitted. Occasionally a nurse asked them their ages, but the fact that they were ten years of age and under didn't seem to cause any alarm.

Bending rules went against my lifelong way of doing things, but I no longer cared.

After five weeks of virtually nothing but water, Dave was placed on a liquid formula that went into the tube in his neck and directly into his stomach. A few days later the formula was recalled by the government because of improper packaging. Dave was begun on a new formula which he had trouble digesting. For the next couple of days, Dave vomited after each meal.

The nurses tried everything to help Dave keep the nourishment down, but the only solution seemed to be to allow the formula to go down by the flow of gravity. A nurse attached the formula container to his feeding tube, pulled the tube up over her head, and the fluid slowly oozed down the tube into his stomach. This often took up to 45 minutes as each nurse took the stance of the Statue of Liberty just to protect Dave from the incessant vomiting episodes.

Now every afternoon Dave was placed in a chair so he could learn to sit up again. The first week his head drifted and hung down on his chest as if he had no muscle control at all. This concerned me because of the right-sided paralysis. I wondered if he was suffering from a paralysis that would prevent him from holding his head erect, but Dr. Emery said it wasn't unusual and his neck would get stronger. "After all, his head weighs 25 pounds," he told me. By the following week Dave had improved and was holding his head nearly erect.

I had improved, too. I was getting braver about asking Dr. Emery questions, and every day I came up with a new one for him to answer. Although his answers sometimes made me feel dumb, I continued asking. I didn't have the Intensive Care nurses to run interference for me any longer.

Although Dave's neck was stronger, he still had no more control over the rest of his body. The nurses tied a sheet around his waist to keep him from slipping out of the chair, but he slid down anyway. The weight of his body seemed to drag him down, and the two to three hours that they left him sitting only increased the likelihood of his slipping out.

It took two nurses to put him into a chair and two to get him out. I was helpless while I waited for them to put him back to bed. I ached for him. Healthy people couldn't even be expected to sit in one position for two to three hours, perhaps not even for fifteen minutes before they would start to wiggle. The nurses, however, would not put Dave back to bed until they felt he had been up a sufficient amount of time.

Yvonne came up for another visit. She, Bonita, and I went to Dea's Drive-in restaurant for lunch and discussed Dave's condition. Yvonne said she wished I would transfer Dave to the Veterans Hospital where he might get better care.

As I munched my french fries, I explained how inconvenient it would be for us all to visit him there. "I don't want him that far away. And I certainly don't want to take him away from Dr. Emery." Yvonne brushed away the tears that were sliding down her cheek.

I was surprised at how easily I made decisions now. Before Dave's accident, I rarely made any decisions without checking with Dave first. Now I found myself in a strange situation, sometimes in the middle, between two families. This position wasn't always popular, either.

When Dave's parents were in disagreement with me on hiring an attorney, I acted with my family's wishes. I hired one. When some of my relatives wanted Dave transferred to another hospital, I ended up on Dave's family's side. They, too, wanted him kept at Valley General. There were many situations like this, and in all of them I had to take one side or the other according to what I felt was right for us. I didn't want to make enemies, but if I did – so be it.

One afternoon on my way home to get the children, I stopped at a grocery store to get a few items. As I put the bags in the car I remembered the cleaners where I had taken Dave's coat. It was located across the parking lot. I put the bags in the back seat of the car and went through my purse for the claim ticket. Today's date was written on it. It was ready now!

I remembered when I left the coat at the cleaners. If this jacket comes out without shrinking,, I had told myself, I will look at it as a sign from God that Dave will get well. Now was the day of reckoning.

I took a deep breath, said a silent prayer, and walked across the parking lot to the cleaners.

I handed the claim ticket to the clerk and while she was looking through the racks of clothes I asked, "How did it turn out?" I hated surprises, and if it was going to be bad news, I hoped to hear it before I saw a badly-damaged coat.

"I don't know," the woman answered. "I didn't bag it." She brought the jacket to the cash register and hung it on a hook in front of me. I handed her the money and while she was making change, I peered cautiously under the plastic covering. The jacket looked spotless. I pulled the sheeting up higher and looked closely over the front of the coat. I couldn't believe it. There wasn't a spot on it, and it hadn't shrunk at all. It was beautiful!

As I carried the jacket to the car, I remembered Dave's watch. Now I couldn't wait to get home and look at his watch. If it was still running on its battery pack, I felt that would be another sign that Dave would recover. I had never been superstitious, and I don't know that I was now. All I wanted was a sign from God.

The minute I got home, I went to the bedroom and pulled out the envelope containing the watch. I looked at the second hand as it clicked slowly around. Dave always took pride in having a watch that kept good time, and all his watch seemed to need was an adjustment of the date. Otherwise it was keeping perfect time.

The watch had made it through the accident along with the jacket. Dave just had to make it, too.

Although the nurses were successful in getting the formula to stay down, his protein level remained dangerously low. The doctor ordered a blood transfusion. A pint was administered, but another check of his blood showed the protein level still low. The doctor then ordered a solution of pure protein to be administered by IV. Dave received a quart.

Dr. Barrett said a tube would have to be inserted directly into Dave's stomach if his protein count didn't improve soon. Almost immediately it improved.

Then that Sunday morning Dave pulled the feeding tube out of his neck. Another tube was inserted, but this one had to go into his nose once again. The incision in his neck closed the moment the tube was removed and the tube could not be reinserted without a minor surgical procedure.

Just out of curiosity, I asked one of the nurses if I could give Dave a drink of water with a straw. He had not had anything by mouth since before the accident. The nurse brought me a cup and a straw. I ran some water into the cup from the sink.

Dave had no difficulty sucking the water through the straw and the nurse then brought in some apple juice from the nurses' refrigerator. He literally gulped it down.

On April 16, after he pulled the feeding tube from his nose for the third time, I began to wonder if this was his way of protesting any more feeding tubes. One of the nurses must have thought the same thing, and she decided to try him on a "fractured jaw diet." This consisted of all liquids.

Dave's appetite was incredible. He had been consuming 300 cc. by tube feeding, but now on the liquid diet he was taking 500 cc. at each meal. He couldn't get the food in fast enough. He had been starving to death.

Except for breakfast (I couldn't get the children off to school before Dave received his first meal of the day), I helped him with his meals, and his protein count came up rapidly to an acceptable level. Now Dave had to learn to eat with his left hand.

I couldn't help but be surprised by Dave's lack of interest. I excused it, however, with the knowledge that he was waking up from the coma. A nurse had told me people rarely snapped suddenly out of a coma. Instead recovery is usually frustratingly slow.

When the nurses got Dave up, he sat quietly in a chair. Unless a magazine was put in front of him, he would stare straight ahead into space. When they pulled a table in front of him and put a magazine on it, he would leaf through it. Was he really looking at the pictures? I could never be sure.

The only time Dave showed a reaction was when I entered the room, and when I brought the children in each evening to see him. He also reacted well to his meal trays. He continued to eat as if famished. Other than that he spent his days as if in a trance.

Sometimes it was heartbreaking for me to watch him, but I wanted so much to believe that he was getting well that I tried not to think any negative thoughts. *Every*thing and *any*body around him must be pleasant and positive, I thought. That especially meant me!

When Dave was in bed I would ask him questions, "Do you want to get up and sit in the chair, Dave? If you do squeeze my hand." Usually I felt the gentle pressure from his thumb.

When he was sitting in the chair I asked, "Do you want to go back to bed? If you do squeeze my hand." Sometimes I would feel two short squeezes against my hand.

One day Dr. Emery covered the hole in Dave's trach as he said, "He looks like he wants to talk." Dave just continued lying there, perfectly still, staring at the doctor. Dave's communication was limited to squeezing hands.

One night a fellow employee from the bakery came in. This was the first time he had seen Dave since the accident. Aunt Phyllis and Uncle Vonnie arrived and the three of them talked while I sat near Dave and listened. As Dave's friend started to leave, his visit lasting about ten minutes, he leaned toward Dave and said, "See you later, okay?" Dave nodded his head.

Phyllis, Vonnie, and I were elated at this response from Dave. Dave's friend must have wondered how we could show so much happiness about someone merely nodding his head!

Bill Folk brought in a TV. Whatever went on in Dave's mind was a question-mark to us all, but we tried anything we thought might jolt him awake faster. When the TV was turned on, he seemed to be watching it. Or was he only attracted to movement? Even though I tuned in on shows he would normally have watched at home, I couldn't be sure he was actually watching them and understanding.

For the first two months of Dave's hospitalization I never saw anyone give him physical therapy. There was, in fact, no therapy facility within the hospital. In the latter part of April a therapist was called in from outside. By now Dave's right arm was drawn tightly against his chest in a contracture from lack of use. And, too, the muscles and tendons in his fingers were shrinking and his fingers were tightly clenched.

The therapist worked on his hand, arm, and leg. The constant movement of his left leg that had been present – and unexplained – since the day of the accident proved to have been therapeutic. It had kept this leg strong during the long months that he was bedridden. Very little therapy was needed to increase its use.

The therapist began teaching Dave to stand up. He had to learn to support himself on his legs once again. After two months of being flat on his back, he had no balance at all. However, within a few days the therapist had Dave working at the rail outside Dave's room. Dave couldn't support himself on his right leg nor could he move it. The therapist stood behind him holding him firmly so he wouldn't fall, pushed his right leg forward with his own right foot, supported his right knee so it wouldn't bend, and then told Dave to take a step with his left leg.

I felt the tears burn my eyes as I watched Dave struggle to regain his ability to walk. Dave had been so strong before. How could it be so difficult, such a simple thing, walking – something Dave and I had always taken for granted?

Still, in my heart I expected him to recover and before the year was out to be blazing down the highway in his truck. Watching him now, struggling to learn to walk again, I probably should have known better.

Julie, the nine-year-old girl in ICU, was doing much better now. She was released from ICU before Dave. Her illness turned out to be a rare form of cancer which had attacked a portion of bone on the top of her head. After surgery she progressed quite rapidly. She, too, would have a plate inserted in her head where the bone had been removed.

One afternoon Julie's mother peered in the doorway, "Julie has something to tell you." I stood up as I saw Julie propelling her wheelchair to the doorway, and then I saw the curly, blond wig which covered her shaved head. She looked like Shirley Temple in those early movies. "Hi, Julie," I said.

In a shy voice she said, "I just wanted to tell you I have been praying for your husband."

"Well, thank you, Julie. That's very nice of you."

She smiled and then her mother, who had been standing behind the wheelchair, turned the chair from the doorway and they headed toward the solarium, where Julie spent her days trying to catch up on her school work. I realized she would never know how many prayers I had said for her, too.

Dave's jaws had healed and the braces were ready to come off, a simple procedure compared to the other surgical processes that he had had to endure. At last Dave would be able to open his mouth if he could get it open after having it wired shut for a month!

It was April 25, a little over two months since the accident. I arrived that morning to find a cork sticking out of Dave's trach. A nurse was standing near him when I walked in. "He's been talking," she said.

After she put in the cork, she asked him to make some sounds and he had mimicked her exactly. Then she asked him, "Would you like to talk to Dr. Emery?" Dave answered, "Yes, I would like to talk to Dr. Emery." She was surpised to hear so much come out of Dave's mouth all at once that she ran out to get Dr. Emery from the nurses' station, where he had been filling out charts.

The first thing Dr. Emery said was, "What's your wife's name, David?" And Dave answered, "Sharon." The nurse didn't tell me what else Dr. Emery asked or if that was all he was interested in finding out. So many people seemed to be concerned about whether Dave would remember me. I knew he remembered me since that day in ICU when he reached out for me.

Later that morning my happiness became tinged with a bit of disappointment. Dave refused to do any more talking for anyone, including me.

I spent the rest of the day asking Dave questions, but I still couldn't get him to talk in sentences. The only way I could get him to answer me was to tell him to open his mouth first and then say the word. "Dave, open your mouth and tell me our dog's name." He correctly answered, "Cinders." We had only had Cinders for two years so I felt this was a good indication there was no great loss of memory. In fact there was nothing I could find that he didn't have at least a one-word response to. Except for the two weeks before the accident and the two months just past, his memory seemed to be totally intact. And it was a blessing, that he had no memory of what he had just been through.

Pastor Wickman was one of our first visitors that day. He had come to the hospital often throughout the past two months and he was surprised with the news that Dave was talking. As Pastor Wickman left the hospital that afternoon he said, "It's a miracle! It's nothing but a miracle!"

X

On April 27 Dave began eating solid foods. It was clear as he shoved food into his mouth that his table manners were in need of restoration. Gulping down his first solid food in weeks, he looked like a wild animal tearing away at its freshly-killed game. But I was happy to see him do anything, no matter how he did it.

After I left the coffee shop that afternoon, a nurse brushed past me. "I hear your husband is going home next week," she said. I looked at her as she hurried on, and I wondered who she was. I couldn't remember seeing her before, and certainly no one had mentioned the possibility of Dave's going home. I watched her as she turned toward west wing. She must be mistaken. She probably thought I was someone else. I went on back to Dave's room on north wing. I knew none of the nurses on west wing.

On April 28 the trach was removed and dressings were placed over the opening to keep it clean during the healing process.

Now it was time to remove Dave's urinary catheter. But when the nurse tried to get it out, she couldn't. She called Dr. Manning but he was gone; his associate came, instead. The nurse pulled the curtain around Dave's bed. Another nurse joined them. I retreated to the hall. I watched two sets of nurses' shoes and one pair of doctor's shoes moving beneath the curtain. Why was it taking so long? I didn't think it should be such a difficult procedure to remove a catheter. Then both nurses left the room and the doctor right behind them. One nurse whispered to me as she brushed by, "We're going to have to get another instrument – we can't get it out." I watched after them as they disappeared behind the counter of the nurses' station to the supply room.

I walked up to the curtain surrounding Dave's bed, peered inside to see how he was, and saw him lying there – holding the catheter in his hand. As far as I could tell, removal was complete. I told the nurse, who in turn told the doctor. He went back to his office.

With the few hints that Dave might possibly be released sometime soon, I decided to approach Dr. Emery with the question, "When will he be able to come home?"

"Oh, he's still not out of the woods," he aswered.

That night I awoke around 2 a.m., suddenly remembering an insurance brochure in the file box that might tell me how many days insurance coverage we had. Wide awake, I couldn't go back to sleep until I found that handbook.

I turned on the light, located the book, and sat down on the bed. I had no idea where to look and I just began skimming over the pages. I knew there was a limit to days allowed in a hospital, but it hadn't occurred

81

to me until now that it might affect us.

"Seventy days" brought me wide awake. Right there, in print, it said Dave had seventy days hospitalization and *no* convalescent coverage. And *this was the 69th day!*

The next morning Yvonne called me from Mama's house. None of us knew she was planning to visit and the surprise could not be more welcome than it was now. She said she would meet me at the hospital.

Later, as I explained to Yvonne about the insurance coverage, Dr. Emery walked in. "Well," he asked, "What's it going to be, The Village (a convalescent facility) or home?" I was stunned for a moment at the question.

"Ho-home," I stammered. "We don't have coverage for convalescent care." I told him how hard I was willing to work on Dave's recovery. "Dave and I are used to hard work," I said. Furthermore, Yvonne had nursing experience and she was going to stay with us for a while, if Dave could come home.

"He's ready to go whenever you're ready to take him," he said, and he walked out of the room. My mouth dropped open and I turned to look at Yvonne who was standing there smiling. How had Dave gotten "out of the woods" overnight? We had lots of work ahead of us!

Yvonne and I made a list of all the medical supplies we would need: a large box of pads, a urinal, a commode, a plastic sheet to cover the mattress of a hide-a-bed that I was planning to purchase. We needed gauze for cleaning the hole in his neck. We needed a wheelchair.

That afternoon Yvonne and I went shopping. The following day we ran into a snag. Dr. Emergy had neglected to sign Dave's discharge papers and the nurse said Dave couldn't leave until it was signed.

We sat around that afternoon waiting while the nurse tried to track down Dr. Emery at all the other hospitals in Portland where he was on staff. She finally found him – he was in surgery.

The head nurse told us to go ahead and take Dave home. She said she would handle the paperwork and have Dr. Emery sign the next time he came in. On the way out she told me to stop at the ophthalmologist's office. "I left a note on his desk a few weeks ago to come down and check David's eyes again, but he hasn't done it yet," she said angrily. I told her I would take Dave by.

Bill Folk arrived just as we were stashing the final remnants of Dave's personal things into a bag. I gave Yvonne the keys to my car and asked her to bring it up to the emergency room door where it would be easier to get Dave loaded. Bill and Yvonne left together, Bill carrying his TV to his own car. They were then going to meet me in emergency.

Accompanied by a nurse's aide, I took Dave to the doctor's office. With Dave sitting in his wheelchair in the doorway of the doctor's office, the doctor took a small flashlight and looked into Dave's eyes. "Yes, yes. I can see very clearly now. The optic nerve has been destroyed." He said it as if this information were utterly trivial. This was a stunning blow. The doctor stood up and I quickly thanked him for his time.

Swallowing back the tears, I refused to believe what this doctor had just said. One day he said everything was all right. Now he coldly stated that the optic nerve been destroyed. I never knew who I could trust or on what day they could be believed. Dave was a truck driver and he needed both eyes. This had to be a mistake! If he could make a mistake on the first diagnosis, he certainly could make another. I just had to make myself believe that he was wrong.

Silently I pushed Dave's wheelchair to the emergency room as the nurse walked beside us.

Getting Dave into my car was like stuffing toothpaste back into the tube. With Bill working from the driver's side, Yvonne, the nurse, and I worked from the passenger side. Because of his unprotected brain, we had to be careful that Dave didn't hit his head on the frame of the car. I pulled the wheelchair away when Yvonne and the nurse got Dave into a standing position. They pivoted him slowly, and then sat him carefully down on the seat. After getting his legs in and buckling the seatbelt around him, we were on our way.

Bill waved and went to his car. Yvonne climbed into the back seat of my car. We set out on our journey which would at last bring Dave to the destination he had started out for 70 days ago.

I felt confident that everything would work out for us. I had heard about a group of nurses that were available on-call to help families who care for invalids in their home. As soon as I got Dave home I planned to call them and enlist whatever aid they might have for us. I was certain I would be able to get Dave well.

Dave's parents met us with a borrowed wheelchair as we pulled into the driveway.

It was sad to see Cinders walk over and sniff at Dave. Over two months ago, she had run down the long driveway to greet him each morning when he arrived home from work. Now she didn't remember him. Of course, he smelled of the hospital rather than of diesel.

But the children would be home from school in a little while and everything would be back to normal soon.

At least that's what I thought.

XI

Something seemed to click inside Dave as I pulled the car into the garage. Almost before the car was stopped Dave tried to open the door and get out. He was so passive at the hospital, never trying to initiate anything, but now the ride home seemed to have been a stimulus. This day, May 2, was a new beginning for us.

Our home was easily accessible in some ways, but it held some problems. The bottom floor was comprised of a family room and a laundry room with an unfinished bathroom. The garage was adjacent and there were no stairs to hinder getting Dave in and out.

The upstairs level contained the kitchen, bathroom, bedrooms, living room and dining room. For now and until Dave could get up the full flight of stairs to the living area, we were going to live in the basement.

I decided against a hospital bed because of its limited use. The new hide-a-bed I purchased the day before could be opened out at night and folded up during the day, and it was big enough for me to sleep with Dave; I couldn't risk leaving him alone, at least not at the present time.

Dave was still incontinent and would be for some time. Therefore, I covered the mattress and pillow with plastic coverings.

Near the bed I placed a big overstuffed chair with a soft cushion. I remembered the many hours he had spent on that hard chair at the hospital, and I promised myself never to leave him for more than one hour at a time in any one position.

Dave still couldn't move himself from one position to another, so I planned to turn him every two hours throughout the night. This, I hoped, would help those bedsores to heal.

Dr. Emery placed Dave on Dilantin, an anti-seizure medication, and the sedative Phenobarbital. Dave had to take these two pills three times a day for the rest of his life, Dr. Emery had said. I lived in fear of forgetting even one of those pills. I didn't have the slightest idea what to do should Dave have a seizure and I didn't want to learn by experience.

My fear of forgetting something prompted me to make up a daily schedule. Periodically throughout the day I could glance at the chart and know exactly what needed to be done next.

The first night Yvonne and I were surprised by the sudden appearance of my four uncles – Bill, Dennis, and Vonnie, who were my mother's brothers, and Don, my uncle by marriage. They brought a toilet, sink, and medicine cabinet and promptly went to work installing the fixtures in our unfinished bathroom in the basement. They pounded nails, and they pounded on pipes.

In no time at all the four of them bid us adieu and filed out the door.

I was ever so grateful, but at the same time I asked God, How will I ever be able to repay everyone?

For the rest of the week Yvonne helped me learn my routine for the time when I would be left alone. It still took two people to move Dave; I couldn't do it by myself yet. His paralyzed right side was dead weight, and when he was standing it tended to pull him to the right, forcing him off balance. I put the overstuffed chair at an angle by his side of the bed and all we had to do was bring him to a standing position, pivot him to the left and allow him to drop down into the chair. Even yet he couldn't take so much as one step.

Once while he was still in the hospital a nurse became over-confident and tried to transfer him to a chair by herself. She was on his left side and was holding on to his arm when he began leaning to the right. She wasn't strong enough to pull him back to a standing position, so she just had to allow him to drop to the floor. She said she went down with him to cushion his fall, then she called out for help. After that none of the nurses tried to handle him alone.

Even though I had Yvonne helping me now, I knew that was going to stop eventually. She had a husband and children who needed her at home in California. All my other friends and relatives also had families and responsibilities. It didn't seem right for me to ask them to do more for me; they had done so much already.

A few days after Dave's arrival home, the head nurse of north wing called. She volunteered to spend the afternoon with Dave while I did some shopping. I was surprised that someone I knew so little would offer to spend her day off doing extra nursing duties.

I explained to her that Yvonne was staying with me, and that for now all I wanted to do was spend a little time at home. I felt I could finally catch my breath after rushing to the hospital every morning to spend the entire day. Even with all the work at home, I felt as if I had suddenly been given a vacation. I told her how kind it was for her to offer, and I appreciated it very much.

She said, "Many people want to help you, so be sure and take them up on the offer." Then she added, "I know what it's like never to be free of that kind of responsibility. I have a retarded daughter and no one ever relieved me."

I had made so many plans that I was certain I would never feel resentful with Dave's care. I was exuding confidence.

I was pleased when the visiting nurse arrived. She, I thought, would be my source of relief. I showed her through the house while Yvonne took care of Dave. I explained that the therapist had scheduled us for therapy once a week and that I would be taught to perform the exercises on Dave.

The nurse's face was expressionless. She (like Dr. Emery) was another tall, glum-looking person. Her graying hair was pulled tightly into a bun, which made her countenance even more stern. I showed her the rail my uncle Bill had put up along one wall for Dave to use in learning to balance. I showed her the pulley-like contraption that I had attached to a doorframe; when Dave's hands were placed into the two gloves, he could pull his own right arm up by pulling down with his left. I showed her how I had hooked up a small hose to the bathroom basin, so that with a wooden chair sitting over the drain on the floor, I had an improvised shower.

The nurse complimented me on my organization and said that everything looked fine. When she left I just assumed she, or another nurse, would be dropping in on me periodically, or perhaps just giving me a call if only to make sure my standards didn't drop. However, I never saw this nurse or any other one again. Perhaps I was too efficient!

I didn't call the nurses' association again. I became so wrapped up with Dave's care that I actually forgot about them until many months later. From the doctors and other experts I had met, I just assumed they expected Dave to have a rapid recovery and didn't need more extensive care than I could provide. No one told me otherwise, and I assumed if I needed more help it would have automatically been provided. After all, Dave had spent two a and a half months in the hospital and we certainly weren't unknown aliens.

Many years later I learned Dave could have received some sort of physical therapy through the Veterans Hospital, but this possibility was never suggested to me by the doctor or therapist. Unfortunately I didn't think about it myself because I was expecting Dave to progress by leaps and bounds.

I did, however, get bold at one point. Dave had always done the repairs on our TV, and when I brought him home from the hospital the set had blown a fuse. I called a friend whose husband had done some TV work for other people in the area. Dave had also learned some of his TV repair from this man, and since this man was a friend I fully expected him to be willing to repair our TV.

I never heard from the couple again. Perhaps I was a little too aggressive, I thought. Then I realized that everything had been handled for me throughout Dave's hospitalization without my asking anyone for anything. My house was cleaned, my lawn was mowed, and my flowerbeds weeded. God certainly knew what I needed before I did, I realized. I decided then and there that I would try to refrain from asking for favors unless it became an emergency. Anyway, I knew I had to learn to stand on my own two feet – at least until Dave was well again.

I no longer had the time to read as I did while Dave was hospitalized and I was grateful for the time I had already spent reading up on other injured people. However, the one question remained in my mind, *What keeps a family together under such strain?*

The only stories I could find were not actually applicable to us, however. They were about brain-injured children or young adults who had never been married. There were none written about families who experienced a devastating injury to the breadwinner. I wondered how wives coped under such circumstances, and how the adjustment is made with the children.

All I could find were miracles, miracles, miracles. Everyone who wrote a book told of miraculous recoveries. Those that were less than miraculous were stories of single people, or of couples who eventually divorced because their lives had changed – they were different people. It could have been depressing but I refused to allow myself to become discouraged. If God brought us this far, He could certainly do more.

On the fourth day Yvonne went back home. We were on our own.

I was now in charge of the family in every way. I didn't have the nurses at the hospital to take over when I got tired, and I didn't have regular babysitters to care for the children every day. It was now all up to me. I had never been entirely responsible for anyone – not even for myself – and now I had four people depending on me!

Dave was so helpless and I felt so inadequate. What if the house caught on fire? The children were upstairs in their bedrooms at night and I was downstairs with Dave. I wondered who I would give priority to if a fire did occur. If I tried to get Dave out first, the children might be trapped upstairs. If I made my way upstairs to get the children first, Dave could possibly burn to death in the basement. We were a long way from the main highway and there were no water hydrants nearby – only our well. I felt the tears sting my eyes at the thought. But I kept telling myself that God had taken care of us this long, He certainly wouldn't stop now.

I knew I had to be strong. But sometimes I got so *tired* of being strong. When people complimented me on my strength, it only caused me embarassment. *I was doing what I had to do!*

I met a friend at the store. She said, "I really admire you for all you have done since Dave's accident – I couldn't have done it."

"Yes, you could," I replied. "If you had to, you could."

She skeptically shook her head.

Now that Dave was home, it was all sinking in. I had to push all fearful thoughts out of my mind, but I realized I couldn't fool myself. I was in a potentially dangerous situation and I had to stay on guard constantly for the sake of us all.

But soon I found I didn't have time to worry. Each day I rushed to squeeze in all the necessary chores: prepare meals, clean the house, care for the children, do Dave's therapy, make sure the animals were fed. And then try to get enough rest.

Each morning the children dressed for school and then came down to the family room to watch morning cartoons on TV (which I called a repairman to fix). It was at times like this that I enlisted the aid of the children while I went upstairs to make breakfast. They were responsible for taking care of any of Dave's needs until I came back downstairs again.

After the children left for school I sandwiched Dave's therapy between visitors. Every day for the next two months we had at least one visitor. And I took advantage of anyone who happened to drop in.

Although Dave rarely spoke it was good for him to be around people and everyone seemed to enjoy talking to him, helping him recover. I would leave him and his visitors to their one-sided conversations while I went upstairs to load the dishwasher, gather a load of laundry, and start lunch or dinner depending on what time of the day they were visiting.

One day as I cleansed and redressed the hole in Dave's neck with a fresh strip of gauze, I realized the only illnesses I had every coped with were the "usual childhood diseases." How much more complicated this was than a case of chicken pox!

Still, Dave was not acting at all like himself. He never spoke unless someone asked him a direct question. He had been so active before the accident, but now he lay flat on his back in bed most of the day except when I turned him to different positions or sat him in a chair. He showed no desires, no reactions to anything. Whatever position I left him in, he stayed in – until I moved him to another position. He was as helpless as a baby.

Perhaps this should have been an indication to me of greater problems for our future, but I naively excused it all because I knew he was a highly motivated individual. He was just the strong, silent type.

Dave's incontinence problem became the greatest problem at night. I encouraged him to use the urinal during the day and within a few days, he was staying dry. However, at night it was a different story.

We had a heat wave in May that year and the temperature rose to 92° on the 29th breaking a record. For our part of the country, that's hot! This helped me with Dave's care since all he needed for covers at night was a sheet. Blankets would have added to my constant laundry, and I was thankful they weren't needed at the time.

Lisa and Jan had slumberbags, lighter in weight than a sleeping bag and able to be washed and dried by machine. On my side of the bed, over all the bedding, I placed one of the slumberbags, which I then crawled into.

I had a very rude awakening that first night – early. The shock almost threw me out of bed. I felt something warm soak rapidly into the slumberbag and before Dave even knew he was wet I was out of bed in a flash. While half-asleep I threw off the slumberbag and top sheet. I rolled Dave to one side. I stuffed the wet sheet under him along the length of the bed, put a dry sheet on, rolled Dave over onto the dry side, and pulled the remaining half of the fresh sheet over the plastic mattress cover. I threw the wet sheets into the laundry room, got a clean slumber-bag, and was back into bed almost before I was awake. Some nights I'm sure I must have done this in my sleep, for during those first weeks I rarely got a complete night's rest without being awakened at least once.

My laundry now included several loads of queen-sized sheets to be washed and dried each day, along with both slumberbags.

Within three days after Dave's arrivial home from the hospital, I managed to get his bedsores healed. Since the nurses had been unsuccessful in this endeavor for nearly two months, I chose to use tactics different from theirs. All during the hospital stay he was kept unclothed except for the hospital gowns that he was allowed to wear for the last month. Though he was still incontinent, I dressed him in underwear and pajamas. I purchased disposable pads from the hospital to keep under him, but they were irritating to his skin. Even the sheepskin that the nurses placed beneath him didn't help. However, once he began wearing shorts, he stopped scratching at the scabs and with a bit of ointment, he was soon healed.

It had been two and a half months since they shaved his head, and he was in desperate need of a haircut. Since I hadn't taken him out of the house since his arrival, I was afraid to risk taking him to a barber. I decided to cut it myself. I was used to cutting my own hair, but this was different. When I finished, Dave looked as if I had set a bowl on his head.

Hilda said, "The difference between a good and bad haircut is two or three days." We both laughed.

A few months later when I was able to have Dave's hair professionally cut, the barber told me he would have been glad to come to the hospital or to our home to cut Dave's hair if he had known about the accident. I didn't know I could ask for a barber's services at the hospital and no one mentioned the possibility. Under those circumstances that was the last thing on my mind, and perhaps the doctors and nurses felt the same.

I rented all of the physical therapy equipment – the pulley, a four-pod cane, and portable pedals that attached to the wheelchair. Along with my duties as round-the-clock nurse, I became a full-time physical therapist.

After Yvonne left, Hilda came over twice a day to help me get Dave out of bed and then put him back again. Within a couple of days Dave was strong enough that I was able to transfer him from bed to chair without any help at all. Dave was as determined as I for him to become self-sufficient again.

Each morning after the children left for school, I attached the pedals to his wheelchair. Dave must have put many miles on that contraption as he pedaled each morning while I brought order to the family room. He had kept his left leg strong while in the hospital and this was helping now. His left leg did the work and his right leg just went along for the ride. But it, too, eventually became stronger.

In the afternoon as he lay in bed, I worked on his arm by pulling it down to his side. It had tightened up across his chest, bent at the elbow, and it wouldn't stay straight when it was pulled down. It acted as if it was on an invisible spring. As soon as I had it straightened out and let go of it, it would slowly pull back up across his chest once again. The only way to keep his arm down for any length of time was to stretch it out, put a pillow across it, and then sit down gently on the pillow. This was easier than trying to hold it down with the strength of my arms alone – in fact, it took absolutely no effort at all.

The pulley helped to loosen his shoulder joint, though the exercise was extremely painful. This was the only time Dave reacted to pain. As his arm went up, he would flinch, screw his face up in agony, and through clenched teeth say, "Ow!. . .Ow!. . .Ow!" Rather than continue this exercise, I often cut it short. I learned how difficult it is for a family member to help a person adequately in therapy. Occasionally those first few days, Dave's parents helped with his balancing exercise. Rather than force Dave to use his cane, Ken would have Dave drape is arm around his neck which caused Dave to lean on him. "I would rather have Dave use his cane," I said. "He's leaning on you."

"He's not leaning much," Ken would answer. Ken had never accompanied us to the physical therapy sessions nor did he get any instruction from the therapist. To me, leaning seemed to be counterproductive.

However, I found the arm exercise even worse. It would have been easier for me not to force him at all, to protect him from all the pain. I didn't want to watch him suffer, but I gritted my teeth and we continued our daily work-outs. If he was ever going to recover, I knew he had to do his exercises.

Muscle spasms were a regular problem in his right arm. The slightest movement could send it into agonizing pain. His right leg was spastic and would shake uncontrollably when Dave was sitting, unless his foot were placed in a precise location. To stop the shaking, I would move his foot slightly to one side and then to the other, a fraction of an inch at a time, until I found that position where it would rest quietly. Later on, when we began taking him to church, he was known to shake an entire pew with just that one leg.

Dave's fingers were tightly clenched. I had to work each day to loosen the joints and straighten each finger out. His wrist was bent, too, and his hand dropped forward and was useless to him.

When the children were home in the evening, we all worked on the problem of balance. By the second week, Dave had gained enough strength to be able to take steps at the rail, but only in one direction. He grasped the rail with his left hand and I walked slowly beside him, holding on to his right arm in support. When we reached the end of the rail, I had one of the children bring the wheelchair to us. I pivoted Dave, he sat down in the chair, and we went back to the beginning of the rail to start over again. This exercise could only be done when I had help, and the children took turns bringing up the wheelchair.

At mealtime I propped Dave up on the bed with a pillow at his back and one pressed against him on both sides. This helped him learn to balance without any other support. Sometimes he would start to lean to the right because of the weight of his paralyzed side. I watched him throughout meals so that I could prop him back up should he begin to lean to the right. His feet touched the floor, giving him a little more support than the pillows would have done alone. This became another important exercise that was incorporated three times into our daily schedule.

The thought that Dave might stay like this never occurred to me. I learned to live in blocks of time. It was only natural for Dave to recover, I thought. And all I was living for was the end of the year when he would be well again. I never considered the possibility that he might not recover.

I kept track of all the insurance checks, but none were coded "Major Medical." So many people, even the insurance clerk at the hospital, had told me we were covered by major medical so I continued watching for the checks. I decided to call the insurance company again.

A man answered the phone. "Oh, you don't have major medical," he said. "There's a third party clause. When someone else causes the accident, you don't get major medical. We *do* have a letter from you stating this was a two car accident, don't we?"

"Yes, you do," I sighed. Although I understood what I was hearing, I found it difficult to believe. I had tried to stay on top of everything, cover all the bases, as they say. It seemed to have done me no good. Even those people who were supposed to be in a position to advise me proved not to have the facts either.

I called my attorney, Mr. Dyer. Over the next couple of months, Mr. Dyer tried to get the insurance company to cover more medical costs, at least until we knew how much they were going to amount to altogether. The insurance company was adamant. The third-party clause was legal and binding.

XII

Head injuries are complicated to understand and difficult to give a prognosis for. Dave was expected to have some change in personality, but the exact alteration could not be predicted. Each person is different. Every injury is also different.

No one explained to me that the frontal lobe, where Dave received the direct blow, was the motivational center. Years ago it was accepted practice for doctors to perform lobotomies on violent or uncontrollable mental patients. In this procedure, a portion of the frontal lobe of the brain is surgically removed, making an uncontrollable person become docile.

Everything that had happened to Dave was all the more frustrating because his memory was intact. His mind and body had changed. He had to learn to live in a paralyzed body and think with a mind that was different from what he remembered it to have been. Dave rarely communicated these frustrations in those early days, but he struggled in private with them just the same.

I was aware, of course, of the obvious physical problems he had. Then, throughout the following months, I also became aware of the other changes. The first markedly different response I noticed was crying. He cried when he was happy and he cried when he was sad. It took me completely by surprise, for it wasn't like Dave at all. Eventually, however, I became used to it, and I tried to help others learn to accept it.

During Dave's hospitalization most of the information I received came from the nurses. Now I no longer had them to depend on, so I turned to Paul, the physical therapist, who became my informant.

Hilda accompanied me to our first therapy session, which was one week after discharge. Paul put Dave through an exam to see how well he could sit, stand, balance, and then he showed me the tricks to handling Dave without exposing him to too much danger. I remembered the nurse in the hospital who lost control of Dave and went down with him to the floor. "It's okay if he falls," Paul said. "Just don't let him hit his head." This phrase went through my mind so many times, I lost count.

Paul taught me how to dress Dave, and how to teach Dave to dress himself with just his left hand. Paul taught us how to go up and down stairs and how to bring Dave to a standing position after sitting him on the floor, and he also demonstrated the best exercises to loosen the contracture in his right arm.

I arrived home that afternoon thoroughly exhausted from the effort of getting Dave in and out of the car and from the anxiety of having him out of the house for the first time. Dave was exhausted, too. He was still quite weak and not used to the strenuous maneuvers Paul had just put him through.

I had asked Hilda to go with me to that first session, but the following week I didn't ask anyone, in the hope that someone would volunteer. We had visitors every day and usually during the time that we were scheduled for therapy. I took it for granted that someone was bound to come by. The children were all in school and wouldn't be home until we returned that afternoon. I assumed everyone knew we had a standing appointment at this time every week; and perhaps that's why no one came.

I began preparing Dave for the journey. He was so thin that nothing in his closet fit, so I dressed him in a clean pair of pajamas. No one was going to see him but the therapist, after all.

I wheeled Dave to the car and told him we would be going alone. "Now, you're going to have to help me. Do you think we can do it alone?" Dave nodded his head, Yes. I had always depended on him in the past and I discovered I had retreated into that habit. If he had shaken his head, No, I would have gone back into the house and called the therapist to cancel the appointment. Instead, we were on our way!

I buckled Dave's seatbelt and shut the car door. Then I took the wheelchair to the back of the car and struggled to get it loaded. I had to raise it almost waist high to reach the level of the door. Within a couple of weeks my muscles were developed enough that I could load the wheelchair quite effortlessly, but at first it was a real battle.

We got to Paul's office, I remembered he once told me that if I ever had to bring Dave in alone I should drive up in front of the building and honk the horn. "I will come out and help you bring him in." I opted for that solution to the problem.

As I pulled up to a side window, I could see Paul working over another patient. I beeped the horn and waited for him to look up and see the car. He didn't, and we waited. I honked again, more loudly. The horn blared, but Paul didn't even flinch as he continued massaging his patient's back. I waited a few more seconds and then honked the horn one last time. Still he didn't look up.

"Well, Dave, it looks like we're going to have to do it ourselves. Do you think we can?" Dave nodded. I started the engine and pulled the car into the parking lot at the rear of the building.

I got out of the car, walked around to get the wheelchair. But before I opened the door Dave had opened his door and was leaning out. "Dave!" I yelled, running to him. "Wait a minute! I have to get the wheelchair out first!" I noticed he had unhooked his seatbelt, so I buckled him back up and shut the door. If he were going to try again, unbuckling the seatbelt ought to slow him down.

Before I could get to the back of the car, however, he had the seatbelt unfastened, and the door opened, and again he was leaning out. I raced around, buckled his seatbelt once again, punched down the lock on the door, and slammed it firmly shut. "Please, wait!" I ran to the back of the car, opened the hatch, and began pulling the wheelchair out, but again Dave was leaning out of the car and struggling to get his legs to the pavement. *What if he falls out?*

I ran back to Dave once again and buckled him up, locked the door, shut it, and said through gritted teeth, "Don't you get out again!" At the back of the car I grabbed the wheelchair, and gave it a yank. It bounced to the pavement just as Dave had his door unlocked, and he was beginning to lean out again as I roared up with the wheelchair.

I helped him come to a standing position, pivoted him, and helped him sit down in the chair. It was plain to see that Dave was highly motivated to walk, and I was equally eager to help him. There wasn't anything I wouldn't do to accomplish this goal.

When we entered Paul's office, he looked up, "Well, Sharon – why didn't you honk? I would have come out to help you."

"Oh, we managed; it wasn't easy, but we did it."

Paul pushed the wheelchair over to a table and laid Dave down on it. In a moment I had forgotten about the incident in the parking lot; as I observed Paul, I was intent upon learning how to help Dave through his daily exercises.

"Why is Dave paralyzed on the right side?" I asked. "Shouldn't it be on the left?"

"Yes, an injury to the right side of his brain *should* have affected the left side of his body. I asked Dr. Emery about it the other day because I was curious, too," Paul replied.

"What did he say?"

"He said, 'Paradoxically it shouldn't *be*.'"

"That's all he said?"

"That's all." Paul continued straightening Dave's fingers, one finger at a time. He pulled against the palm of Dave's hands as he tried to relax the contracture of Dave's wrist. While he worked, he talked about other patients he was doing therapy on, quadriplegics and paraplegics.

I knew these people had suffered paralysis from a neck or back injury; a head injury usually didn't complicate the problem for them. I didn't understand this at the time, and I began to probe with all kinds of questions: When did their accidents happen, and how long will it take them to recover?

When Paul mentioned a young man who had broken his neck in a swimming accident, I latched onto the subject. Paul patiently answered my usual questions, but then he said, "Sharon, don't ever compare."

I didn't understand it then, but Paul must have been reading my mind. Much later I came to see that he had given me one of the most important pieces of advice that would affect Dave and me for the rest of our lives.

During those early days, I wondered why Dr. Emery hadn't sent Dave to a rehabilitation facility. The only conclusion I could come to was that the other people who were sent were worse-off than Dave. Dr. Emery must be expecting Dave to recover completely, I thought, or he would never have left his therapy up to me to do alone. Paraplegics must be worse, I thought. Then Paul cut into my thoughts, "Hemiplegia, like Dave has, is much worse than being a paraplegic."

There was a bigger question in my mind. Do I believe the physical therapist, or the neurosurgeon? Although I didn't present the problem to Dr. Emery, I assumed he was doing everything necessary for Dave since he was an expert in injuries like this. Dr. Emery would send Dave to a rehabilitation center, if Dave needed one. Dave obviously didn't.

Some time later I learned how wrong I was. *Anyone* injured as Dave had been *must* be placed in extensive and expert rehabilitation classes to enable them to recover as quickly and completely as they can. Families aren't capable of giving that care.

XIII

I didn't have any more trouble getting Dave to our therapy sessions, though no one ever went with us again either. Somehow Dave began to understand that he had to help me by being cooperative, instead of trying to do it all by himself.

Compared to the weeks Dave had spent in the hospital, he was now progressing by leaps and bounds at home. I was excited by my expectations for his recovery. I called Dr. Emery and told him the bedsores were healed; and I told him how Dave could answer correctly any question asked him. I showed Dave pictures of family members; we pored over albums of pictures that he had taken while in the Air Force; I quizzed him about Tennessee Walking horses and he answered as if he was puzzled at why I would ask such simple questions. "Sure, I remember," he would say.

I asked the doctor, while I had him on the phone, "How soon will he be able to resume a normal physical relationship?"

"As soon as he has the desire," he said. Since I was still terrified of this man, I didn't want to risk offending him by disputing this simplistic response. If that's all there was to it, I wondered, why are there healthy people – at least people who haven't suffered a head injury – who have the desire, but can't function normally?

In many ways Dave was like an infant; I felt more like his mother than like his wife. It was as if he had reverted back to his childhood and was growing up all over again. Although I believed the doctor to be all-knowing in Dave's recovery, in this case I remained skeptical. This would be a wait-and-see situation.

Dave and I had two viewpoints on eating. He lived to eat, and I ate to live. He liked to cook, and I liked to cook only when I was in the mood. Now, however, I enjoyed bringing Dave his meals and watching him gain weight. He looked like a concentration camp survivor, with his ribcage showing and the skin on his buttocks hanging in folds. He didn't have an ounce of fat on him.

He was ravenous! Well, I thought, from now on there will be no more cold cereal that had left the cafeteria hot; and no more soft-boiled eggs. I made his breakfasts the way he enjoyed them – everything fried. After his two-month fast, his mind seemed to be completely on food, more than ever before. He'd once had a weight problem, but now my main concern was fattening him up a bit so he didn't look like a walking skeleton. He certainly had no weight problem now.

One problem he did have was that of eating with his left hand, but he managed to get most of the contents of the spoon into his mouth. Dribbles of food left a path up his shirt-front, however, as he struggled to learn to eat all over again. I knew he had to learn these things by practice, and I had to force myself to leave him alone during meals; sometimes the urge to help him became too great. He couldn't handle a knife and fork with one hand, so I stepped in.

One month after discharge, Dave had a follow-up appointment with Dr. Emery. Dave's strength and endurance were still limited, and I presumed the doctor would take that into consideration. After all Dave had been through, the doctor wouldn't make Dave wait long. How wrong I was! We spent two hours in the waiting room before we were ushered in to see the doctor.

Julie had an appointment the same day. I was happy to see the smiling faces of Julie and her father as they sat down in the chairs next to Dave's wheelchair. Julie's father and I got into a discussion on disability insurance. "If only we had taken out that disability policy last fall," I said. "But instead we decided to put in a swimming pool and take out the policy next year. Now, that $500-a-month disability payment looks awfully good."

Julie's father said, "We could never live on $500 a month."

"Five hundred dollars is better than nothing," I concluded. He nodded.

I had looked forward to this visit, with the hope of hearing some encouraging words from the doctor. Why, I don't know, for he had never been one to try to encourage me before. "Well, how are things going?" he asked.

"Fine," I answered. *Say something,* I told myself. But every time I met Dr. Emery, I got tongue-tied and my memory began to malfunction.

"Do you have any questions?"

I came to hear great statements of expectations for Dave; I expected the doctor to examine him carefully, and say, "Ohh . . . Ahh . . ." I didn't know enough about Dave's condition to have formulated questions, and those I did ask were answered by the physical therapist. I couldn't think of a question now if my life depended on it. "No," I managed to say.

Dr. Emery leaned back in his chair and stared into a corner across the room. I waited. Was he through? Should I excuse myself and take Dave home?

At last Dr. Emery started talking. He told about a meeting he had attended at Valley General Hospital just after Dave's discharge. The last five discharges are discussed at this meeting by all doctors on staff; Dave's chart was among those pulled.

The physician who was head-of-staff began with Dave's records; they became so involved with it they never did get to any of the other patients, he said. I could tell Dr. Emery was pleased about this incident; he must be pleased with Dave's recovery, too. Another feather in Dr. Emery's cap, I thought, as I mumbled. "That's wonderful."

I sat in awe of this man; he *was* a genius. Someone had said he was

98

the best doctor this side of Mount Hood.

Then Dr. Emery gave me something to reach for; at last he offered a speculation. In the past he had never said a word about how he expected Dave to recover. The last memory I had of his telling me anything was, "He's still not out of the woods, yet."

Now Dr. Emery said, "He'll be up and around in the next couple of months." I was astonished to have a date predicted, excited at the prospect of seeing Dave walk. It wasn't that I was doubting it would happen; I had just never put a date on when it would occur. Now at least I had a time schedule.

Dave sat through the entire session in silence as if we were talking about someone else.

Dr. Emery rose from his chair, walked over to Dave's wheelchair, and maneuvered it toward the door. I followed them down the hall, fully expecting Dr. Emery to relinquish the chair to me once we had arrived at the entrance to the waiting room, a room overflowing with other patients. But instead, he opened the door and wheeled Dave right on through. I wanted to hide my face from those other people who had been waiting two hours to see the doctor. It was embarrassing for me to watch as the doctor wheeled Dave to the front door and out onto the sidewalk. I wondered if the other patients thought Dr. Emery was leaving.

Oh, well, this was his idea, not mine. I rushed ahead to the parking lot as the doctor pushed Dave down the sidewalk.

I didn't want to take Dr. Emery away from his other patients any longer than necessary so I thanked him and reached down to help Dave stand up so I could get him into the car. Dr. Emery stood by the door of the car and watched until I had Dave safely buckled in the seat. He then went back to his office as I prepared to load the wheelchair.

Dr. Emery was special in another way; someone had told me about his bout with cancer three years before Dave's accident. Dr. Emery knew what it was like to be a patient. Perhaps that's why I found it so difficult to complain or question Dave's recovery. *Who was I to complain?* Dr. Emery was himself a living miracle.

As I jumped into the car I realized what a struggle it was to take Dave anywhere. I always arrived home from our outings completely spent. I put Dave to bed for a nap, and I sagged into a chair.

The generosity of our friends, relatives, and community continued shining through as a check for $430 was presented to us from Powell Valley Covenant Church.

Several of my aunts and uncles, my sister Bonita, and her husband Bill, came out to weed the flowerbeds and mow the lawn. Bill Folk had handled the tedious yardwork while Dave was hospitalized though I never asked him. They all did what had to be done without putting me on the spot to engage and direct them.

Each weekend throughout the entire summer relatives assembled for planting the garden, maintaining it, and sustaining it through harvest. I knew this would please Dave to have his garden producing as if he had done it himself.

We all tried to keep things as normal as possible; we even manipulated some sort of normalcy in a chaotic situation.

The night before the accident Dave had left a pair of loafers sitting in the bathroom in a corner. I passed by those shoes every day, but I left them where Dave had put them. As relatives worked and cleaned around the house, no one ever moved those shoes. One day Phyllis said, "Whenever I go to your house, I look for Dave's shoes in the bathroom. When I helped clean one day, I picked up the shoes, cleaned under them, and put them back." Neither she nor anyone else could bring themselves to put the shoes back into the closet. "We're waiting for Dave to get well, so he can do it himself."

Somehow I felt the same way, and the shoes didn't get back into the closet until Dave came home. I put them away then, but I remember the silent ritual we all fell into. By putting Dave's shoes away, we might have broken the spell of his recovery. Not one of us could bring ourselves to be that person who would cause it by moving the shoes.

Then problems began to develop; Cinders came in heat. I kept her shut in the garage fully expecting her confinement to last three weeks. When Mama came over to help with some yard work, she let Cinders out. As we spent the afternoon waiting for Cinders to come back to the house, I realized I was to blame. I had neglected to tell Mama that Cinders was to be confined to the garage. All I could do was hope for the best.

Cinders returned; a couple of months later she had eight puppies to feed and tend to. Four weeks later, *I* had eight puppies to feed and tend to; they were growing rapidly and needing more nourishment than Cinders could supply. Besides, I suspect she was tired of the responsibility and wanted some relief.

Those little mouths were like vacuum cleaners, scooping up the food I put down for them. One day I ran out of their regular regimen. In desperation, I heated a can of pea soup in the hope they would eat it. I needn't have been concerned, I realized in amazement, watching them gobble it up so fast that I don't believe they even tasted it.

When they were six weeks old, I placed an ad in the paper and each little puppy went to a kind and loving family. So ended that responsibility.

It was during those gardening "parties" that I explained to the fellows another problem, one I was anticipating. Just above us on the hill where our home stood, there was a field of broccoli with what seemed like hundreds of little troughs between rows, aimed directly at the house.

Dave had dug trenches along the upper portion of the yard, to keep us from being nearly washed away when the fall and winter rains came. The trenches diverted the water around the yard to a drainage ditch under the driveway, which then took the run-off into the creek at the base of the hill. Now Dave could no longer dig those trenches, and I didn't have time, with the amount of work I had to do for Dave's care.

But the men pitched in and did it for me. Afterwards, I went into the living room, where Dave was lying on the sofa. I was feeling pleased with myself for having thought of cleaning out the trenches so far ahead of time. "Well, we're all set for winter. The trenches are all dug out," I said.

"I clean them out five or six times a year," he answered. Although Dave rarely talked and it was good to hear him rattle off a whole sentence at once, I didn't relish hearing this one. All I could do was pray for a dry winter.

Bonita's son, Dan, eased the load a bit for me that summer, when he moved in to spend the next three months until college started that fall. I had spent a month alone with Dave, and now it was a comfort to have another adult in the house, to know that there was someone to leave Dave with when I had to do the marketing, and to have someone closer to my age to talk to.

Dave could talk, but he rarely did. Even though we had company every day for short visits, I still grew hungry for adult conversation. Moreover, Dan entertained the children and got into regular Monopoly games with Steve. He brought some normalcy into our house when nothing was really normal.

Still, I fully understood I was the only one who could be entirely responsible; the only person who could oversee it all; I couldn't drop it onto Dan's shoulders completely, no matter how much I would have wanted to – not even for the hour or two that it took me to get our weekly groceries. All the time Dave was in the back of my mind and I knew I had to hurry back. Even when I was asleep, I was on edge, ready for any crisis, any disaster.

I found I could never be entirely prepared, however. It was a shock to us all when Cinders was killed shortly after all her puppies had been given away. Dave and the children cried. I brushed away a tear of sorrow, and plunged headlong into my daily chores. The crushing in my chest was a reminder of our latest grief.

Whenever I took Dave out into the sunshine, I checked the dilation of his pupils. They both got smaller in the bright light, and promptly got bigger when I took him inside the darkened house. I still didn't believe the ophthalmologtist had made a correct diagnosis. Both of Dave's eyes looked normal to me and reacted together.

I covered Dave's left eye with my hand. "Can you see now?"

"No," he responded.

I remained puzzled.

On our first follow-up visit to see Dr. Barrett I decided to ask him about Dave's eye, even though his field was plastic surgery and not ophthalmology. Until now I hadn't mentioned any of this to either Dr. Barrett or Dr. Emery, and I suddenly felt compelled to tell Dr. Barrett. He was easier to talk to.

Dr. Barrett looked into Dave's eye. "A healthy optic nerve is pink," said Dr. Barrett. "One that has been destroyed is white. David's is white." I swallowed hard at that announcement, blinking back tears as Dr. Barrett said, "David, I wish I could give you a pill to snap you out of this." Though he couldn't wish for that any more than I did, I heard the compassion coming through his voice. This was one of the kindest doctors I had ever met. Other doctors may have empathy for their patients, but rarely do they verbalize it. It was nice to hear Dr. Barrett express his feelings.

"What did he hit to have caused so much damage to his face, but not to leave a bruise?" I asked. Somehow, with Dr. Barrett I began to think up questions.

"The other doctors and I have discussed it, but we don't know. We just don't know." Dr. Barrett checked over Dave's right arm, trying to get reflexes. He was concerned about Dave's wrist. It was bent at a right angle. "We can do surgery on his wrist," he said. "We can take the strong tendons in the inside of his wrist and transfer them to the back of his arm. This will force his wrist back rather than inward. That can be decided at a later date, however."

Dr. Barrett and Dr. Emery were like day and night. The inspection Dr. Barrett gave Dave was what I had expected from Dr. Emery. Dr. Emery, however didn't leave his chair the entire visit, except when he got up to wheel Dave out of the office. Dr. Barrett checked Dave over very carefully. I asked Dr. Barrett, "Will you be helping with the surgery when Dave has the plate put in?"

"I can," he answered, "if you want me to."

"I do."

On the drive home I thought about what Dave might have hit at the moment of impact. The right side of his face was crushed and the car came at him from the left. Dave had to have been looking to the left. Bill Folk said he and Dave talked about what they would do if they were ever involved in a collision. They agreed that they would brace themselves for the impact. Dave had bent the steering wheel in half. The windshield was shattered, but not broken out. He must have hit the wildshield with the right side of his head, I concluded. The question of why he didn't have any bruises on his face would remain, however.

Dave had been on his way home. He had a lot to live for, and somehow nothing was going to prevent him from getting there.

XIV

I heard about a young father in our community. He had a wife and two small sons. In the spring of 1972 he learned he had cancer. His doctor acknowledged the condition to be far advanced and inoperable. After exploratory surgery, the doctor sent him home to await the inevitable outcome – death. The young man was not going to give in easily, however. He and his wife approached the elders of their church and hoped for a miracle. The elders anointed the man with oil and prayed over him according to scripture and asked the Lord to heal him.

I had just brought Dave home from the hospital when I heard about this young family. I was full of hope and inspiration for all of us. Not only was Dave going to recover, but this other man would overcome his bout with cancer. We just had to have enough faith, and that was something I had a great supply of.

A few months later I learned the young father had died. I was shocked and bereaved even though I didn't know this couple. I remembered how I felt when I feared Dave was going to die, and now I felt guilty that my husband had survived and this other man had not. I was grateful to have my husband home with me, but I wondered why Dave had been given back to us and another man had been taken from his family. I didn't know how I could ever begin to understand all of this; the point, the purpose, the answers.

That weekend in July, Dan went to the beach with some friends. I, too, felt the boredom of being cooped up in the house all day long. Dave and I spent grueling hours in therapy, rebuilding muscles, and learning to stand straight and tall with a cane. Instinctively, we began pushing each other to our limits. "Is there anything you would like to do that you don't think you can? Maybe I can help you."

"Yes. I want to go upstairs." That should have been obvious to me, I thought. The basement had never been used much except as a playroom for the children, and Dave had not been upstairs since he came home.

I had given Dan the master bedroom. The children also slept upstairs; going upstairs would bring another grain of normalcy to our lives. I realized how much I yearned to be upstairs, too; to look out the front windows and see Mount Hood as the sun changed the snow from white to pink, sometimes to purple, and to watch the clouds settle over the peak, making it look as if it were preparing to become once again an active volcano.

I guided Dave as we walked toward the staircase. He reached for the rail and I took his cane to the front entry landing. I walked behind him as he held the rail which was on his left side. He reached for the cane as we neared the landing and then I glanced up at the next flight of stairs. *The rail was now on his right! Oh, no. I'd forgotten about the rail being on the other side of the wall.* "Dave, we'd better go back down. The rail's on the wrong side. I forgot, Dave; I'm sorry." Just then the phone began to ring.

As the phone continued ringing Dave insisted, "Yes, we can. I want to go upstairs!" The ringing of the phone was irritating, but I couldn't risk leaving Dave to answer it. Dave shouted, "Go answer the phone!"

"Whoever it is can call back," I shouted right back. "Are you *sure* we can do this?" I still trusted Dave's instinct more than my own.

"Yes! I want to go upstairs." Dave reached out for the wall on his left and then I realized that going back down the stairs we had just ascended would be as hard as going up the rest of the way. In either case the rail was going to be on his right! I rushed up the stairs with the cane and placed it at the top of the stairwell.

I took my position behind Dave as he began to climb. He stepped up with his left leg and then slowly brought his right leg up onto the stair. His balance was so bad that he would teeter with even the slightest movement and I hung on to him in sheer terror. These steps were much steeper and the heavy carpeting added to the danger of slipping or of his losing his balance. Each step upward separated us by two stairs, thereby making him even that much taller than I. He already was a foot taller, and this increased it by another half-foot or more.

I looked up and saw him towering high above me and suddenly I realized I had no control over him. I remembered the words from Paul, "It's okay if he falls, but don't let him hit his head." Now there was a danger of his flipping backward, right over my head. I supported him in the only way I knew, by putting my right hand on the rail, my left firmly against the wall, pressing my head against his buttocks. I put all my concentration on climbing those stairs.

"Don't push! Don't push!" Dave shouted. Through gritted teeth I shouted right back at him, "I have to!" I was trying to keep him balanced, but didn't realize I was throwing him off balance by pushing so hard. all I could think of was the danger of his falling over backward. Finally we managed to reach the landing. I helped Dave to the sofa in the living room.

And then I collapsed onto the floor in a heap, and started laughing. Dave glared at me. "How can you laugh at a time like this?"

"Would you rather I cried?" He didn't answer. I knew Dave's condition was no laughing matter, and the resulting situation I was in was certainly not funny. Now that we were upstairs, however, I could not help but see the humor of the near disaster on the stairs. If a stranger had peered in the doorway at us, I'm sure he would have been confused as to why we were climbing the staircase the way we were. It just struck me as funny.

Later that afternoon I called my uncle Bill and asked him if he would move the railing from the family room wall to the stairway.

By the time Dan came home the following day, I had made the decision to move back into the master bedroom and move Dan downstairs to the family room. My uncles installed the rail and Dave was now able to get up and down stairs with my help.

We made an adjustment to Paul's instructions on climbing stairs. Paul wanted Dave to start down with his strong left leg, but Dave's weaker right leg consistently became caught on the stair and he couldn't bring it down. I chose to have him step down on his weak right leg and then lock his right knee for support. Then he brought his left leg down on the stair beside the right one. It worked!

Dave enjoyed being upstairs. The first thing he wanted to do was rummage through the refrigerator. He said he didn't want anything; I think he just wanted the satisfaction of doing it once again – perhaps to check out what was in there in case he did want something later. Since he had very little balance, I had to follow him and hold on to him wherever he went.

I wasn't used to telling Dave what to do and I found it hard to take over the role of being in command. I wanted so desperately to have Dave back the way he had once been and I believed he was no different than the man I remembered just before the accident. Even in his present condition, I still trusted his choices over anyone else's.

Slowly, however, I was beginning to evolve into someone else; someone a little more independent; someone who was becoming a risk-taker. I had always been fearful of making mistakes. Rather than expecting to learn from my mistakes, I thought of myself as a failure whenever I made one. I learned that from my mother. Rather than take an unnecessary risk, she would try not to go ahead with the task, or ask someone else who was more capable.

There was a part of that in me, and another part that didn't want to relinquish a challenge to someone else.

Going through a change was also difficult for me. I hated the transition that change brought about; it was painful and required effort. But Dave's condition brought out something more in me. I was willing to try anything and take the chance that whatever I did could be the motivational force to make Dave get well that much faster.

Dave was seeing a "new" me, too. Sometimes he wasn't so sure he liked what he saw.

The "world" we lived in was dictated by our religious beliefs. The husband is the head of the family; he makes the decisions; he's the authority figure. I had always willingly gone along with this lifestyle.

Dave was much more worldly than I; his common sense was better developed. I respected his intelligence, and was thankful to have him as my husband; someone I could count on, and someone I could lean on.

But now my budding strength had come into full bloom. I vowed to take over the reins of our household until Dave was fully capable of having them back. My great lack of self-esteem began to transform. I could, and would, do anything for Dave.

Dave was lying on the sofa one afternoon as usual. I was fixing lunch, peeking in at him occasionally. He didn't have enough strength in his body to sit at the kitchen table so I brought a tray into the living room for him. He looked at me and said, "You've changed, and I don't like the change."

I was taken by surprise as I set the tray down in front of him. But I said, "That goes both ways. You've changed and I don't like your change any better." Dave didn't respond to this statement, and just focused in on the lunch in front of him. Food could make him forget anything.

I realized that I wasn't the girl he had married, and there was a possibility I never would be again. At the age of 28 I had suddenly become someone else. Dave was no longer the man I once knew, either. I didn't know it then but those beautiful, golden years before the accident would never return. Even now they seemed light years away, as if it all had happened in another lifetime. Our lives were permanently and irreversibly changed.

I don't know if I could have faced the knowledge of that during those first years after the accident. As stubborn as I was I'm certain if someone had told me, I would not have believed it. I remained tightly clinging to hope.

In many ways I was blinded by Dave's continued and rapid progress. After being on a catheter for so long, I just assumed it would be a matter of time before he regained bladder control. By the middle of July he had perfect bladder control and near-perfect bowel control. Taking him out of the house was less a challenge now since I didn't have those two problems on my mind.

Can you imagine how I feared being in the middle of town with no bathrooms nearby and having Dave in urgent need of one? That would lead us to the nearest gas station. For handicapped people, and others with physical problems of various kinds, finding a restroom while shopping can be a major problem – and there are not always gas stations located nearby! For the first time in my life I became aware of the obstacles that face the disabled every day.

However, we tried not to let obstacles get in our way. My uncle and aunt arrived from Denver; another aunt came from Nebraska; and an uncle from Los Angeles. All my mother's brothers and sisters living in Portland planned a family gathering at the airport to meet those arriving. I wasn't about to be left out. The activity and stimulus were just what Dave needed. Although there are wheelchairs at the airport, Dave refused to be put into one. He wanted to walk from the main door to each gate. I relinquished Dave at the airport to my uncles and they took over his responsibility while we were there.

At home Dave had refused to use the wheelchair. I put it in a corner, under the assumption he would change his mind after he saw how difficult it was to get from one place to another. Just to go to the bathroom, he had to have someone walk behind him holding him erect since he still had poor balance. But Dave continued to insist that he wanted to walk wherever he had to go, no matter how far the distance or how long it would take him to get there. His steps were agonizingly slow, and I tried to control my impatience. In a wheelchair I could have him at the destination in much less time than it took him to walk it. However, I couldn't change his mind; so I did as he wanted, and eventually gave the wheelchair back to the people who had lent it to us.

Dave didn't like giving in to his paralysis, and he was determined to walk. He didn't want to be dependent on people, and he struggled hard for this renewal of his independence, a quality of his personality that was so familiar before the accident.

I was determined to stimulate him with a new situation at least once a week. Sometimes I forgot about past disasters, and plodded ahead towards getting us into another pickle.

One afternoon while Dan was out for the day, I was working on Dave's fingers, trying to get them to loosen up and straighten out. When he yawned or tensed up his fingers drew up into a fist; his arm was spastic and it was impossible to keep his fingers relaxed and unflexed. "Is there something you would like to do that you don't think you can?" I had forgotten how much trouble we had climbing the stairs that first day, and I was determined still to help Dave do things that were important to him.

"Yes, I want to take a bath." My mind flashed a picture of how wonderful I felt while soaking in the tub; I couldn't imagine spending my life only taking showers and never getting into a bathtub. That was where I did a lot of reading while languishing in steaming water and oils.

I prepared the water for Dave's first tub bath. But as I helped Dave sit down in the tub, I had an immediate premonition of trouble.

We had a glass shower door which could be pulled to the extreme right or left, but either direction it was pulled it would be in Dave's way when he got out. He could not get hold of the side of the tub to pull himself out; the glass door was directly beside his elbow.

Paul had instructed me on getting Dave off the floor and I had successfully accomplished the task. All I had to do was stand in front of him, put my right foot in front of his right foot so it wouldn't slip, place my hands under his arms and pull him forward toward me. With this action, Dave would automatically begin to rise until he was in a standing position. I had strength I never knew I had before. Now, I realized I couldn't use that maneuver to get Dave to a standing position. There was barely enough room for Dave in the tub and certainly none for me.

I studied the bathtub. Dave couldn't use his right arm; it would be of no help to him at all. He had to stand up with only the use of his left arm. I pushed the glass to either side of the tub, and asked Dave to try to pull himself to a standing position. He couldn't do it. The porcelain was getting harder by the minute and he was getting eager to get out.

I ran the water out to eliminate any drag from its weight on Dave's body. I placed a towel beneath his feet to allow for friction, so his feet wouldn't slip. Nothing seemed to help, however. Dave struggled, and I felt a stab of helplessness.

I remembered Paul telling me, "If he ever falls and you can't get him up, call the fire department. They handle situations like that." I knew Dave would be furious at such an event, but I thought I had no other choice. "Dave, I'm going to have to call the fire department to get you out." He virtually exploded. He couldn't talk much yet, but he could certainly swear. Each curse came out between sobs and sputters as he cried, tears running down his cheeks. The sobs, sputters, and tears were normal reactions to everything, but the profanity was unusual. "Shh, shh. Okay, I won't call the fire department, but you'll have to try to help me." He nodded.

This time I got into the back of the tub with one foot on either side of him in a straddle. I pushed him forward until his knees were bent which allowed enough room for me to stand solidly behind him. He grasped the side of the tub as I began to push against him, and almost miraculously he began to rise up.

I kept pushing until he reached up and grabbed the shower nozzle. He then pulled himself into a standing position. I kept holding him until he was standing solidly upright.

I couldn't believe I had done what I did. He was standing! I grabbed the towel and helped Dave step out of the tub. I made a silent agreement with myself that this was the last bath until he could get out by himself. Showers could get him just as clean, and they were much easier.

As closely as I tried to monitor him, he did things without my knowledge. While cooking meals, I would come in to the living room to find him in a different chair than when I had left. *I thought I put him in the other chair. How did he get to this one?* Sometimes I left him on the sofa only to find him in a chair when I returned from a minute or two in the kitchen. "How did you get here?"

"I walked,"" he replied.

"You shouldn't try to walk unless someone is around to help." I might as well have remained silent; he paid very little attention to my suggestions.

One afternoon as I was getting lunch, Dave was sitting on the sofa in the living room, watching TV. Suddenly I heard a loud thud which virtually shook the house. It sounded like an explosion; I glanced into the living room. Dave was gone!

I turned toward the screen door which led out onto the deck; it was open. The deck was a full flight of stairs to the ground. I flew to the door visualizing Dave lying in a heap at the foot of the stairs. Paul's words came at me, "It's okay if he falls, but don't let him hit his head." A fall like this would most certainly kill him.

I could hear whimpering as I neared the doorway, and then I saw him lying on the deck, trying desperately to get to his feet. He lay there on his side, helplessly squirming. I kneeled down and maneuvered him to a sitting position so I could help him up. He had tried to go outside, but could not manage even one stair without someone to help him keep his balance. I helped him to his feet, and then back to the living room. He sobbed and sputtered as he sank down in the chair and I scolded him, "Don't ever do that again." I checked him over and could see nothing but an abrasion on his elbow.

A few days later I was in the kitchen again when I glanced up to see Dave walking toward me through the doorway. I nearly gasped, but I managed to keep myself in check. I didn't want to scare Dave and cause him to lose his balance. He had an intent expression on his face as he concentrated on his careful steps.

As he entered the kitchen, he looked at the countertop as if he was going to lean against it, but it was on his right side. I could tell he was much too far away from it to even try it, and I began to walk slowly toward him. As I neared him, he began leaning to the right as if in slow motion. There was a startled look on his face as he suddenly realized he was going to fall. I rushed to him and tried to push him back up, but it was too late. I had to let him go down as gently as I could.

He dropped slowly to the floor with me holding on to his right arm and going to the floor with him. He let loose with profanity and tears as I sat down beside him. I waited while he cried, stammered and sputtered. He couldn't be of any help to me while he was so angry, so I had to wait it out.

Once he had cooled off, I helped him stand. Though he was angry at what he considered failure, I was pleased. His ability to walk was increasing day by day and it wouldn't be long before he would be walking by himself again.

XV

Every day brought new problems. I came down with 24-hour flu. The nausea left me reeling and I kept my post near Dave by lying on the floor beside the sofa where he lay.

Other things, besides me, began to break down, too. I had been so dependent on Dave to fix everything with an electrical function, and now I felt lost. The dryer broke; the kitchen sink clogged; the lawnmower gave its last sputter and died.

I had to learn to delegate. I didn't want to impose on the same person all the time to do my repairs, and I couldn't bring myself to call a repairman. I called my brother-in-law Bill to repair the dryer. I called my uncle Bill to unclog the sink.

That spring when it was time to move the cattle, I called those who knew how to move livestock. But October brought me another problem.

On October 31 our cow had a calf. This added another living thing for me to take care of. I had never been a cow-hand in the past and I didn't want to become one. Our little calf was a bull, and I knew enough about them to know he would have to be turned into a steer; our goal for him was to end up in our freezer. I knew something had to be done soon. At the time of Dave's accident we were buying milk from a friend who raised a small herd of milk cows. I called him and asked if he would come over and turn our baby bull into a steer. I knew I would be forever grateful to all those people who not only did things for me without asking, but also those who willingly helped me when I asked.

Mr. Dyer, our attorney, also became a friend as the months passed. "Please call me Les," he said (as his protectiveness seemed to increase toward us.)

The circumstances surrounding the accident became, after the fact, more complex. We had started a suit against the man who hit Dave, but soon learned he received a re-call letter from the manufacturer of his car two months after the accident. The major effort for recalling these cars was started the month of the accident, and the information regarding the accident pointed to this automobile defect.

Les said the man who owned the car had property, but a lawsuit would merely ruin him financially. We would recover very little in the end. The suit was dropped, and another drawn up against the manufacturer of the car that hit Dave.

I didn't look forward to a legal battle, but I felt it was my duty to Dave and our children to follow through with it. If I didn't do everything possible, I feared I might always wish I had. Les said it would cost up to $7,000.

I thought it through. That was a lot of money, but I felt I had to take the risk. Money couldn't bring Dave back to the man he once was, nor be a replacement for his right arm and leg, nor restore the damaged portion of his brain. It could, however, make life a little easier for him to endure.

In addition, we filed a second suit. This one was against the highway department for not maintaining highway safety on that section of highway, where innocent drivers should have been protected from the dangerous curve. A divider could have bounced the car away from the on-coming traffic rather than directing it into its path.

Money was more important to me now than before. We had to have enough to pay legal costs after the medical bills were all covered.

The secretary of Dave's union called. He wanted to know how much longer the insurance company would have to pay out on Dave's medical bills. "They're getting on my back," he said.

I was infuriated by that remark; Dave was supposed to be covered by this company no matter how much it cost. They were supposed to be with us in a time of need. They were supposed to help me, rather than cause me further anguish. At least that was what I thought. This was the man who told me the second day after the accident, "Don't get an attorney. You can't afford one, and you probably won't need one."

Trying to keep my anger under control, I explained how seriously Dave had been injured. I remembered Dave had always considered this man a friend, but this was the first phone call he had made about Dave and it was only because the insurance company was on his back, as he put it.

After listening to me describe Dave's condition and pending lawsuit he said, "I remember telling you not to settle too fast."

I said nothing in response to this statement; he had said nothing of the kind. It was principally because of him that I didn't get an attorney right away. That, in turn, caused another problem.

When I did hire Les to represent us legally, he went to the junk yard where the other car had been taken after the accident. I kept Dave's car at a friend's home, and didn't consider the ramifications of losing the other car at the junk yard. Les said it had been entirely dismantled within that month, and he couldn't find a scrap of evidence that it had even existed. If I had hired Les immediately after the accident, this problem would not have developed. Now how could we verify the defect that caused the accident? It would have to be proven to a jury by other means.

"The insurance company is lucky in one respect," I said to the union secretary. "Since the wreck was a two-car accident, they don't have to pay the major medical. They're getting off easy on this one, and I'm having to pay more."

He answered, "Well, you do have to admit they paid a large portion

112

of the bills."

"Yes, I guess I do have to admit that. But I still don't like it. I don't like taking the money from the insurance company, and I wish none of this had ever happened. But, I think you should realize I have no control over the mounting medical costs. Coverage is part of the insurance benefits you worked so hard to provide for Dave's union." When we said good-bye, I don't think he liked me any better than I liked him. We never heard from him again.

If Dave had caused the accident the insurance company would have been out much more money – the major medical which amounted to an additional $25,000.

Les suggested I check over each hospital statement to be sure we weren't accidently being charged for more than Dave received. After I began scanning the long pages of equipment used, bandaids and dressings applied, treatments administered I realized there was no possible way I could detect an error. I paid the hospital without question the amount that was listed on the bottom of the invoice.

I continued trying to add further stimulus to Dave's life by taking him back to church. In the past months Lisa and Jan were either picked up by a family who lived nearby and attended our church, or else they spent the weekend with Bonita. I realized now it was time for us to start back as a family.

The congregation greeted us warmly. It was plain that they were glad to see Dave; they had spent many Sundays praying for his recovery and now they could see the result. Nearly everyone felt Dave was a living miracle.

Friends from church called me occasionally. "You must be so happy," they would say. I reluctantly said I was; I couldn't bring myself to admit to the constant ache in my heart. My strong, handsome husband was terribly crippled, and I didn't see how anyone could expect me to be happy about that. They did, however. They expected me to be happy just to have him alive and breathing no matter what condition he was in. My beliefs were different than that; there were some things worse than death.

The moment I stepped into the church building and sat down in the last row next to Dave and the children, I felt a tug at my throat and the ache in my heart. The organ music filled the room and the rush of tears dropped uncontrollably onto my cheeks. I had always had so much control over my emotions, but now they took over.

I tried to think of other things, happier times. When Pastor Wickman announced a song for the congregation, I helped Dave to his feet. As I opened my mouth to sing the lovely hymns that had always given me comfort, I couldn't make a sound. The songs reminded me of the pain and suffering surrounding the entire world, rather than of the beauty I had always seen.

Even at home I found myself bombarded with painful memories. Healthy people on the Christian Sunday morning radio programs reminded us to count our blessings and be ever mindful of the wonderful things that were happening to us every day. Dave's disability was always forefront in my mind. How could I learn to be thankful for that?

And the TV commercial that always cut into my faraway thoughts, "When you have your health, you have everything." That was something I couldn't agree with more, but I didn't want to be reminded every day. Rather than all of this making me appreciate my own health, I just focused in more on Dave's disability and my growing disappointment in the rate of his progress. It was agonizingly slow.

Still, by the end of September Dave had proved Dr. Emery's prediction correct. He was walking and needed only a cane for support.

Our next appointment with Dr. Emery was at the end of September. I walked slowly behind Dave as he made his way down the long hall toward Dr. Emery's office. Dr. Emery's nurse stepped into the doorway of her office, and I looked up to see Dr. Emery standing near the end of the hall outside his office door. The two of them were watching Dave as he limped slowly toward Dr. Emery. I was pleased that Dave had reached the doctor's door without any help from me to steady him.

Then Dr. Emery broke the silence, "Well, David . . . All I've got to say is you've got a good nurse." What a compliment, coming from Dr. Emery, I thought.

The three of us went into Dr. Emery's office and sat down. "Do you have any questions," Dr. Emery asked.

This time I was a little more prepared than I usually was when I met the doctor. "Yes," I responded. "When are you going to put the plate in?" There was a long pause as Dr. Emery gazed at the wall and leaned further back in his chair. "Will it be soon?"

"Yes," he answered. Again a long pause.

"Are you waiting until he's ready?"

"Yes." The conversation seemed to be over. I managed to get caught up in a multiple choice set of questions and nearly ended up answering my own questions.

I mentioned Dave's eye and the fact that Dr. Barrett had confirmed the damaged optic nerve. With that information Dr. Emery rose from his chair and as he walked toward Dave, he pulled a small flashlight from his pocket. He looked into Dave's eye. He nodded his head as he walked back to his desk; he then reconfirmed Dr. Barrett's diagnosis. Although Dave's right eye looked healthy and identical to his left one, he would never be able to see out of it again. The optic nerve no longer functioned.

Dr. Emery sat back down at his desk, and pointed to a book on a shelf

114

near a bookcase where I was sitting. "Bring me that book." I got the book from the shelf and handed it to him. He opened it to a picture of a cross-section of a brain.

Dr. Emery pointed to the base of the brain where there is a cross-over point. The impact of the accident forced Dave's brain to the back of his skull and the added damaged occurred on the left side. This caused the right-handed paralysis, he said.

I realized then if he had only suffered the frontal lobe injury, he very likely would not have been paralyzed at all. Dr. Emery handed me back the book and I set it back on the shelf.

He then started talking about Julie. He explained how he discovered the deterioration of her skull; how the cancer had caused it to become paper-thin. A slight blow to the head from a fall or tumble while playing could have killed her. Here was another patient Dr. Emery had saved. I knew I couldn't have gotten a better doctor if I had asked for anyone special. I remembered how Dr. Emery had been at Valley General Hospital when Dave was brought in. There was even the possibility that Dave might have been taken to another hospital where another doctor would have cared for him. Dr. Emery was the best, I thought, and I was so glad that Dave's path crossed with his.

Throughout the months Dave had been complaining about his vision, "Do we have a black and white TV or one with color?" When I told him it was a color set, he responded he could only see in black and white. One evening while we were watching the news I asked, "What color tie does the newsman have on?" Dave answered correctly, "Red." I couldn't understand this, and Dave couldn't reason it out either.

Since he began talking more, I noticed his thought capacity was limited. His intelligence seemed the same, but he was slow to respond. It was a mental struggle for him to try to reason something out, or to communicate more than one sentence at a time. His attention span was limited and in mid-sentence, if something distracted him, he would forget what he was going to say.

If we were outside and he began to tell me something at the moment an airplane went over (or a truck drove by), he would fasten his eyes on the moving object or search the skies overhead. "What were you saying, Dave?" He would look perplexed and give a helpless shrug of his shoulders, "I don't remember."

While he was watching TV he could start a sentence, a sudden noise from the television program could grab his attention, and I knew he would never remember what he was going to say.

When I knew he was going to be stopped midsentence, I wanted to say, "Keep talking . . . keep talking," but that was just as distracting for him. It was terribly frustrating for me to listen to half-sentences, knowing he would never remember what had been so important just a moment or two before.

There wasn't much to do about his memory, but I did complain to the doctors about his vision. The ophthalmologist prescribed reading glasses. There wasn't a thing he could do about the color perception, but since his vision was 20/40 in his left eye, the glasses would help him read a little. With vision as bad as that there was a great possibility he would never drive again – not even our own car. He understood this and he refused to believe it. In one breath he would say, "I can see just fine." In the next breath he would say, "I can't see anything, everything is so dark." Even in the brightest sunlight he complained of the dark; yet at the same time, he shaded his eye from the brightness.

He began his days moaning and groaning, and ended them the same way. When I asked, "What's wrong?" he responded, "Nothing," and went back to the groaning once again.

Dan enrolled for the fall term at college and moved back home. The children started school, and we no longer had our daily visitors. They came fewer and farther between. When I cleaned the bedroom, Dave would call my name over and over until I came to see what he wanted. When I got to him and asked him what he needed, he would say, "I just wanted to know what you were doing." This repeated itself over and over throughout the months. I couldn't ignore him because he might truly need something.

He said one day, "I'm sick and you have to take care of me." What a strange thing for him to say, I thought. This didn't sound like him at all. In eleven years he only took off one night's work for being sick. He went to work whether he was sick or not.

I responded, "I don't have to do anything I don't want to do." As usual, he had no reply. Anything more than a couple of sentences were difficult for him to follow in his mind.

Still trying to stimulate him, I took him and the children to see the "Sound of Music" at a theater in Portland.

Dave reveled in the huge screen and then sobbed quietly that he could see color. He was happy. After a few minutes he grew irritated. The picture went from color to black and white, he said, and remained that way for the duration of the movie. It was frustrating for me since I sat beside him and watched the entire movie in color. I wondered what his brain was doing to him that caused colors to appear and then disappear.

During the wedding scene he began to cry. He cried whether he was happy or sad. At home I encouraged the children to ignore him when he cried during TV programs, and I did the same. Now, however, it was impossible to do. People started to stare. I passed him tissues to blow his nose. "Come on, Dave. Let's go outside for a minute," I said, reaching for his arm, but he pushed my hand away.

"No! No! No!" His sobs became louder and he dabbed at his nose. The organ music became louder; the children were sinking into their seats from embarrassment.

"Come on, Dave. Just for a minute." I reached for his arm again, but he pushed me away again as me sputtered, "No!" By now the organ music was drowning Dave out and the gawking people were turning back to the movie. I sank back in my seat and realized I would have to sit this one out. There was no way to get him to leave without making a bigger scene then he was making now.

The rest of the movie was less emotional for Dave, and we managed to get through it with no more tears. I was exhausted and angry; angry at myself for not anticipating this problem before we came. From now on I knew I would have to check all future movies for sadness and violence or anything that might bring out Dave's enthusiasm. Anything shocking or surprising would bring him to attention with loud ooh's and other exclamations of equal intensity.

Later Dave admitted his own feelings. "All I do is cry," he said between sobs.

As much as I wanted to help Dave, to help him reach his full potential, I realized there was no time left for me.

In the past my life had revolved around Dave and the children. All I wanted out of life was to have a family and a successful marriage. Now I felt as if the doctors expected me to put everything into Dave's recovery. None of them seemed to realize I was a human being, too, and needed to have some time to myself, an hour or two a week just to indulge myself in something frivolous.

I felt guilty when I wasn't giving Dave my all. That seemed to be my only purpose in life now, to make Dave well. I would do backward flips if I thought that was what society expected out of me. Now I felt the doctors pressuring me, although none of them said they expected me to do what I was doing. Somehow I sensed, however, that this was what everyone expected. It was my duty "in sickness and in health," they must be saying.

Whenever I left Dave with the children while I spent an hour at the store doing my weekly shopping, I felt the urgency to get back home. I rarely left Dave except when it was absolutely necessary, and he wanted me with him every moment of the day.

XVI

Winter came early that year. The cold east wind blew hard and steady. Snow fell and then we had freezing rain. The ground froze and then there would be a sudden thaw a few days later. The earth rose and buckled; the driveway turned into a quagmire.

I listened for weather reports. Our driveway was so long that it was impossible to get an oil truck in to refill the barrel during a thaw, so I had to be alert for a freeze that lasted long enough to harden the ground. When it was solidly frozen, I called the oil company for a delivery.

After watching holes and ruts form from the shifting earth during each thaw, I ordered a load of gravel; the smallest load they would deliver. I hoped to fill the worst spots and hope for the best through the rest of the winter.

I hated spending money on gravel, but immediately I could tell this small load wasn't going to be enough. It was like a bandaid on a large wound. Ken confirmed my feelings when he called and told me to have another load delivered.

What a disaster! The man who delivered this one drove too high against the side of the driveway, making tire grooves nearly half its length. He almost high-centered his truck; at the turn-around he was forced to dump his load. Now I had a bigger problem than chuck-holes in the driveway. There was an immense pile of gravel blocking the entrance to the cul-de-sac in the front of the house. I could scoot around it with my small foreign car, but any larger one was in danger of being swallowed up by the ditch on one side or the soft, muddy ground on the other. The driver drove away leaving me a shovel in one hand and the silent plea, "Now what do I do?"

Ken couldn't help me because of a heart condition, he said. I enlisted Steve after school; we shoveled gravel all the rest of the day.

I shoveled the gravel into a wheelbarrow and Steve wheeled it over to a hole and dumped it. Steve brought the wheelbarrow back, and I filled it up again. As I waited puffing and panting for Steve to return with the wheelbarrow, I thought perhaps it would be easier for me to push the wheelbarrow, and have Steve do the shoveling.

But the moment I picked up the loaded wheelbarrow a shot of pain ran through the small of my back. I gingerly placed the wheelbarrow back down on the ground. "Well, Steve, it looks like you're going to have to push the wheelbarrow," I said, reaching for the shovel. By evening we had made just a small dent in the large gravel pile. Too exhausted to shovel even one more load, we walked back to the house where I thought through my predicament.

We entered the house where Dave and the girls were monitoring one another. At first I was not sure who was more responsible, but by now I had to admit it was Lisa and Jan hands down. Dave was sitting in front of the TV watching a situation comedy. Although it didn't get easier to accept, I was getting used to Dave's disinterest in what went on around him. He couldn't have cared less about the gravel in the driveway.

The following morning I remembered another gravel company that Dave had worked for before we were married. I placed a call to them and asked for my third load of gravel. "I also have a load of gravel blocking my driveway that will have to be smoothed out," I told them.

The man said he would be happy to come out but, "The county has stopped all truck travel in Clackamas County until road conditions improve." This was turning out to be one of the worst winters on record. Until things got better, he said, he couldn't be of any help. I hung up the phone and made up my mind what I was going to do. *Nothing.*

Until I could get some help, I was not about to risk injuring my back from trying to shovel gravel. Since I could get in and out without difficulty, I decided to put the problem out of my mind.

That wasn't as easy to do as I had hoped, however. The evening of Lisa's birthday, a car came bolting down the driveway toward the house. I saw the headlights as they flashed in odd angles against the night sky. The car pitched into the ditch along the driveway; it shot up out of the ditch; then it came to rest down in the ditch again. I went to the front door and walked out into the cold, dark evening to meet Lisa's Sunday school teacher. She wanted to surprise Lisa with a birthday cake.

I felt so helpless. Normally, Dave would have pulled this woman's car out of the ditch without giving it a second thought. He was now in front of the TV without a care in the world. I was relieved when Mrs. Alcorn said her husband would come over and get the car out. We went into the house where she made the call.

I felt terrible after Mr. and Mrs. Alcorn left. I had to do something to keep other people from driving down our driveway and having the same thing happen. I called Uncle Bill and asked if he would put a barricade at the entrance to the driveway.

The following morning there was a large saw-horse blocking the driveway with a sign, "Do Not Enter."

Dr. Emery's nurse called and told me they had just scheduled Dave for surgery on November 28. At last he would have the plate put in. I wouldn't have to worry about Dave's head being so fragile after that. I looked forward to getting this latest operation over with.

Coincidentally the children's school arranged a benefit spaghetti dinner for that same evening. The proceeds were to be used to help defray medical expenses. Although I explained that we did have insurance, the people in charge insisted they wanted to do this for us anyway.

Although the evening was cold, the weather held and we were free from ice and snow for a while. I assumed Dave must be doing very well to be considered stable enough to endure this surgical procedure.

A hard plastic shield was inserted to protect his vulnerable brain. Another incision was made, using the same surgical site as before, from ear to ear across the top of his head. The flap was pulled forward and the plastic was heated and molded to fit the area. Dr. Emery said the procedure would take about three hours, so I decided to wait in the hall outside the surgical suite until Dave was taken to his room. Waiting in this hospital brought back old memories, but it wasn't as difficult as the first time around. I expected Dave to be back in his room by noon, and I could be home when the children arrived from school.

I'd neglected to bring a book to read so I was forced to flip through the antiquated periodicals sitting on a small book rack in the hall of the west wing. The hospital didn't have any formal waiting rooms except for the coffee shop and the solarium, and they were both in another part of the hospital. I wanted to be nearby so I would know when surgery was over. I glanced at my watch; four hours had passed since Dr. Emery had taken Dave in.

A nurse came out the door, and walked toward me. "Dr. Emery asked me to tell you everything is going fine." I thanked her and she went back through the swinging doors. I was surprised that Dr. Emery had even given me a thought.

Occasionally I paced the floor, held a brief conversation with the nursing supervisor who remembered me from the time before; by now I knew most of the nurses at the hospital. Occasionally I tried to focus my attention back on the magazine articles, but I was unsuccessful. The fourth hour was turning into five.

Just then another nurse came out the door. She said, "Dr. Emery wanted me to tell you he is finishing up and everything's fine." Back she went into the surgical suite.

Dave slept the rest of the day in a drug-induced stupor, but by evening he was coming around; the pain was very severe. The nurse said he couldn't have any pain medication until he was fully out of the anesthesia.

I picked up the children from school and they went to a friend's home to spend the evening and attend the spaghetti dinner. I went back to stay with Dave for the evening.

Bonita and her husband, Bill, attended the benefit dinner and then dropped by the hospital late that night on their way home. We were presented with a scrapbook containing the signatures of all who attended, and a check for $1,050. I was stunned at the continued concern for us throughout the community and astonished to learn that over one thousand people attended the dinner. Their generosity was overwhelming.

Bonita said the school ran out of dessert and someone had to go to the store to buy more pies. I was sure that the Lord was smiling on all those people as they waited in line out in the cold night air.

It upset me the following morning when I arrived to find Dave in excruciating pain. I held his hand as he moaned and groaned; I felt so helpless. There wasn't a thing I could do for him.

Then Dr. Emery arrived. "Dave's got a terrible headache," I told him, in the hope he would give him a good, strong pain-killer.

"I wonder why," he answered as he strode over to Dave's bedside. He left as he always did. "Well, okay," he said, and he was gone out the door.

When I saw a nurse give Dave a Tylenol tablet which they seemed to be doling out sparingly, I asked her if she could give Dave something stronger. She said they couldn't, because they wanted him to stay as alert as possible. Dave would have to suffer through it.

I realized what a protection the coma had been for both Dave and me. I had never seen him suffer until now, and it was nearly as bad as if I were going through it myself.

This time Dave was in a ward with three other patients. The nurses still allowed me to spend my days with Dave, and I tried to be useful by helping the other patients when I could.

One of the men was an Iranian college student who had been stabbed in the stomach. His name was Nasser. He had very few visitors and the language barrier prevented communication between him and the nurses. One morning a nurse put a small basin, a glass of water, a toothbrush, and toothpaste on the table in front of him. She walked away without saying a word.

I had spent enough time in the hospital to recognize the puzzled look on his face as he pondered over what to do with all the utensils sitting in front of him. With hand motions, I managed to show him that he was to brush his teeth. His face lit up in comprehension.

Nasser managed to get across to me one afternoon that he wanted his bed elevated. I had been reprimanded for elevating Dave's bed the day following surgery. Dave was supposed to stay flat that first day. I wasn't going to take any more chances at getting yelled at, so I peeked into several rooms until I found the head nurse for west wing. "May I raise Nasser's bed?"

I didn't know this nurse as well as I knew many of the others, and she had never been too friendly since Dave's admittance this time. She was standing with her back to the door. She didn't even turn around as she said, "You can do anything you want with him. In fact you can take him home with you."

I didn't answer this statement as I retreated back to Dave's room to roll Nasser's bed up. Apparently something was bothering this nurse, but I didn't know what. One thing I knew for certain, I wasn't going home with any more patients than I came in with. I had my hands full as it was.

Dr. Emery had said Dave could go home in a couple of days. I arrived that third morning to find Dave hallucinating. As he cried he explained through his sobs that his dad was lying in the bed next to his. Then he pointed to Nasser and said he was his brother-in-law.

Dave could get up and walk now, so I took him out into the hall to get him away from the people whom he thought were his relatives. We sat down on a windowseat which looked out into the courtyard near ICU. I explained who each patient was and tried to make him understand that he didn't know any of them; it was all his imagination.

A nurse passed, came back, and asked if she could help. Dave was sputtering by now, but I knew by experience that nothing would help until he got this out of his system. I told the nurse he was okay, and he began to get himself under control; he dabbed at his eyes with a tissue.

We must have looked strange; Dave with his large white turban wrapped tightly around his shaved head, dressed in a bathrobe and sobbing his heart out. All I could do was reassure him, and in a few minutes he was composed enough to go back to his room and face his roommates as the strangers they actually were.

I had to get Dr. Emery to sign Dave's release and I didn't want a repeat of the last time. I watched for him to arrive throughout the entire morning, but I never saw a sign of him. I finally managed to track him down in the coffee shop as he sat down to eat his lunch.

He was sitting alone so I walked over and sat down in a chair across the table from him. I explained the change in Dave's mental state, while Dr. Emery listened and ate at the same time. I was afraid Dr. Emery wouldn't let Dave go home, but he didn't seem at all surprised. He didn't give me any explanations as to why Dave was acting so strangely, nor did I ask. I just assumed since Dr. Emery wasn't concerned, I shouldn't be either. From talking to other people I had heard that the third day after surgery is often the worst, and I assumed that was what was wrong with Dave. Tomorrow he will be better, I thought; and he was.

I took Dave home that afternoon and his hallucinations stopped almost immediately – perhaps just from the familiarity of home surroundings.

The pain around his incision was intense, but within a few days he began to bounce back. The swelling went down rapidly. I noticed his forehead looked different. The right side didn't have a rounded shape like the left. I thought it was due to the skin stretching from swelling, and it would eventually relax and shrink back to normal. I soon learned this was not the case.

Ten days after surgery I took Dave to Dr. Emery's office to have the stitches removed. The doctor looked quizzically at Dave's forehead and then said, "Well, David, you're going to have a forehead with character." I knew then my discomfort about the shape of his forehead had been warranted. It wasn't going to shrink back.

Dr. Emery said the swelling during surgery prevented him from making an exact shape because of the intricate and precise cutting of the plate. He was unable to see the problem at the time and there was no way of doing anything about it now. Dr. Barrett was never in surgery with Dr. Emery as I had assumed he would be. Apparently, I was not adamant enough about requesting his presence. Dr. Emery still intimidated me and I wasn't about to ask him why Dr. Barrett wasn't there. It wouldn't have changed anything anyway.

Dave recovered very quickly. He said, however, if he had known it was going to be so painful he never would have allowed the surgery. No one was going to do any more surgery on him again, he said.

I welcomed the continued visits from Bill and Louise Folk, Sunday dinners at my mother's or Bonita's, and an occasional outing with other friends or relatives. I felt it important to keep Dave stimulated, and equally as important was getting out of the house myself.

Although Dave could talk in sentences, he rarely did. He usually answered in simple sentences, and more often with just the word yes or no. Anything he said was in groups of threes, "Yes, yes, yes." When I asked him to do something he didn't want to do he would say, "I don't want to! I don't want to! I don't want to!"

His ability to walk was improving every day and he no longer needed a cane while in the house. When I wanted to go shopping and suggested leaving him with someone, he would vehemently protest. However, he didn't mind staying with either of the three children or Bill Folk.

By the end of the year he was getting around well enough by himself that I did risk leaving him alone for the time it took to do the marketing. Though I worried about him when he was alone, he accepted it more easily than when I planned for someone to stay with him.

He could put together the makings for a simple lunch and sometimes that kept him occupied the short time I was away. He hated to have me leave him, but accepted my absence since I was going after food to restock the cupboards. He was terribly possessive of me, but food came next in line after me in his thoughts, so I could get away from him with the reminder that we needed groceries.

He was quick tempered with the children, but at the same time enjoyed having them nearby. The television became the main problem between them. When Dave worked nights I let the children watch most of the children's programs in the evenings. Now Dave was interested in other programs and insisted they watch what he wanted. There didn't seem to be an answer to this problem. In the past Dave would have watched the children's programs with them, but now he seemed to take delight in learning which program they wanted to watch so he could insist the channel be changed.

The children didn't know how to react to their father and neither did I. He looked like the same person, but his moods were unpredictable. There was a cruel streak showing up in him, but he let no one else see it except the children and me. It was only when we were alone that he

124

displayed this new personality. I couldn't understand what was going on with him unless he was taking his anger out on the children – anger at being crippled, anger at what had happened to him. That had to be the only answer, I thought.

Dave was becoming more independent. He could dress himself, although it was a struggle to put clothes on with one hand, especially hard to get a sock on. He even learned how to tie his shoes by using the right hand just a little to stabilize the bow. He had movement in his arm but his fingers were useless. He could also take showers without assistance. The one thing he couldn't do was clip his own nails.

He learned to shave himself again, but invariably he left gashes on his cheek or straggling whiskers on his neck. Paul said, "Don't be surprised if he doesn't shave the right side of his face at all. Many stroke patients actually forget that side even exists." Fortunately, Dave didn't forget about his right side; it was just his vision that brought him problems. He couldn't see well enough to shave; but he was determined to try.

He was good natured when I said, "Let's go back into the bathroom and see if I can get the whiskers you missed." Without a word, he limped along, following me obediently.

Many people thought our lives had been momentarily interrupted during Dave's hospital stay, and then suddenly put back the same as before the accideent. That's what they thought. In reality, the nightmare continued for me.

Dave was like a caricature of himself. Everything about him was twisted just a bit, not enough to make people believe that there was something wrong with him mentally or emotionally, but just enough to make life miserable for those of us who had to live with him.

He had always been calm during a crisis and could take over any situation no matter how difficult. He was still calm; a little too calm. Nothing affected him or caused him alarm. The only time he showed concern was when he thought his next meal might be late.

When I took Dave to see the doctors, he sat in silence, as if completely uninterested; in fact, he wasn't interested, not in the least.

When we visited Les about the pending lawsuit, Dave became restless. He was interested in only one thing – going home. If we were left alone for a few minutes he would whisper, "I wanna go home. I wanna go home. I wanna go home." The minute the doctor or lawyer returned, Dave would be back on his good behavior again, and I know they all thought he was following the conversation with great interest.

As Christmas neared I tried to forget about the trenches. I felt I had to trust they were dug out well enough in the fall that they would get us through the winter months and the heavy rains. However, I didn't realize how the rain compounded with the snow, deep freezes, and recurrent thaws would affect the absorbing ability of the ground.

I awoke in the middle of the night to the sound: *drip, drip, drip.* I could tell water was dripping into the house somewhere, but I couldn't imagine where. It would be impossible for me to do anything about it in the middle of the night even if I could find the source, so I tried to go back to sleep. That was impossible, too.

By morning the heavy rain had changed to occasional showers. The dripping had stopped. I got the children off to school and got Dave into position in front of the TV. Then the phone rang. It was Sharon Meier.

I told her about the dripping noise I had heard during the night, and how it kept me awake. "I'm worried about the trenches," I said.

"Oh, you just think up things to worry about," she said. I admitted this bad habit and we both laughed. I promised I would stop worrying.

After hanging up the phone, I picked up a load of laundry to take downstairs. When I reached the laundry room, I saw water all over the floor. My heart stopped. We had never had water come into the living area of the house before.

A couple of years before the accident, I had to wake Dave up at nine o'clock at night to dig out the trenches. After a heavy rain they had filled up with soft topsoil, and water was seeping into the garage. That was as bad as it had ever become. There was carpeting on the family room floor which would be destroyed if it got wet. The water now was just a few feet from the family room.

I steeled myself, and then opened the garage door for a look. Water was everywhere. The trenches had to be full, and it was essential to dig them out as soon as possible. I looked outside and saw the rain coming down harder. The ground wasn't absorbing any more and it was all running down the hill into our home. It wouldn't stop coming into the house until it stopped raining, which didn't seem too likely right now.

I went back into the house and called Bonita. I asked her to send Dan over when he got out of college for the day. I needed someone a little stronger than Steve to help me. With the three of us working we might be able to successfully divert the water. I then called Sharon Meier and told her my worries weren't unjustified. She said, "I'm sorry."

I put on my rain hat and an old coat; then my boots and gloves. I left Dave by himself and told him I would be outside digging trenches. He looked away from the TV program, nodded his head, and then turned back to the TV again. It was obvious he wasn't concerned, I thought, feeling a bit sorry for myself. *I'd cry if I had time, but I don't.* I went to the garage to get a shovel and then up to the edge of our property.

Some of the trenches were still clear, but the farmer that rented this field from Dave's parents had run his tractor through in the fall. A couple of turns at the end of the field next to our home filled up the trenches with soil. It hadn't done a bit of good to dig the trenches in the summer because the farmer filled them up in the fall when he cut the broccoli.

As I dug, the rain soaked through my coat and into my clothes. The mud was hard to dig; it looked a little like pea soup and shoveled the same way. It would cling and then drip slowly off the shovel. As I pulled out a shovelful of mud, I then needed another shovel to scrape the mud off the first one.

By the time Dan came and Steve was home from school, I had a good start on the trenches. Steve and Dan each took a shovel and the three of us built blockades to divert the water to a dip in the pasture where the water would then flow to the creek. We dug more blockades to divert the rest of the water into the woods behind our house. We packed shovelsful of mud on top of mud to make some parts of the trenches a little higher in spots. We dug out two hundred feet of trenches, one foot wide, one foot deep.

While I was digging, Lisa called out that I was wanted on the phone. I angrily pushed the shovel into the ground until it stood solidly upright. I was cold and wet. But most of all I was irritated at the interruption. Right now the trenches were uppermost in my mind. I dripped my way through the kitchen to the phone and picked up the receiver.

A woman on the other end of the line said she had a box of food to deliver to us. She said she couldn't get past the barricade at the entrance of the driveway. "No, of course you can't," I answered. I wanted to say, "And that's the point," but I didn't. I explained that the driveway was impassable.

"Well, I'm calling from your neighbor's house and I'm in a hurry. Would you come get this box of food now so that I can be on my way. I have some other things to do." She explained exactly where she was, and I recalled that to be approximately a quarter of a mile away. I told the woman I would be right there. As I hung up the phone, I realized how tired I was. I didn't feel like picking up anything from anyone. I'd been shoveling mud all day long.

So far, this was the third box of food that had been collected and delivered to us during the holiday season. I appreciated the thought, but this one came at a very inopportune time. I waved to Dan and Steve, "Be right back," and jumped into my little car. I zipped down the driveway between the deep holes and ruts, and then out onto the main highway. When I brought the box of groceries back to the house, I gave it to Lisa and Jan to unload while I went back to help in the trenches.

By dark we had the trenches completely taken care of and the garage was beginning to dry out. I mopped up the laundry room floor and we were finished. By bedtime we were dried out ourselves and Dan left for home. It was an exhausting day, but we managed to get through it successfully. I felt a small measure of satisfaction in between the aches and pains.

Trouble seemed to come at me in waves. The gravel company sent a truck out with a load of gravel as soon as the county would allow them in. The man who brought this load started at the cul-de-sac and then drove forward, spreading the gravel evenly down the road. He did a beautiful job. Then as he neared the center of the driveway, the right wheel dropped off into the culvert. Now in the middle of our driveway we had a dump truck lodged with no room to drive around it – not even enough room for my own little car.

I'd taken Dave and the children shopping that afternoon, and when we arrived home the truck was lying at an angle across the driveway. We couldn't get to the house. I drove into Dave's parents' driveway and we waited for the man to have someone come pull him out.

As the other truck arrived, darkness was setting in. The two men didn't have much daylight left to work in, so they hurriedly tied a cable onto the crippled vehicle and the other end to the axle of the rescue truck. As the rescue truck pulled on the crippled vehicle, the cable quivered, and the axle snapped.

I now had two broken dump trucks in the driveway. It was too dark by now to do any more work so they left the retrieval of the two trucks until morning when a semi-trailer truck would be brought out to retrieve them both.

Dave couldn't walk very well in the gravel, and at night when he couldn't see, it was virtually impossible for him to make his way down the driveway. Ken and I walked on both sides of him as we carefully led him down our long driveway to the house. The air was cold and biting, but the tension of the moment kept us warm.

The following morning the semi, carrying a caterpillar, was brought out. With the cat they smoothed out the gravel, and repaired the bent culvert. Within the hour the driveway was in perfect shape, and the trucks were on their way for repair.

I felt guilty about this incident even though I knew I wasn't responsible. The gravel company didn't even send me a bill – not even for the gravel.

Christmas was coming and we needed a tree. Getting the Christmas tree had always been Dave's job, but this year I was on my own. I remembered a neighbor who had some trees for sale. The only problem was that we had to cut it ourselves.

The trees were clumped together. Steve and I searched for what we considered the prettiest tree on the lot. When we finally made our choice, Steve began sawing it down. My job was to pull on the tree to keep the branches out of Steve's face. After a few minutes we traded places; Steve held the tree out of my face while I lay on the ground and sawed.

I began my first thrust forward and the saw stuck. I pulled back and tried again, but it stuck again. After several more tries, we decided Steve was going to have to do the honors or we would be there all night. For some reason unknown to me, Steve could make the saw work.

The owner of the tree farm walked up. He had a puzzled look on his face as he said, "You're going to put *that* tree in your car?" Steve stopped sawing and looked up.

I looked at the car and then back to the man, "Sure, I think it will fit.

We don't have far to go, anyway." He just shook his head and motioned for Steve to get up. The man got down on the ground and finished cutting the tree for us.

After the tree was cut and pulled over to the car, I could see there was indeed a problem. It looked as long as the car or more. Steve and our neighbor pushed and pulled the tree until it was wedged into the back of our car. Half of the tree hung out the back, but we had such a short distance to drive, I wasn't worried. I knew it was stuck in there tight.

When we got home Steve and I dragged the tree up the full flight of back stairs to the living room. Then we struggled, pulled, tugged, and propped until the tree was standing gallantly straight and tall in the front window. I was proud! Steve and I had done it all by ourselves; well, almost.

From the bedroom closet I pulled out the box containing all our ornaments. The children and I decorated the tree with all the lights and globes I had stored away from previous years and we put our precious angel with the china head at the very top. The children also added paper decorations they had made at school and glittered ones they made at home, and then we finished it off with a thick layer of tinsel.

The tree fell down the next day.

I was glad we always got our tree at least a week in advance; it would probably take that long to figure out how to keep it up. It had looked so easy when Dave did it.

I crawled under the tree while Steve pushed against the tree trunk. With some adjustments on the tree stand, I managed to screw the tree trunk in a little tighter, and we finally got the tree to stay up. I didn't get it standing as straight and tall as Dave would have – it definitely *leaned* – but at least it was standing. And fortunately, not one of the ornaments was broken.

Anonymous gifts came pouring in for the children. As Christmas drew closer, the stack got higher under our leaning tree. It was heartwarming to see so much kindness in one year's time. The concern that was exhibited right after the accident was happening all over again. People brought over more food, boxes of groceries. Checks came in the mail with Christmas cards. I answered each one personally to let everyone know how much we appreciated everything.

I decided that if we ever won that lawsuit, all the money donated to us would be paid back to someone else in a predicament like ours. This was the only way I knew to pay the community back for all they had done for us.

The children said this was the best Christmas ever. The thoughtfulness of the people in our community warmed my heart; I had to agree.

However, I did look forward to an end to 1972. I thought things could never be any worse. How wrong I was I would soon come to know.

XVII

After the plate was put in and after our December follow-up visit at Dr. Emery's office, Dave was not scheduled for any more appointments. Dr. Barrett was still considering the surgery on Dave's arm, which he later decided against because of increased movement in Dave's right hand.

At this time I hadn't felt abandoned by the medical profession – at least not yet.

Dr. Barrett ordered a brace for Dave's shoe and another one to straighten out his right wrist and fingers. Although some function was returning to Dave's arm, his wrist was still bent and his fingers struggled against the drawing-up reflex the spasticity caused.

I hoped the brace would increase his ability to walk. He had worn off the toe of his right shoe, dragging his foot whenever he took a step. Eventually, because of the persistent pressure against his big toe, his toenail came off. The brace helped bring his foot up as he raised his foot to take a step, eliminating that problem.

None of the doctors gave suggestions for Dave's rehabilitation. After the books I had read, I knew stimulus was vital for Dave's eventual recovery. However, I did feel despair that the year was nearing its end, and Dave hadn't recovered as I had expected him to. This knowledge only drove me harder. He *had* to get well.

I continued to take him to visit friends and relatives as often as I could without wearing out our welcome. Dave was never satisfied, however. He was always eager to leave when I mentioned going for a drive, but he didn't want to stay in any one place for longer than a few minutes. He wanted to keep going.

While visiting Bonita on occasion, Dave would get restless after a minute, go out to the car, and honk the horn.

I'd jump, grab my purse, yell "Gotta go!" and run out the door to the car so the neighbors wouldn't be disturbed. Only when Dave saw me would he stop honking, and there was no way I could prevent him from doing it again. I just had to stay prepared.

Dave was distressing in many ways, and he continued to confuse me. His memory seemed intact when I pressed him for details about his past flying experiences, horse training knowledge, and even world events. Except for those two weeks preceding the accident and the entire hospitalization, Dave was just like he was before the accident. One of the things that had drawn me to Dave when we first met was that he had a well-rounded knowledge of just about everything. Once again I began to turn to him for advice and to depend on his judgment. Occasionally, I noticed a problem, though.

Dave had taken electronics in college and understood it well. However, one day he asked me if we had to have a color TV to get color reception. *What a strange thing to ask*, I thought; especially for Dave! That was a question I might have asked him in years past.

About a year before the accident Dave had taken two old engines that didn't run and built one that did. He then put it into his 1956 pickup truck. A friend of his told him he was crazy to tackle such a project; he had never done anything like it before.

I was concerned the day when he brought home that final missing piece. He put the key in the ignition and turned it. I expected silence, and then a wrench would go flying across the garage from Dave's anger, but instead the engine started right up. I think I was just as proud of him at that accomplishment as he was of himself.

When Bonita's younger son, Mike, began rebuilding an engine for his car a little more than a year after Dave's accident, he expected some advice from Dave. Dave and I were sitting with Bonita at the kitchen table when Mike asked about a particular part.

Dave's face went blank for a moment. Then he said, "I don't know, Mike," and shook his head.

Mike said, "But you had to have done it when you put in your engine."

"Mike, I don't know!" Mike's shoulders drooped as he turned and walked back to the garage. But a moment later Dave got up and went out to the garage, where he correctly instructed Mike and solved the problem.

Information seemed to be filed away in Dave's brain just waiting for one of us to need it. Until we pressed him for it, however, Dave showed no ability to share it.

One afternoon I left Dave in the car while I went into a store to get a few items. When I came out of the store I passed a woman parked a few spaces away with the hood of her car up. Just then I saw Dave feeling his way unsteadily around the front of our car as he struggled to step over the curb near the car. I rushed up to him, "What are you doing?"

He replied, "I'm going to help that woman with her car."

"I'm sure she can get someone else to help her," I answered, as I helped him back to his seat. Dave had enough trouble just standing on his feet when he was outside on unfamiliar ground; I wasn't so sure he could safely help anyone do anything. I knew I couldn't help him much since I was completely ignorant about mechanical things – most certainly cars.

Sometimes he didn't give it a thought as he struggled to help someone. This was so much like he was before the accident. Then there were other times when he seemed to have a mental block and couldn't remember things that in the past he would have taken for granted.

I knew Dave would never be able to write with his right hand again, so I encouraged him to learn with his left. Those first months we received social security checks he could only make an X for his signature. Two witnesses had to sign that they had actually seen him make this mark before I could deposit the check into our account.

132

He hated to write with his left hand, however, and only did so under extreme pressure from me. He eventually learned to sign his name because he realized how often a signature was needed on documents, but he absolutely refused to spend any time practicing to make it better.

For ten months I did therapy on him three times a day, massaging and bending his fingers, straightening his arm out of its insistent curve, and trying to keep his shoulder joint loose. Dave built up the strength in his legs by pedaling every day on the pedals which I hooked on to a chair.

Winter was over and spring was showing its face with the daffodils and tulips that were adding bright splashes of red and yellow to a colorless, drab terrain. Winter had released its hold, and I looked forward to spring with a renewed sense of hope. Another block of time had been added to my life.

I saw an item in the *Oregonian*, our daily paper, about an adaptive physical education class for rehabilitating the handicapped at Mt. Hood Community College. The course was set up by the Department of Vocational Rehabilitaiotn (DVR) and was to be made available to all disabled adults in the community.

At our next therapy session I showed the article to Paul. "What do you think of something like this for Dave?"

Paul glanced at it quickly as if he were already familiar with it and said, "I can't compete with that. Yes, I think you should enroll Dave in the class." That was all I needed.

I went right home that afternoon and called for an appointment to talk to the instructor. Anyone admitted to the class, the article said, would have to be accepted by the college.

Although Dave was walking, he wasn't too steady on his feet. He leaned heavily on his cane, dragged his right foot, and his arm was drawn up to his chest – this was caused by the unrelenting spasticity. His vision was a major problem. His depth perception was bad and he would stumble into curbs if I didn't warn him. When he approached a curb he had to stop, think first which foot he was supposed to step up with so his right leg wouldn't buckle and collapse; then he locked his right knee, and made a somewhat wobbly step with his left foot to the curb. Then he dragged his stiff right leg up next to his left one and planted it firmly and decisively next to his right leg in an attempt to maintain his balance. Everything he did, including walking, took determination, thought and effort. A small stone or hole in a sidewalk blended into the pavement and he walked in fear that his next step could send him sprawling to the ground.

He was fearful of parking lots, worrying about approaching cars as we crossed traffic lanes. "Don't worry, Dave," I would say. "They'll have to hit me first." But that was no consolation to him.

"I'm not worried about you getting hit," he would answer. "I just don't

133

want them to hit me." I laughed, but the look on his face made me realize he was serious. For him it certainly was no laughing matter.

I knew Dave wasn't well enough to become employed, but this P.E. class seemed to be the only answer for us. Dr. Emery never mentioned anything other than the physical therapist one day a week, and all my phone calls to agencies for the handicapped were fruitless.

From that first week home from the hospital I began looking for help from agencies in the area, but I couldn't seem to make any of them aware of me. The visiting nurses never showed up, and the other agencies said they only gave aid to children under eighteen years of age.

Dr. Emery worked so hard to help Dave survive that accident. I wondered why and for what. There didn't seem to be anyone to help us through the long rehabilitative process. Then with the knowledge of this new adaptive P.E. class, I saw a glimmer of hope again.

The class was held five days a week, for one to two hours each day, and the cost was just $15 a term.

I guided Dave through the college gymnasium to the P.E. office and gave his name to the woman at the desk who introduced herself as the instructor for the Adaptive P.E. class. Then a man walked up, introduced himself as Mr. Frank, the counselor. He asked Dave to come with him to his office. Mr. Frank didn't include me in the invitation, so I sat down in a chair against the wall, and waited.

After several minutes had passed, I began to get restless. It took effort to communicate with Dave. He rarely answered questions with more than a yes or no response. In fact, I thought, I'm not even sure he knows why we're here. Immediately I became angry at myself for allowing Dave to go with the counselor without me.

A few minutes later Mr. Frank brought Dave back, laid a piece of paper on the instructor's desk, and announced that Dave was not well enough to participate in the class. He said the class's purpose was to help people who were nearly ready to return to the job market; Dave, he said, was clearly not one of them.

Mr. Frank called another name and took the next potential student to his office. I hadn't said a word. I was speechless.

I stood there wondering, *Well, what do I do now?* This class had been my only hope; it was essential that Dave be admitted.

The moment we got home, I went directly to the phone. I explained the problem to Paul. "Now what?"

"Try again," he answered. "If you still can't get him in, give me another call and I'll see what I can do." Whew! I hung up the phone with a determination growing deep inside me. I was going to get Dave into that class if it was the last thing I did. I called the college and made another appointment to see the counselor, Mr. Frank.

This time Mr. Frank met with Dave and me at the same time. He listened as I poured out my story and how important this class was if

134

Dave was going to have any further recovery. I'm not sure how I got through to him, but at the end of our meeting he said Dave could be admitted to the class. With a sigh of relief I took Dave home.

Dave's first day of class was March 28, 1973. It turned out to be everything I had hoped for – and more.

The first ten weeks Dave worked out each morning on a universal gym lifting weights with both his arms and legs. While he did his exercises, I waited in the car and read the morning paper, sewed a hem on a skirt, or worked my way through a novel. One morning each week I drove to the nearest grocery store that opened at eight o'clock, and bought my weekly supply of groceries. After Dave had attended several class sessions, he asked me to come in and see what he was doing.

When I arrived that morning with Dave, the instructor walked over, we said good morning to one another, and she asked Dave to do ten sit-ups on the slantboard.

As the instructor walked away, Dave sat down and began the exercises, "One . . . two . . . five . . . ten." He struggled to get to his feet. What in the world was he doing, I wondered. I *knew* he could count.

"Dave, you didn't do ten." He ignored me as he limped over to a bench and sat down to do leg-lifts. The instructor passed by as she headed toward another student, "Did you do ten?" Dave smiled and nodded.

A flood of thoughts whirled through my mind. *He didn't do ten, he did four!* "Dave," I whispered. "You are only hurting yourself when you don't do what you're supposed to." But he acted as if he hadn't heard me, as he began demonstrating the leg-lifts. He reminded me of a six-year-old trying to impress his mother by showing her around his first grade room.

Perhaps this was just a part of the pattern. At least he did four sit-ups. At home I couldn't get him to do any. Four or five weren't as good as ten, but they were better than none at all. I couldn't bring myself to snitch on him to the instructor. I decided to see if she was bright enough to find it out for herself. If he succeeded in keeping it from her, it would just prove how ingenious he still was.

Before the class was over I did mention to the instructor a similar problem I had with Dave. "He has no motivation," I told her. "I can't understand it. He was very active before the accident, and now all he wants to do is sit around and watch TV."

"If he was highly active before the accident," she responded, "he'll probably be just the opposite now."

I hoped she was wrong.

Following the ten weeks of exercise was a ten-week swimming session. Dave had gained a lot of weight, and his balance was quite precarious. Getting into the pool was no problem. He could just fall in. Getting out was something else. It took three people to get him safely to his feet. As he attempted to climb out of the pool one person grabbed his right arm and Dave grabbed the rail with his left. One other person was in place below him in the water; his right foot was positioned on the steps as he struggled up the ladder; a third person helped steady him as he stepped onto the concrete at the pool edge.

The instructor said he would swim in a circle since he could only paddle with his left arm and left leg. He would be like a canoe with one paddle, she said. He proved this theory wrong, however. Without difficulty he swam from one side of the pool to the other.

For someone like Dave, this was excellent therapy. The water protected him from falling and hurting himself. The buoyancy allowed him to bob all around and at the same time he could float upright in complete safety.

Nevertheless, although Dave had been a good swimmer, it was different now. In the past he showed very little fear of anything. Now he was afraid of cars, he was afraid of falling, and he was even afraid of being splashed with water. The other students in the class were active and played rowdy games of basketball. Dave hated the swimming class, but to please me, he attended.

The third ten-week session was held at a bowling alley, where the students tried to throw a bowling ball hard enough to strike the pins at the end of the alley. His lack of balance affected Dave and all he could throw were gutter balls. I was reminded of the time, a few years after our marriage, when he was awarded the trophy for the most improved bowler of the year. Now each day's failure was another reminder of how much he had lost – how much we had all lost! This was the first time since the accident I actually saw depression cross his face. He looked so discouraged.

I tried to keep encouraging him, "You'll get better. You just need practice." I motioned to a quadriplegic student in a wheelchair at the next alley. "At least you can throw the ball. You can even pick it up without help, he can't."

"I know," Dave responded with a sigh. "I really am grateful. I realize I could be in worse shape." I'm not sure if Dave and I believed this or just tried to continue convincing ourselves that we really were well off. I could look at someone in a wheelchair and feel gratitude that Dave could walk. But then I could look at a strong, healthy man and feel angry. It didn't seem fair that Dave was the one who had been hurt so badly in that wreck. He hadn't even caused the accident, but he was the one who would suffer for it the rest of his life.

There were so many what-if's again. If he hadn't had a head injury, he wouldn't have been injured at all. If the injury hadn't been so hard, his brain wouldn't have been damaged in the back, causing the paralysis. If the injury hadn't occurred to the frontal lobe of his brain, he might have had a stronger determination to recover, and there wouldn't be the personality changes or the mood variations. In fact, if he had lived twenty-five years earlier and had this kind of accident, he might be dead.

Sometimes I thought death would have been a blessing. I wondered, where does God leave off and doctors take over?

Since I was ten years old I have suffered from painful and debilitating menstrual cramps. For two days each month I suffered from the unrelenting pain that even pain pills could not ease. The advent of birth control pills allowed me a reprieve from the pain. And, once a year I had to keep an appointment with our family doctor, Dr. Manning, who would renew my prescription for another year.

After the examination Dr. Manning sat down to write out the prescription. He then tore the slip of paper from the pad, stood up, and as he reached for the doorknob he asked, "How's Dave?"

I watched Dr. Manning open the door, "Oh, he's slowly getting better, but progress is very slow. He's in an adaptive P.E. class at the college now."

Dr. Manning replied, "he'll probably have to be institutionalized." With that he retreated from the room, closing the door behind him.

I was surprised at this statement. I never considered the probability that Dave would be institutionalized. I knew Dr. Manning hadn't seen Dave since he lay comatose in the hospital. He certainly didn't understand the progress Dave had made since that time.

And, Dr. Emery never suggested the possibility of Dave going anywhere but home, except for suggesting the convalescent facility the day before Dave was discharged from the hospital. I pushed Dr. Manning's words right out of my mind. As long as Dave had me, he would never go into an institution.

I didn't anticipate, however, what a drain Dave would be on my physical and mental health. It wasn't necessarily a matter of how much determination I had. Depression would eventually remove determination from my soul, leaving barely a shell of a person behind.

XVIII

I couldn't bring myself to face another year of digging trenches and caring for livestock. In the summertime one little fly bite could cause a steer to raise its tail in the air and head for the nearest fence. I had spent too many days chasing and herding cattle before Dave's accident to want to face it alone now.

The upkeep of six acres was too much. Every moment of my waking hours were spent on Dave's recovery, and I was no longer interested in the place we called "Our Dream House." That was another time which no longer existed. I had important decisions to make and I couldn't allow sentiment to interfere.

Neither Dave nor the children were pleased with my decision, but it seemed the only thing we could do. I had to sell.

I put the house and acreage up for sale. I sold all the cattle except for our little calf that was born the previous fall. Uncle Bill took him home to raise for slaughter. Bill, Peggy, and their children christened him Herfie and treated him like a pet. That turned out to be a mistake when time came that he was ready to go to the slaughterhouse.

I sold Dave's hay-hauling truck. And I sold the pickup Dave had so lovingly rebuilt.

I remember my feelings when Dave was lying in the hospital in a coma. Although I hoped I wouldn't have to do it, I vowed to sell the house to help him recover – if we needed the money. We had a beautiful place. I loved being able to look at Mount Hood every day (when there was no cloud cover) and see the snow-covered peak as the sun rose in the morning, casting behind it a lavender-pink backdrop. I had almost begun to take that view for granted.

I loved beautiful things – clothes and furniture. The accident, however, had changed me. I didn't care about *things* any longer. They could all be lost in the flash of an eye – a fire, a tornado. We had been financially comfortable before Dave's accident. I had possessions I never dreamed I would have. All of it held a different meaning the moment of Dave's accident.

I wished I had "stopped to smell the roses" more often. I wished I hadn't been in such a hurry to get through life. I wished I could have the opportunity to live the eleven years of my marriage over again and I would have savored every second. Money no longer meant anything to me, nor did all my possessions. My family was priceless; they were the things I didn't want to lose.

The next step in Dave's recovery was a house that wouldn't require so much maintenance; a house with all the rooms on one level and with level ground outside for Dave to walk safely on for exercise. I wanted a house that a wheelchair could get around easily in, if Dave ever needed one again.

Now I was up and down the stairs a dozen times a day, lugging up clean laundry, or packing up sacks of groceries. Just to answer the front door, I had to go down a half a flight of stairs. Sometimes in my hurry to get downstairs, I would slip on the edge of a stair and then found myself sliding down the rest of the staircase on my back. I awoke the next morning with only aching muscles, but it angered me anyway.

I began searching through the classified ads of the *Oregonian*. In the meantime I sold our house. The family who bought it had one month to vacate their own home. They had livestock to move onto our property as soon as we found a place to move into, and could relinquish our house. The pressure was on.

A neighbor just above us on the hill had an acre for sale. The land was level, and if I bought it, a house could be built on the property to our specifications. This would be a big undertaking, I realized – to hire a contractor to build us a house.

I chose to continue looking for a house that was already constructed. I contacted real estate offices and pored over the classified ads. Eventually, I found a house that looked almost perfect. It had only one stair; otherwise the floorplan was all on one level.

My mother suggested I have one of my uncles come over and look the house over to be sure it had no hidden defects. Before I could get anyone to look at it, the house was sold. And there wasn't another house like it in the area.

The only solution seemed to build a house in the filbert orchard on the hill. I had to apply for a new loan through the Veteran's Loan office. I had to get a letter from the doctor that we were transferring the loan because of a medical need, otherwise we might have been turned down. As usual, I was terrified of all the paperwork, meetings with the loan officer (by myself). In the back of my mind, I was afraid we might be turned down because of Dave's health. Perhaps we weren't a good enough risk; they might be afraid we couldn't afford to pay the money back.

Since the family who bought our home had to get out of their's immediately, I chose to find a house for us to rent. One of my uncles had apartments and I became a bit too confident in being able to obtain one. He said it was okay, but called me back a short time later and said his wife didn't want to rent to relatives.

Back to the classified ads. Unfortunately, I couldn't find anyone who would rent to a family with three children for just three months.

I mentioned our plight to the real estate agent who sold our home; she offered to rent us a little two-bedroom home not far away. It was nestled on the main street of the little town of Boring.

Uncle Bill offered to store most of our furniture in his garage since the rental house was so small. We ended up filling half of Bill and Peggy's garage and part of their basement with chairs, a sofa, appliances,

140

and assorted boxes of dishes and other paraphernalia.

The day we moved brought friends and relatives over to help. We planned to make many trips with the pickup trucks they brought with them, and with all the willing hands we hoped to have the work done in record time.

Someone called my attention to a truck pulling into the driveway. I looked out the living room window to see a semi-trailer truck coming down the driveway. The word "Wonderbread" was emblazoned across the side. We all stopped packing boxes and stood in the living room as Bill Folk drove the truck up the door. As Bill jumped from the truck he said, "I got permission to bring the truck out to help you move." With this truck one trip was all that was needed.

The following three months we spent in that little house in Boring were rough. We were in the middle of a lumber town with log trucks and dump trucks barreling past our front door all hours of the day and night. The noise was horrible after living on six quiet acres for so long.

The bedrooms were small; we had wall to wall beds. In the summertime, big black ants tried to take possession from us. I had to keep the kitchen scrupulously free of crumbs or the ants would file in while we were gone, only to scatter through cracks and crevices in the walls when we returned. It made us all shudder when we entered and saw those ugly insects – all except Dave. Nothing bothered him!

We had been there a few weeks when Steve came down with pleurisy. It lasted six weeks. His first attack came one weekend while he was staying with my mother. She and Bonita's husband, Bill, took him to the emergency room of a hospital close to my mother's home. There the physician treated Steve for possible food poisoning or appendicitis, and they made him vomit.

Steve sat on the examining table and rapidly sucked in shallow breaths. The doctor scolded him for doing this saying, "You'll hyperventilate if you breathe like that." I arrived then and took Steve home with me along with a bag of medications the doctor had prescribed.

A few years previously I had suffered a bout with pleurisy. I watched Steve as he lay on the sofa struggling to get air into his lungs. I remembered how I could only get short, shallow breaths. It was a Saturday afternoon. I decided to call Dr. Manning at his home.

Dr. Manning answered his phone, and I explained the incident at the emergency room. "I think he has pleurisy," I told the doctor.

Dr. Manning said, "Don't give him any more of the medication you were given, and bring him right in to the emergency room. I'll meet you there." I bundled Steve up and drove him to Valley General Hospital. Dr. Manning was already there when we arrived.

Dr. Manning ordered x-rays and gave me a diagnosis for Steve's condition, "He has pleurisy." He placed Steve on antibiotics and sent us home.

Steve lost ten pounds over the next five weeks trying to fight off the attack of pleurisy. It was a stubborn case. Finally Dr. Manning said, "If he isn't better by next week, I'll have to aspirate the fluid with a needle." Steve suddenly began to improve, and by the sixth week he was completely recovered.

At last I was beginning to take charge of the lives of my children and my husband. In the past I silently allowed people to make decisions for me, to tell me what was best for us, to run my entire world. No more, I decided. Just because a doctor has spent many years going to medical school doesn't mean he has the answers to everything. One doctor, I found, couldn't diagnose a case of pleurisy.

In the past I took any doctor's suggestions without question. But now I realized that doctors were not infallible. I had learned that there were times when I would have to look out for my family and take over from the experts. I might not have spent so many years in school, but I knew what was right for us.

The contractor who began construction on our new home didn't agree with the way I did things, but I did it my way anyway. The money we received from the sale of our home and property, I put into the building of our new house. The contractor said that was a big mistake; he said I should invest it in something else. I argued that I didn't want high mortgage payments while living on social security checks.

While studying the blueprint of the house, I asked for more cupboards and closets. The contractor wanted us to have more floor space. He finally gave in a little and put two small closets in areas that would have been boarded up anyway.

Dave had taken up cooking before we moved. He was a disaster waiting to happen in the kitchen. He used dishtowels rather than potholders to remove a pan from a hot burner. By now all my dishtowels had either been burned up completely or were close to destruction.

I tried to be patient. I didn't want to discourage Dave from helping in the kitchen since this was the only task he was motivated to handle. I knew, however, I had to try to make the kitchen as safe for him as possible. I didn't want him to burn the house down if there was a way to prevent it.

With Chef Dave in mind, I picked out a ceramic-top range for the kitchen. The burners were not as hot as the conventional stove and a dishtowel would be less likely to catch fire unless it was left lying on top. I chose this type of stove for its flat surface, too, with no burner wells to worry about. Dave, it seemed, spilled something under the burners whenever he cooked.

One day he placed a glass bowl from the refrigerator directly onto a red-hot burner. The bowl contained oyster stew. The glass shattered from the intense heat and hot milk went everywhere, under the stove and into all the burner wells.

I hoped to eliminate this problem with the ceramic top range, but my contractor continually argued against it. "You don't want that," he would say. "They break."

"I do too want it," I insisted.

After three months of listening to him tell me what a bad choice I had made, we accepted delivery of the ceramic top range. I arrived at the house that night to find the contractor and his wife with all the lights out, standing in the kitchen in front of the stove, waiting in quiet anticipation for the burners to begin to glow.

I wasn't sorry with my decision. Contrary to all negative statements, the ceramic top did not break. We had no more burned dishtowels, and spills could be wiped up in an instant without having to dig around in cracks and crevices.

Although the Adaptive P.E. class was good exercise for Dave, he hated going to class. He continued doing as few exercises as he could get by with, and he was always in a hurry to get back home again.

While at home he sat around watching TV, bickering with the children, complaining that they wouldn't mind him. Moreover, Dave was resentful of any attention I gave the children and wanted me all to himself. This wasn't like him at all. In fact, the children had been an important part of his life before the accident. Now I found myself playing the intermediary. Usually, I sided with the children because Dave's demands were so childish and unreasonable. While he gave orders for chores that the children were supposed to do, he sat watching TV for the entire day and did nothing to help out around the house.

He began smoking, a habit he had successfully quit eight years before. He smoked incessantly. The children and I hated the smell and the smoke burned our throats. However, he wouldn't stop.

He burned holes in his shirts, in the legs of his trousers, in sofa and chair cushions, and in the car seats. When I pleaded with him to stop, he didn't refuse, he just sat and took longer puffs. When we sat down for a meal, he would light a cigarette. The smoke would curl and drift in front of my nose, and across my plate. If I got up and moved, the smoke would follow me to the other side of the table.

When we all climbed into the car for a drive, Dave would immediately light up a cigarette and choke us all out. He flicked the ashes out the car window and invariably the lighted ash would blow back into the lap of the child sitting directly behind him. He seemed to take pleasure in causing us discomfort, and eventually we learned to suffer in silence. It did no good to complain; he would only smoke that much more.

One day I became intensely angry at him for smoking. He had been sitting day after day filling the house with stale tobacco odors and rarely moving from in front of the TV except to go to the bathroom. He was doing absolutely nothing around the house to help out. Suddenly I just couldn't take it any more. I watched him inhale deeply and then slowly blow smoke around the room. I walked over to him, took the cigarette out of his hand, and stubbed it out in the ashtray.

I got a reaction out of him that time. He jerked his head around and with a flash of anger in his eye, he said, "You do that again, and I'll knock you clear across the room!"

I glared right back, and between clenched teeth I told him, "Go ahead and try! I can run faster than you!" That was the end of the conversation. He lit up another cigarette and his attention was drawn back to the TV. I left the room. This was the first time he had made an angry response in a confrontation since the accident. In a way, I was pleased that he reacted, but I grew increasingly angry at the "smokestack" that sat on my sofa every day.

He had been gaining weight since his discharge from the hospital. He was nearly fifty pounds overweight and showed no sign of slowing down. He ate the three meals a day that I cooked, and between meals he snacked. He had an incredible appetite. He never showed any signs of feeling satisfied; he *always* wanted more to eat.

He gulped down candy bars that he bought at the store near our little rental house. I took him back to see Dr. Emery. He put Dave on a high-protein, low carbohydrate diet.

Dr. Emery said Dave could have anything on the diet and as large a portion as he desired, the larger the better, he said. "How can he lose weight on that?" I asked. Dave was already on a similar diet, eating as much as he wanted of everything in the house.

Dr. Emery said he could lose weight *if* he stuck to the diet. The look Dr. Emery gave me made me feel guilty. I wondered if he thought I was forcing Dave to eat. The tone of his voice sounded irritated, as if he blamed me for Dave's weight gain.

I was concerned when I took Dave home. I talked to friends who had tried the diet. "He can't fail to lose weight," they said. "It takes a couple of weeks, but it's a good diet." It seemed strange, however, that all the people I knew who had been on the diet were still overweight.

It turned out just as I suspected. Dave added this new diet to his secret clutches of candy. He stuffed high-protein foods in his mouth until he could hold no more – then he squeezed the candy in for dessert.

I decided to cut down on the meals I was presenting to Dave each day. Since he could put together breakfast for himself, he fried a couple of eggs and toasted some bread. Lunch was not much of a problem for him to organize. I insisted he make these meals on his own. From the first day that he was able to make his wants known, he had insisted on three square meals every day. If I didn't make the meals big enough, he searched through the cupboards until he gathered enough items to make his meal complete.

I told him I would take care of the children's meals from now on, and I would cook dinner in the evening. However, the rest of the day was up to him. "If you intend to eat, you're going to have to fix it yourself."

I was getting more forceful as the days went on. He began taking care of his meals without complaint. For the first time in over a year he was actually doing something around the house. Since he appreciated the final result, he took great pride in putting together his meals.

He wasn't very neat, however. The kitchen was always a disaster when he finished. He wouldn't clean up after himself. He didn't refuse to, he just didn't. He left salt, crumbs, grease, and sticky-goo all over the countertops and the kitchen table.

Whatever he spilled onto the floor was then ground into the vinyl as he walked about the kitchen adding the finishing touches to his meal. Since he had to use his left hand for everything, he would dribble mayonnaise or catsup as he dipped or poured them from the jar or bottle. I kept having to remind myself, *This is great therapy.*

He couldn't pour liquids because of his depth perception. As he tried to pour milk into a cup, it would run over the side of the glass, across the countertop, down the front of the cupboard, and onto the floor. He didn't try to clean it up, nor did he tell me it was there. Luck was with me the days I came across something just after he spilled it. Other days I came across whatever he had spilled only after it had seeped under the breadbox, or glued two important documents together.

When I cooked a roast for dinner with the anticipation of having leftovers, I usually found it ground up for lunch meat the next morning. Dave got up all hours of the night, usually three or four in the morning, and he would grind up any leftovers for sandwich meat. I wasn't too crazy about his ground-up concoctions since I never knew exactly what he put into it, so Dave ended up having the pleasure of finishing the roast by himself.

Although I was angry at Dave for never realizing how much extra work he caused me when he didn't clean up what he spilled, I felt sympathy for the person he had become. In the past I had been the one who let the dishes pile high in the sink until *he* did them. The man he had now become was a stranger, not only to me, but to himself, also. Sometimes I wondered how much of Dave really existed.

At last I persuaded him to smoke outside. "You need the exercise," I told him. Instead of sitting in front of the TV every moment of the day, he would light up a cigarette and go outside and literally watch the world go by.

Occasionally when I was out of the house, a salesman would call. Whatever the man had to sell, Dave would buy. One day I picked up the mail and discovered a contract for five magazine subscriptions – magazines we had never bought before. Dave had verbally agreed to the contract by phone a couple of days before. I sent a letter back to the company, "My husband is not able to contract business." The magazines were cancelled.

When a storm window salesman called, Dave asked him to come over. We couldn't afford storm doors and windows, but that didn't matter to him. If the salesman told Dave it was a good buy, or how essential it was for everyone, Dave was convinced. He agreed with everyone about anything!

Since Dave was in charge of cooking his own lunch, I allowed the extravagance of TV dinners. They're expensive, but not as messy as putting together a meal from scratch. All he had to do was pop the dinner tray into the oven, and he did leave the kitchen slightly cleaner.

Whenever we shopped together, I watched him carefully as we went through the baking section so he wouldn't fill the cart with cake mixes of every flavor and style. Invariably he would find the rotten tomato in the produce section and dented cans were the only ones he ever put into the basket. If I was looking for dented cans and getting them at a bargain, I wouldn't have cared. But that wasn't the case.

He tossed heavy cans of baked beans or bottles of catsup onto the loaves of bread before I could rescue them. I always went home with at least part of one loaf of bread smashed. Then I found the rotten tomato only after we had arrived home and I was unloading the groceries. I needed eyes in the back of my head and two extra arms. Whenever I turned my head, he dropped something we didn't need into the basket. When I picked the item out of the basket to return it to the shelf, Dave spied another item he wanted. Before I could get back to the basket, he had already dropped it in.

Dave always took charge of the grocery cart the moment we entered the store. He leaned on it as we walked up and down the aisles. Since his depth perception was so poor, I walked with my hand behind my back; otherwise, he ran the car into my heels.

His peripheral vision was not much better. One shopping day as he rounded a corner he and another man crashed their shopping carts together. As much as Dave wanted to drive again, I wondered how it would be possible for him to see well enough to drive a car, when he couldn't even maneuver a shopping cart too well.

Dave had the theory that if a little is good, a lot is better. In the produce department he picked out enough broccoli to feed us every day for the entire week. One afternoon when we approached the check-out counter, Dave left to sit on the bench while I got checked out. As I stood in line while the lady in front of me got her groceries bagged, a woman walked up behind me and said, "What are you going to do with all that fish?"

"What fish?" She was pointing to the front of the basket. I took a few steps back, looked in and saw three large packages of red snapper. I smiled. "My husband must have put them in." By this time Dave was sitting in a corner nowhere to be seen. I didn't know what to tell this woman, but I said, "I'm really not sure what we're going to do with them. I do have a good recipe for batter-fried fish, though." That seemed to satisfy her as she stepped back to her own basket.

Another day a man walked past my overloaded cart. "Women sure know how to spend their husband's paycheck," he said. I smiled. *If he only know! Most of the stuff in this basket was put here by* my *husband!*

It was at the check-out counter that the clerk held up a can, made a strange face, and said, "Is this good?" I looked up to see her holding a can of escargot.

"I don't know. My husband put that in. He also likes pickled pig's feet."

She made an even funnier face and said, "Oh, yuck!"

As the weeks and months progressed I realized if this was what Dr. Emery meant by a "change in personality," I needed help – desperately.

I mentioned to Mr. Frank, the DVR counselor, that problems were beginning to surface and I didn't know how to handle them. He suggested enrolling Dave in a two-week testing program at a rehabilitation facility in Portland. "I can also set up a series of seven sessions for you with the psychiatrist."

"That would be great," I responded. "The sooner the better."

The following Monday Dave and I were scheduled to appear at the rehab center. Dave would be an outpatient. Every morning I drove him the twenty-five mile trip to the center, taking the same freeway on which his accident had occurred.

I hated driving more than anything. I only drove out of necessity, to get from one place to another. I never drove just for the sake of going for a drive or to look at scenery. In those days the speed limit was 70 mph and my little car would shudder and shake at that speed as if it was going to fall into a pile of bolts on the highway. Even at the lower speed of 60 mph, I was frightened and held tight to the steering wheel with a near-death grip. Dave had always handled the driving, and even then I often panicked and screamed when other drivers made careless maneuvers towards us.

I would never have driven this route every day, twice a day, if I didn't think it was vital for my sanity and our marriage.

Twenty-five miles is a long way to drive without removing your hands from the wheel at least once, but the first few days I drove into Portland, I think I did just that. My palms became moist and wet with perspiration. I was too afraid to let go of the wheel and dry them off on my lap; I feared I would lose control of the car. I also feared losing control if I *didn't* wipe off my hands. Fortunately we arrived safely each day.

It was at this rehab center that I met Dr. Vale. She was a small woman with short, blond hair, about the age of thirty. She told me to have a seat in her office. She closed the door, sat down at her desk, and then began asking questions about my family and the accident. I talked while she scribbled furiously on a yellow legal pad.

After nearly a half an hour I realized she had barely looked away from this pad of paper as she continued to write. I wondered if she was writing a letter home since she rarely spoke while I explained in detail as much as I could recall about our problems. I made a point to say, "But I don't want help out of my marriage. I want help with it."

At the beginning of another session on the following day, Dr. Vale mentioned how she and several women friends had moved a piano to her home. "That must have taken a lot of muscle," I said.

She pointed to her head and said, "Not muscle, we used this." I assumed they didn't move the piano with their heads, but instead used their brains; but I didn't ask. She went on, "Women don't need men." I didn't understand what she meant by that remark, and still I didn't ask for clarification. I wanted to say that I wasn't interested in "men" either; all I wanted was my husband back. Still I remained silent. I didn't want to offend her.

The rest of my session went much like the first day, Dr. Vale scribbling furiously on her yellow pad while I talked.

Throughout my life I tried to look at the brighter side of situations no matter how bad they might look. I still tried to do this even when I became discouraged with Dave's recovery. I wanted to believe that there was still hope. When I met Dr. Vale that morning I said, "I am grateful that Dave isn't any worse. We are having problems, but thank goodness he isn't violent." I went on to tell her about a couple I had heard about. The husband had suffered a head injury, but had become a terror, even actually pointing a gun at his wife. "At least Dave isn't like that," I concluded.

Dr. Vale answered, "You're no better off than they." I wasn't at all prepared for that statement. I said very little for the rest of the session. When it was over Dr. Vale walked me to the door.

"It's been eighteen months since the accident," she said. "I had another patient who was injured in the same way Dave was. He reached a plateau at eighteen months. He stopped progressing. Dave won't get any better. Why don't you put him in a boarding home and forget him?" She must have noticed the shocked look on my face as she said, "Oh, I know how you feel. I had a puppy dog one time that I had to get rid of."

She's comparing my husband to her dog? Perhaps that was the psychological way to view relationships, but I didn't see the connection. Not only did I drive home with sweaty palms – I drove home with tears streaming down my cheeks. How could she be so cruel? She wasn't helping me at all.

The following day I drew on some inner resources when I met with Dr. Vale. "If you put a normal person in a closet or a small room and never allow them to come out for stimulation, won't they deteriorate?"

"Yes, of course," she answered.

"And . . . if you put a handicapped person in a stimulating environment, won't they progress? Isn't that human nature?"

"Well, yes. But we just don't know that much about the brain."

"That's my point," I answered. Dr. Vale looked exasperated, but she didn't say anything further about Dave's rehabilitation.

Well, that's it, I thought. I refuse to go back again. Together Dr. Vale and I had accomplished absolutely nothing.

Much later Dr. Vale wrote a letter to Les, our attorney, and described me as an "uncooperative patient." Perhaps that's why no further suggestions were made by the rehab facility to help in Dave's recovery. I refused to put him in a boarding home and forget him, so they chose to think I was uncooperative.

Each afternoon I drove back into Portland, picked up Dave from his testing session, and drove home again. At the end of the two weeks, I knew no more about Dave than I did when we began.

It seemed it wasn't entirely the accident that caused the most obstacles in my life, but rather the "system." Society was inflicting more pain than a direct injury could. And there was always another painful incident just around the corner.

I had come to believe there was no one I could talk to who could understand, not even my closest friends. When I mentioned, "Dave won't do anything around the house anymore," my friend would say, "Oh, I know just what you mean. My husband won't do anything either."

Although people meant well when comparing their husbands to mine, I began to realize they didn't fully understand what I was talking about.

I wanted to tell them it was their own fault for having married a slob, or someone lazy, but I didn't. In many cases this just continued to remind me of how much I had lost. Dave *did* help out before. I married an extremely capable man who could clean house better than I, who could take care of the children better than I, and at the same time hold down a full-time job and squeeze in hundreds of hobbies in his spare time. *Now* he was different, and I didn't know how to adjust to that change.

I couldn't find anyone who understood my problems, nor could I find anyone to help me through the experience. My hope was turning to complete desperation.

Our new home was finished in September. Bill Folk brought the big Wonderbread truck over again to help us move. The gang who helped us move out of the house, came over to help us move into this one. I worried throughout those three months that something would prevent the loan from going through, but the money was dispersed without a hitch when final inspection was made on the house.

I was busy in a different way now. There were no more trenches to dig, but having a new home brought new responsibilities. A landscaper gave me a bid for $1,800 to plant grass and shrubs in the front yard. At that price, I decided to do it myself. After digging so many ditches, I figured I could handle digging holes for shrubbery.

The day I rented the roller to press the grass seeds into the ground, I came down with a bad cold. Steve and I took turns pushing the roller while I alternated the chore with blowing my nose. I fell into bed that night completely exhausted but with a warm feeling of accomplishment accomplished by the warmth of fever. I planted shrubs and flowering bulbs and turned my thoughts to spring, when color would fill the yard.

School started just after we moved, and the warm September winds began to blow, bringing the familiar feel of autumn to the air. The smell of the new wood mingled with the strong aroma of new carpeting, all intoxicating. Everything felt right about this house. I was certain the decision to sell our other place and buy this one had been correct.

Still Dave showed no interest in anything. While the children and I worked in the yard raking and digging, he sat in a lawnchair and watched. His right leg was weak and the spasticity remained, but he could get around without a cane in the house and with a cane outside. He sat silently, not giving suggestions or throwing out complaints. In the past when he saw me digging holes for plants, he would take the shovel out of my hands and finish the work. I was too slow, he said.

I was angry at Dave for never offering to share in the responsibilities, but at the same time I felt sympathy for him. He couldn't help it.

Neither could he escape his handicap. It would follow him wherever he went. *I* could *escape*, however. I knew I could walk out the door and go shopping for a few hours and have some temporary freedom. The temptation to walk out the door and never come back was there, but only as a thought. I knew I could never leave Dave. I loved him too much to leave him to live with this handicap alone.

It took strength to choose to live with Dave. But Dave had no choice; he was trapped in a handicapped body.

I recognized that the temptation to leave was there, hence I could never sit in judgment of those who actually decided on that course of action. It was important for me to find a way to live with something I could not change instead of trying to transform my life into something entirely different.

I continued looking for books about other injured people. How do they keep their marriages together, I wondered, when everything familiar about their personalities had been wrenched away? There had to be a way.

I read every story in all the women's magazines; I poured through book stores. There were numerous inspiring stories about handicapped people, but I still could find nothing about a spouse who was brain-injured. When I asked a doctor, "How do people keep their marriages together under these circumstances?" he said, "They don't. They get divorced." I knew it wasn't true in every case, but no one could show me a documented case that proved it. I continued, therefore, to stumble along on my own.

I was growing weary and depressed. I felt trapped. Since Dave couldn't leave the house unless I drove him, I felt guilty whenever I wanted to spend an hour or two in town by myself. But Dave was as trapped as I was.

Yvonne drove up from California for a short visit. She suggested taking Dave back home with her for a week. Enthusiastically, I jumped at the opportunity of having seven days of freedom, seven days of indulging selfishly in anything I wanted to do. I loved to sew, read, paint ceramics, and take long, leisurely baths. I hadn't been able to enjoy those things since the accident; I felt guilty doing anything that didn't include Dave.

When Yvonne and Dave drove away, I went back into the house, dropped down onto the sofa and went to sleep. The following day after the children left for school, I laid down on the sofa for a nap; instead, I slept the entire day away. And that was how the week went. I woke up long enough each afternoon to get dinner for the children, and then I drifted off to sleep on the sofa again, waking up each evening in time to go to bed, where I dropped off into another deep sleep. I couldn't keep myself awake.

At the end of the week Dave came home wishing I had the energy Yvonne had. I wished I had it, too. He described the visits they took to her friends' homes, a day on Chuck and Yvonne's boat, and the many trips into town. Yvonne had an exciting place to stay. I, on the other hand, had run out of ideas for keeping Dave entertained, and I no longer had the energy to keep up the pace that I did the first year or so.

I continued to drift in and out of depression. Once every few months, I slept for four to seven days at a stretch without feeling a bit rested. The children tiptoed around me and Dave quietly put his meals together without asking for help. I would wake up long enough to clean up the kitchen and throw a load of laundry into the washing machine, then back to bed I went.

The lawsuit nearly drove me crazy. For two years the date was set every two months only to be cancelled three days before convening. I became anxious and tense the moment Les told me the due-date. Court always convened on Monday morning. The pressure followed me throughout the two-month wait and grew in intensity. The days before the scheduled date, the trial would be cancelled after one of the attorneys had filed for an extension.

It was almost like a game to see who would fold first. I would think, *I can't stand this anymore! I can't take another postponement!* Then Les would call again, "It's been delayed again for another two months."

I finally reached a point where I knew I had to get away from Dave for a few hours each week. I continued to feel guilty about it unless I knew it was for a good cause. Les suggested I come in to his office and help with the increasing amount of paperwork that was piling up.

Suddenly I felt a surge of energy and enthusiasm. For one day a week Dave could manage without me for a few hours, I reasoned. And I knew it was not only good for me to be away from him, but it was also good for him as well.

I sorted through the depositions of other cases like ours, through the newspaper and magazine clippings. I organized it all into file folders so Les could find everything without a moment's hesitation when we actually made it to trial. I felt useful and my time was well-spent, so I felt no guilt at leaving Dave alone when I was working on the case. If I had left him alone just for the sake of getting out of the house, I would have been burdened with guilt.

If only I could have an hour or two alone at home without Dave underfoot, I thought. To be able to spend a little time in the house without another soul would be divine. I'd heard about women complaining when their husbands retired. They said it almost drove them crazy not to have any time to themselves. That was exactly how I felt.

I asked Dave's parents to take Dave with them whenever the could, for I thought it would be good for him to be with other people. Dave went with them, but he was angry that I made him go. He only wanted to be with me, he said, at home. Ken and Hilda took him twice, but Dave's anger prevented me from asking them again. It seemed more trouble than it was worth.

Not only had Dave and I experienced great changes, but especially so had Steve. By the second year after the accident, his voice was deepening and a growth of whiskers appeared on his face. By the time he was twelve he was shaving every day. The accident not only forced him into a role of greater responsibility, but also brought about a physical maturity that seemed out of place for his age. He looked older than some of his teachers.

I was grateful to those who spent time with the children. Especially a neighboring family who took Steve on their camping trips and on a two-week vacation to Disneyland. And Bonita, who included the girls in her family circle and took them on shopping trips.

Sometimes, however, these were painful reminders of all we had lost. Perhaps we would never be able to do such things as a family again – like other people. I hoped my children would grow to be grateful receivers, as well as givers. Fortunately, they did. However, I found resentment growing occasionally inside me when I had to accept so much charity. All I wanted was to have Dave well again and have our family back the way it was. I was tired of taking so much.

As I was hurrying to a grocery store one day, I met Debbie coming out the door. She had spent five weeks nursing Dave when he had been discharged from ICU. Nearly everyone I met knew about the accident, and wanted to know how Dave was doing. When Debbie first spoke, I thought that's what she asked. Instead she said, "I didn't ask how David was doing, I wanted to know how *you* are."

I paused as I felt the tears surface. *No one had ever asked me how I was until now.* I managed a terse, "Oh, I'm fine; we're all fine." As I walked into the store, I wasn't sure if my face had betrayed me or not. I certainly wasn't fine, and neither was Dave. I believed that was what people wanted to hear, however. I wasn't sure, if I told everyone exactly how I felt, that it would do any good. People keep telling me how happy I must be to have Dave home and "well" again. That was what I thought they wanted to hear – the stories about how happy I was. If I told Debbie how rotten I really felt, was there anything she could do about it?

Sometimes I wondered if the doctor managed to save Dave only to lose me in the process.

XIX

I was suffocating. Dave would have been happy if I had discarded everything from my life – children, home, and hobbies – to sit by his side, 24 hours a day for the rest of his life. This wasn't like him, to be so possessive. He had been the most responsible, independent, and intelligent man I knew. The children adored him, and I idolized him.

Now Dave drifted along without energy, watching TV hour after hour. Perhaps it's the Phenobarbitol, I thought. It was a sedative and I wondered if this was affecting his motivation. I called Dr. Emery and asked if it could be discontinued. He agreed to stopping the Phenobartital, but again stressed how important it was for Dave to continue the Dilantin which would control any seizures Dave might have as a result of the accident.

There was no change in Dave after the adjustment in his medication. It seemed the sedative had had little effect either way. Even the abrupt cessation caused no signs of withdrawal. His motivational level was exactly the same.

It was October and the rainy weather settled in. The whole world looked gloomy and dreary. The prospect of another winter cooped up with Dave was almost unbearable.

He continued getting up early each morning, fixed his own breakfast about five o'clock, and then sat in front of the TV until eleven when he considered it was time for lunch. He had no desires or purpose in his life. He had been driven to try everything before the accident, and now he only existed. His life had come to an abrupt halt. I couldn't stand to watch him like this.

One day I walked over to the sofa, "Would you please do something?" I told Dave as I stood in front of him.

"What do you want me to do?"

"You could vacuum; or you could load the dishwasher; you could even pick up after yourself. I really don't care what you do, just do something!" I was shouting by now.

Dave leaned forward and struggled to his feet. I was shocked. I'd finally got through to him, I thought. Perhaps I should have gotten angry at him before, and it only took a confrontation to bring him around. When he was at last on his feet, he looked questioningly at me and said, "Now what do you want me to do?"

We both stood looking at one another. Finally, I said, "Oh, do anything you want," and I left the room. A few moments later I walked back into the family room to find Dave sitting on the sofa watching TV. The episode was never mentioned again. And he continued in the same pattern as before.

I read in the Oregonian about a group of volunteers that had just formed at Valley General Hospital. Being a volunteer would be a perfect excuse. I could go to the hospital a few hours every week and since it

153

was for a good cause, Dave wouldn't mind. Les no longer had work for me to do at his office, and I was dreading the long, boring winter. Typically, I had always been a home-body, but now I had cabin-fever.

Within a couple of weeks I had become a hospital volunteer. I fed patients, took them their mail, delivered supplies to ICU, and filed charts in the office. I was scheduled for four hours, one day each week. The children were in school, and Dave managed quite well without me.

While working at the hospital, I met a young woman who said she had a friend who suffered a head injury much like Dave's. We compared notes on the two, and I was grateful Dave wasn't having the on-going seizures as this woman's friend did. She said he and his wife were divorced after the accident; the wife had remarried. Oh, how the pangs of envy hit when she described the happy life this woman now had! Her nightmare was over, I thought. Mine didn't seem to have an end.

One rainy Sunday we were on our way over to Bonita's for dinner. I stepped on the brake as we neared a red light at an intersection. The engine stopped and the entire electrical system on the car went out except for the emergency flashers. I'd been lucky all this time not to have car trouble. Dave had always taken care of the maintenance of all our cars before the accident, and now I panicked. I turned the key in the ignition, but there wasn't a sound. "What's the matter with the car?" Dave gazed out the front window. "Dave! What's the matter with the car?"

"I don't know," he answered and turned his head to look out the side window. The children sat silently in the backseat. I looked around the intersection. There was a gas crisis that year, and I saw a boarded-up gas station on one corner. Another corner was a book store that was closed on Sunday. The only other business at the intersection was a tavern.

"I'm going to call Aunt Bonita," I told the children as I opened the car door to get out. The rain was coming down in torrents as I pulled my coat around me and waited for the cars to pass. Our car was stalled in the outside lane and in order for other cars to pass, they had to swerve around us. No one stopped to help. Of course, on such a stormy day, I didn't blame them. I sloshed across the other four lanes of traffic to the tavern parking lot.

I walked inside and immediately I saw a phone sitting on the counter and a barmaid standing nearby. "May I use your phone? My car is stalled at the intersection." I was standing right in front of the phone on the counter as the barmaid pointed to the wall and said, "The pay phone is over there." I glanced at the phone on the wall and suddenly realized I had left my purse in the car.

"I'm sorry. I guess I left my purse in the car. Could I use this phone right here?"

"You'll have to use the pay phone," she answered. As I started to pull my coat up around me again to go back to the car, I noticed a man who had been sitting at the bar. He stood up, tossed me a dime, and said, "Where's your car?" I pointed to the intersection where my car was sitting with the emergency flashers blinking off and on.

As the stranger walked out the door, I went over to the pay phone and dropped in the dime.

After I reached Bonita she said she would send her husband out to help me. I hung up the phone and walked to the door. The man from the tavern had pushed the car to the intersection and over to the side of the road. He came back to the tavern, jumped into his own car, drove up to the front door as I was walking out. He motioned for me to get in. Normally I would never have climbed into a stranger's car, but on this wet, drippy day, I did.

He drove out of the parking lot and onto the main highway. He pulled up behind my car to let me out. I offered to pay him, but he just shook his head and drove off. How strange, I thought, on a rainy Sunday after church to have a man in a tavern help me when I was stranded, and all the while people driving home from church were passing me by. Someone was looking out for me, I decided.

Bill arrived and took us back to his house, where we had a nice dinner that Bonita had waiting. Then Bill went back to see what he could do about my car, which was still sitting on the side of the road. Together with my uncle, they managed to find out the reason for the stalled car: a 15¢ fuse that had blown out.

While I continued my volunteer duties coupled with my responsibilities at home, the costs of the trial were mounting. Already the medical expenses had whittled away a large portion of the insurance money. I had no idea what it took to take a case to court, but I was learning fast. Depositions had to be taken and court reporters had to be paid. Other attorneys sent Les a bill whenever we required their services, whether it was for their time or for file information from previous cases that were similar to ours. Several times Les flew to another part of the country to compile some necessary information.

The car that hit Dave no longer existed. We were basing our case strictly on witnesses and the recall letter. This would make the case much harder to prove, and Les spent long hours away from his family working on our case.

Mr. Frank suggested Dave be placed in a sheltered workshop for occupational therapy. He needed more than just the exercise of the Adaptive P.E. class. Mr. Frank began setting up appointments for us to inspect each facility – and for each facility to inspect Dave. It would be up to the counselors to make the final decision where Dave would be placed.

Our savings had dropped dangerously low. I knew eventually I would have to begin working, and it looked as if that eventuality was coming closer and closer. Dave was doing fine the four hours I was gone each week. When I left for the hospital he was sitting on the sofa in front of the TV and when I came home, he was still there. I decided to take the risk that he could manage alone while I worked part-time. I began skimming through the want-ads.

It didn't take long before I found a position for a receptionist at a doctor's office. Training would be included, the ad said.

When I arrived for the interview the secretary told me, "There are two doctors in the office. You will answer the phones, take messages, call patients and usher them to the inner office, take EKG's, take chest x-rays and develop them, sterilize instruments, make sure the doctors have their supplies and their offices are clean – and, of course, handle the filing."

Whew! It sounded like a lot to learn, but I looked forward to the new challenge. I knew I needed to be free of Dave and being so busy would prevent me from worrying about him. I just wouldn't have time.

The hours seemed ideal, but they turned into a nightmare. I was to work Mondays and Wednesdays from nine to five, and half days on Saturdays. I had expected it to be a snap once I learned the ropes.

I struggled through Mondays, trying to learn everything, only to forget it all by Wednesday. Working only two and a half days a week did not allow me enough time to learn all the things expected of me. I hadn't anticipated that.

And the phones rang off the hook. I answered the first line just as the second line rang. I put the first person on hold and answered the second. I put the second on hold and went back to the first. When I finished with the first caller and had hung up, the phone would ring again before I had a chance to accept the call from the second line. That went on nearly all day until the answering service automatically took over at five o'clock.

If and when I had a moment between calls, I was supposed to get the patients to the inside holding room and prepare those persons receiving physical examinations for chest x-rays and EKG's. The secretary took over the phones then.

I looked forward to the days when the x-rays had to be filed in a back room. Then I could spend an hour in quiet solitude without the constant jangle of phones. I did wonder about all the duties they wanted me to do, however. X-rays were considered dangerous if the operator wasn't a licensed technician. As usual I decided the doctors must have known what they were doing when they hired an amateur. One of the doctors interviewed me the first day, and he knew I had no experience.

One afternoon while I was at the "community" paper cutter located between our office and another doctor's, I saw a woman who had been hired the same day I was. I noticed her eyes looked glazed as she clipped the best sections of the EKG strip to attach to the patient's chart. I smiled at her, but she seemed lost in thought and when she was through she silently walked away.

The following day she was gone and I never saw her again. I wondered if my face held that same glassy expression. Perhaps I hadn't smiled at all, perhaps I only thought I did. If the shocked look didn't show outwardly, it certainly was present inside.   It took me all day Tuesday to recover from Monday, and all day Thursday to relieve the pressure from Wednesday. I didn't get anything done on those days of recovery, either. I just dropped down beside Dave on the sofa and spent the day asleep while he watched TV. Saturdays were relatively quiet and people didn't seem to get sick on weekends.

Each weekday there was a two-hour wait for most of the patients and the office was still full of waiting people when I left for the day.

I ushered an obviously ill young woman into the x-ray room. She was sneezing and sniffling. "I'm sorry you had to wait so long," I said.

She quickly wiped her nose on a tissue and, sounding as if she were holding her nose, she croaked, "The doctor is so wonderful, it's worth it." I raised my eyebrows in surprise, but said nothing. I didn't think anyone who consistently kept patients waiting for two hours was worth it. Then I remembered my feeling for Dr. Emery. We had waited two hours for him and though I was a bit irritated that Dave had to endure it, I, too, felt it was worth the wait. After all, Dr. Emery had saved Dave's life.

I lasted a little longer than the woman at the paper cutter. I quit in my second month for many reasons. I became discouraged at the lack of respect that the doctors had for their patients and for others they worked with. One doctor would go to the hosptal, not inform them he was there, and not answer his pages. The office staff at the hospital said he would hide once he entered the hospital. Sometimes, we, his own office staff, couldn't track him down. He would tell patients to come in tomorrow, but not write them down in the appointment book and not inform us that the patients were coming. Squeezing extra patients into an already overbooked day was what caused the two-hour backlog.

Another reason I quit was because of the stress the office caused me. It seemed it would be easier to work full time and spread my duties out over a week than try to cram a week's work into two and a half days. Dave was doing fine while I was gone. All he had to do was get his lunch ready, and I insisted he do that while I was home anyway. I knew we could use the extra money that a full-time job would bring.

The third reason I quit was because the doctor didn't seem to care enough about his employees to make sure they got paid. I worked two full months without getting paid. When I brought it to the doctor's attention he said, "You should have reminded me." I thought since I was on the payroll, it was understood that I was to be paid, and I shouldn't have to remind him. I did finally get paid, but not until after I had quit and was no longer working for him. Being forceful was not one of my best attributes.

The final reason I quit was that too much responsibility was required, working in an office and dealing with sick people. Patients would call the office and ask *me* to make a decision for them, "Do you think I am sick enough to need a doctor . . ?" One day while I was all alone in the office a woman called in and said her husband had a temperature of 105°. He was too sick for her to bring to the office. "Do you think I should call an ambulance and take him to the hospital?" she asked. She was asking me, someone who couldn't even make a rational decision for her own family!

After I advised the woman that an ambulance was necessary, I worried for the next several days that my decision had been incorrect and they'd been charged for an unnecessary ambulance ride. It's better to be safe than sorry, I thought. Then suddenly I wondered, *What am I doing here?* I didn't want to spend the rest of my life worrying about other people; I had enough to worry about with my own problems.

When I gave my resignation, the doctor asked why I was quitting. "You're doing so well," he said.

"I'm afraid I'll make a mistake," I answered. Although I explained the woman and the ambulance, he didn't understand.

"Who are you not to make a mistake?" he wanted to know. "Everyone makes mistakes, and you learn from those mistakes." I knew he was right, and I was grateful for the advice, but I had made up my mind. I didn't have enough self-confidence to hold down this kind of a job. I was too close to the medical profession, but my experience was from the viewpoint of a patient and family. I didn't want to cause problems for people who already had enough. I didn't want people to look to me for answers while I was struggling to find answers for myself. Mistakes in a doctor's office could be fatal, I thought.

I explained to Dave that I was preparing to look for a full-time job. Although he could make life difficult, and part of the reason I wanted a job was to get away from him, he made an effort to help out in the only way he could. He said, "I want whatever you want. If you think going to work is the right thing to do, then that's exactly what you should do."

"If I'm gone to work everyday, I'll need help from you," I said. "Will you help out around the house?" He nodded.

Enthusiasm began to grow as I looked through the paper and sorted through my closet for dresses that would be suitable for an office. I had taken shorthand and typing in high school and had worked as a typist at the radio station during my senior year. Moreover, I'd worked for a year as a part-time secretary in a real estate office to ease the financial strain that we'd felt when our home in Boring was under construction. Dave came home every afternoon to care for the children, just as I was leaving for a four-hour afternoon shift. We kissed in the doorway, saying hello and good-bye.

We'd been married six years then, and Steve was just starting kindergarten. Dave had dinner ready every evening when I arrived home, and the children were winding down from an exciting day with their father. Dave made it easy for me to work, but after a year the glamour had worn off, and I was ready to resume my station in our home.

Now my excitement was spilling over onto Dave. He knew how much I wanted to find a comfortable office to work in, and he became just as eager as I that I find the right position. This was going to be the beginning of a career; a role change for Dave and I. And I wouldn't have to worry about Dave during the day because he would be safely tucked away in a sheltered workshop. It was all working out just right, I thought.

Another pleasant diversion entered our lives that year. I took the children down to a neighbor's ceramic shop so they could paint knick-knacks while I worked on a vase that I had started the previous week. As I pulled the car into Palmblad's long driveway, a Great Dane came bounding toward us. I glanced at Steve as his eyes grew wide. The dog followed us to the ceramics shop. As I looked out the rearview mirror I remembered Steve telling me a few weeks before, "When I grow up, I'm going to get a Great Dane." I hadn't given that statement much thought at the time, but now Steve was turned around in his seat gazing fondly at the gangly Great Dane racing us down the driveway.

I settled down in a chair with my vase. All three of the children decided they would stay outside and play rather than paint ceramics. They wanted to be with the dog, whose name turned out to be Duchess.

Mrs. Palmblad told me a friend had brought Duchess over in the hope of finding a home for her. The owners had bought her eight months ago and Duchess was outgrowing their apartment. She had to go.

Mrs. Palmblad said *they* couldn't keep her either. "She's running our dog to death. Daisy's just too old to be chased around like that!"

I gulped as I said, "Please, don't tell Steve." She said she wouldn't. I spent the next hour in the quiet solitude of the shop as I finished my vase, preparing it for firing in the kiln. When I went to gather the children together, Mr. Palmblad was outside with them. I had forgotten to tell Mr. Palmblad that I didn't want a Great Dane. I didn't think about this at the time, however.

A couple of days later as I pulled the car into our road after returning home from the store, I saw Steve standing at the end of our driveway. I knew something was wrong. Steve only met me in the driveway when there was a problem. I stopped the car and rolled down the window.

"Mom, they have to get rid of Duchess. And, Mom, if they don't find someone to take her they're going to take her to the dog pound. Can't we have her? Please, Mom?"

I sat there in the car in silence, except for an enormous sigh. This was what I had hoped wouldn't happen. We didn't need a dog, and especially we didn't need a Great Dane. I had always been the one who took in stray cats or any other animal that was dropped on my doorstep, but this was another matter; a Great Dane was not a small kitten. I knew Steve had reached me when I realized I couldn't be responsible for Duchess going to the pound. "All right," I said. "But, listen. This is just on a trial basis. If she doesn't work out, back she goes!"

By this time Steve was on his bike, pedaling down the road as he yelled back, "Okay!"

The first three nights Duchess spent in the garage next to the twenty-five pound bag of dog food which the Palmblads gave Steve. I watched for problems, but none developed. When Steve brought her into the house, she never knocked anything off, even though her tail was coffee table height. Her manners were unquestionable and she slowly worked her way into the house on a permanent basis and eventually into our hearts. Duchess became another member of our family.

Not long after we moved into our new house, a neighbor asked me to accompany her to a women's nondenominational Bible study which was to be held in the living room of another neighbor's home. Usually I attended only those Bible studies that were held by the church where we worshipped, but this time I made an exception. I looked forward to any *good* excuse to get me out of the house, now that I was between jobs.

My neighbor and I were among the first to arrive, and I watched the room quickly fill with other young mothers. Soon there was only sitting room left on the floor. I especially noticed a young woman in a wheelchair and my curiosity was aroused. Why was she in a wheelchair? Then, as the meeting began, my attention was drawn to the speaker.

I had looked forward to meeting with other Christian women. I was eager to receive some spiritual guidance. And I recognized the speaker from a Christian Women's luncheon I had attended a few years before.

A tragic murder had occurred in our area a few months before, and the speaker brought this to our attention. I listened as she recounted how the tragedy affected all of us in the area. We were all a little more concerned about our children, knowing a teen-age girl had been killed by an unknown assailant.

Then the speaker said that we, as Christians, do not have to worry about this happening to our children. As long as we are Christians, she said, this would not happen to any of our loved ones.

What about the young woman in the wheelchair, I wondered. Is she not a Christian? Can we tell who is a Christian and who is not by the tragedies in their lives? My mind whirled around to Dave.

Then I remembered the woman who asked my aunt, "Was Dave a Christian?" Even the contractor who built our home insinuated we were not Christians. He assumed that because this accident had occurred to Dave, we were obviously not Christians. "Bring Dave to my church," he said, "and he will be healed."

I don't remember my beliefs having a beginning, but I was baptized when I was twelve years old. This only intensified my faith. I felt strongly that if God wanted Dave healed, he could do it in our own home.

During that meeting my mind wandered in frustration. I couldn't understand chasing all over looking for healing that some people presumed was waiting within arm's length for us. Dave had already miraculously survived a terrible head injury. To some it was a miracle that he still lived, or that he was walking and talking.

There were Christians who claimed God blessed them for their faith and were in turn given wealth and good health. Some people explained how children are punished for their parents' sins or that God allows tragedies so He can bring about something good from it. It was also explained to me that people are tested and punished for their own sins, and that was why, some say, disasterous things happen to *certain* people.

Even though I prayed for Dave in the hope he would be healed, nothing dramatic happened. Dave progressed slowly, but not in leaps and bounds as I expected. It was then that I felt guilty and sometimes blamed myself for not having enough faith. If it weren't for me, I chastised myself, Dave would be well again.

Then I remembered Adam and Eve. God didn't want Eve to eat the apple in the Garden of Eden, but He gave her the choice to make the decision for herself. We all are given the choice to live life as we want to, not as God dictates. God could have made us into puppets, but He chose to make us in His own image living a life of free will.

God didn't say that if I had faith in Him, I would not struggle. He didn't say that if I prayed He would protect me from all pain and frustration. That would be wrapping me in cotton batting, and God doesn't do that.

In the Old Testament when Cain killed his brother Abel, God was not happy about it, nor was it something God programmed Cain to do. God knew it would happen, but He didn't *will* it to come about.

In answer to those who felt we were being tested according to the Lord's will, I wondered why He didn't pick people who would have made a greater impact on the religious world rather than "ordinary" people like Dave and I. He could have chosen someone famous who could have brought more glory to God.

I also wondered why God doesn't instantly punish murderers by paralyzing them instead of crippling a child in an accident. If punishing and testing is the Lord's practice, then why do criminals prosper financially – even from their own victims? A criminal isn't immediately caught in the middle of his misdeeds because he has been struck by a paralyzing bolt of lightening.

I concluded that Dave happened to be in the wrong place at the wrong time on that freeway, but not because God chose him to be there. God doesn't build roads nor does He build cars. God doesn't produce powerful chemicals that pollute our water and food supplies, nor does He build nuclear weapons. Man does all of those things.

Dave was given the free will to drive a car on a busy freeway with other people who were also given the same free will. There are both careless people operating automobiles and cars that malfunction due to faulty design or maintenance. And I don't believe God ponders each morning which cars He should crash together just to see what good He can bring from it.

People view an organ transplant as a miracle for the person who received the organ. However, someone had to die to make most of these donations possible. God didn't decide to injure a person in an accident just to give surgeons an organ to transplant into a more-deserving person.

I've also read stories about people who feel they were saved from death after they prayed. Others who are just as strong in their faith have died without God intervening for them.

If simply being a Christian our lives were made safe and secure, all

Christians would automatically be free from the worldly problems that inundate nonbelievers. However, we're all given the same perplexing problems and life-threatening accidents. If I thought I would spend a life of horrible suffering simply because I chose to be a Christian, I'm not so certain I would agree that the reward would be worth it. There is no rhyme or reason that we can understand as to why there is so much suffering and unhappiness in the world except that it came with the gift of free will when God decided to allow mankind to make his own decisions. I know when I became a Christian, I wasn't given a blanket-insurance policy that provided life-long security and wealth instead of trials and torment. I was given the gift of eternal life. Some day there will be no pain or suffering in a place where everyone is united in peace and love.

Death, too, is a fact of life that everyone must face. I don't believe God sets traps on freeways any more than I would consider setting traps for my own children just to see how they get through them, or to see what good could come of it. God must be very sad to hear us describe Him in those terms – as a trap-setter.

Over the years I have prayed for A's on test papers when I was in school, green lights at intersections when I'm in a hurry, and parking spaces near the doorway of the grocery store when it's raining. Nearly every time those prayers have been answered, but the prayers for Dave's healing were not. At least not in the manner I expected.

I believe God can bring miracles into our lives, but I don't believe He is going to grab me from the edge of a cliff if I should choose to jump. Nor will He suspend the law of gravity if I pray and then suddenly change my mind after I jump. Neither does He pull back a speeding car that's out of control in order to bring protection to those inside or in its path.

It is, however, inherent for human beings to see the cause and effect in every situation. The majority of the people on this earth want to have an answer for everything that happens, but there are no answers for everything. We are asked to have a simple faith, a belief that doesn't look for answers. Only at the end of time will we receive the answers we are looking for, and those answers will come from God Himself.

In order to enjoy the wonderful things in life, God knew I had to be exposed to some of the suffering, too. He didn't protect Dave and I, nor did He leave us. He didn't guide my every step or tell me everything to do. Sometimes He gave me a slight nudge, but mostly He allowed me to use the gift He gave me – free will.

After that evening Bible study I spent the following months in a continuing downward spiral as I struggled with life. The Lord didn't stop this suffering, nor did He abandon me. Sometimes I didn't feel Him as closely as I was accustomed, and sometimes He seemed absent – but He wasn't. He was there beside me all the time, and He was giving me the space to learn to live. I had to go all the way down, it seems, in order to come back up.

162

XX

Dave didn't care that his weight was reaching toward 300 pounds; he didn't care about responsibilities; he didn't care that I maintained control over our home and business affairs.

A slight change in his daily routine came with a deck of cards. Instead of spending the entire day in front of the TV, he spent some of his time playing games of solitaire. As for me, I rarely let my frustration surface. I kept it buried, and all the while I persisted in trying to see the silver lining in black thunder clouds.

There were times when Dave was deeply depressed. With tears spilling over he would say, "I can't do anything anymore! I'm no use to anyone!"

"Yes, you are," I declared. "You're very important to the children and me. And you can do things!"

"I can't drive a truck anymore," he replied. "I can't fly a plane anymore . . . I can't even drive my own car."

"I know, I know." My heart ached for him. Next to his family, driving a truck and flying a plane were the most important things in his life. They had been snatched away from him.

When an airplane flew overhead, he would search the skies trying to catch a glimpse of it. "Where is it? Where is it?" I would point to it, giving direction, over there, over there. Dave's vision was now so poor that he couldn't even see a plane flying just above the treetops. In anguish he would sob, "I can't see it. I can't see it."

His depression reached a peak. "It would be best if I just took my hunting rifle and shot myself," he said.

"Don't you dare," I shouted at him. "Don't you ever say anything like that again. After all we've been through, don't you dare commit suicide!"

"I won't. I know I won't go to heaven if I do," he answered. "Suicide is a sin." Thank God, I thought. At least he was rational enough to understand that.

I felt so sorry for Dave, and so sorry for the children. I remembered the pain I endured when my father died. I was eleven years old, just a year older than Steve was at the time of Dave's accident. I *knew* the intensity of the pain the children endured. Losing a parent is excruciating to a child. And they had lost Dave, even though he was still there.

If I felt anger, I didn't know where to focus it. I couldn't feel angry at the man who caused the accident – it wasn't really his fault. I couldn't feel angry at the automobile factory that built the car. *How can I be angry at a building?* Am I angry at cement blocks, at the siding that encompasses the factory, or at the unknown people who built a defective car? Should I be angry at the president of the corporation? Or the board of directors?

I realized all I felt was intense sorrow. A sorrow for what should have been, a sorrow for what would never exist again.

Some days I could push the hopelessness out of my mind. This could go on for months. Then without warning the overwhelming hurt that had been growing for those months would come crashing down on my head.

When that happened, I locked myself in the bathroom, turned on the water in the bathtub to muffle any sounds. I buried my face in a thickly-folded bath towel and sobbed.

Although this torrent of emotion changed nothing, it did allow me to get through another six months or so of more normal living. Both Dave and the children needed me. I had to keep cheerful, and try to help Dave continue to grow. I didn't dare allow depression to take over my personality.

Day-to-day activities were difficult and I stopped forcing myself out to social engagements, although they had been only rare excursions anyway. Since the accident I felt different from other people. Our family was unlike any other family in the area.

On the phone one day a friend told me how difficult her teenage son was becoming. "I wish my husband had been in an accident like Dave's and perhaps it would teach my son a lesson." I was horrified. What a thing to say, I thought. I said nothing in response, but I wished to God that I could trade places with this woman. I would gladly give up my role to take over hers.

I attended another women's Bible study after the memories of the previous one had worn off. Of all things, the scripture lesson for the day was instruction on how to be the perfect Biblical wife. After listening to the leader explain all that a wife *should* be, I couldn't keep silent any longer.

"All of this is good to do," I said, "but wives should learn to become more independent of their husbands for the day they might be left alone without their protection." When I looked around the room and saw the cold, icy stares, I wished I could have bitten my tongue off. The silence was profound.

I knew then that these women didn't want to know what I was talking about. They were going home that very afternoon to fix dinner for husbands who would come home after a long day at the office. They could walk into their houses and close their doors to any unhappiness occurring in the rest of the world.

Chances were great that most of those women would lose their husbands to death or divorce, but none of them wanted to think about it now. Their main goal in life now was how to be the "perfect" Biblical wife. My goal was trying to survive in a role I was totally unprepared for.

We managed to get through the spring months and by June, 1974, I found a job as a bank teller in a savings and loan. The salary was very low, $400 a month, but I was promised a $50 raise after a six-week training period. The bank was located in Gresham, and the short distance to and from work made it all worthwhile. I would be only a ten-minute drive from home.

Mr. Frank placed Dave in the United Cerebral Palsy workshop where Dave would also be put through a training program. Dave and I were

164

both encouraged. At last he had something to look forward to every day; the stimulus would be wonderful, I thought. And I could go to work every morning and not have to worry about him. He would be well cared for.

However, working at the bank was not what I had anticipated. After the six-week training period, I was moved to the Gresham branch. There were no such things as "banker's hours." The doors opened at nine and closed at 5:30, but the tellers didn't necessarily go home at that time. A computer processed all the transactions and we were trained to work on a computer terminal. We typed in the information and the ending cash balances were displayed at the end of the day. Our cash drawers had to balance out exactly to that figure.

Mistakes were made. Sometimes during a busy day, one of the managers would work out of one of the teller's windows. If a wrong key was accidently coded in, the cash balance would be thrown off at the end of the day. During the time I worked there, all the tellers were mothers with children. We helped one another when anyone was off balance. The more help a teller had to find the error, the quicker we could all go home. But many nights I didn't get home until seven.

Some days the computer lines became overloaded and the deposits and withdrawals couldn't be processed as they came in. A few nights like that kept us until nine o'clock. Sometimes just as the doors were locked for the day, the computer came back on and we had to stay and put nearly an entire day's work through before we could go home. If the computer remained off, we did work the following morning in between our regular customers.

I went from one stressful situation at home to another at the bank.

Every morning I took Dave to the workshop, nearly a half-hour drive from home. In the afternoon he caught a bus home. The bus service to our home was one every two hours, so if he missed one he had a two-hour wait for another. Usually Dave arrived home every day just as the children were getting off the school bus.

I was pleased that Dave was learning to ride the bus, a step toward a greater degree of independence for him. And the workshop looked like a definite step up out of his depressing existence.

Dave soon became discouraged with the workshop, however. They told him he would be paid a salary, but he was horrified with his first check. Ten cents an hour to stuff moss into plastic bags, after $5 an hour as a truck driver in 1972! His ego was crushed. He told the other clients at the workshop, "Ten cents! I made five dollars an hour as a truck driver!" They would look at him in incredulity. "Imagine, five dollars an hour," they would say. They were grateful for the ten cents; they couldn't fathom five dollars.

All of this was hard on Dave. His intelligence wasn't impaired, and he spent most of his days pondering over the things he used to do. He didn't want to stuff moss into little plastic bags, he wanted to be a truck driver. *Why couldn't anyone see that?*

When he left his position at the table to go to the bathroom, a counselor would ask, "Where are you going, David?" After a few weeks of being questioned whenever he rose from the chair, he decided he wasn't going to put up with it anymore that day. He walked out to the bus stop.

That only made things worse for him. Each day after that he was watched more closely. The counselors were beginning to show irritation at his lack of cooperation; why didn't he appreciate what they were doing for him? I wondered if any of them truly understood Dave. He wasn't ignorant, but they treated him much as they would a child. And Dave didn't like it one bit.

I must have seen too many Hollywood movies. It seemed that friends and relatives must have, too. Now I was beginning to believe that the counselors and therapists had also seen too many. Death was an inevitable occurrence, but disability is misunderstood. We all seem to have absorbed the misconception that all handicaps can be healed or completely overcome. I thought of it as a soap opera; when enough scenes are worked out, all becomes well once again and everyone lives happily ever after. I never believed things would be less than that. It's inconceivable to have them go on and on.

To cope with an on-going problem is difficult. To know I will never see Dave as he once was; to face each day with an acceptance of what I could not change. Some days I thought this was impossible, but I knew I loved Dave enough to master it. I was determined!

I kept reminding myself, things could be worse. Then I would wonder, *how?* Some people mentioned how lucky Dave was to be alive, but this was no consolation to us. I often thought of death as better than the life Dave was being forced to live. He was only breathing, not actually living.

Living in constant physical pain was the only thing I could imagine to be worse than the condition Dave was in. I thought of the thousands of people who lived in war-ravished countries, the many thousands who were starving to death every day. The fear of bombs, the pain of starvation – I could feel a relation to that suffering, and yet their pain *was* worse.

Dave still had pain in his right arm, but it was a pain that could be relieved by moving his arm to a different position. I was thankful he wasn't living in perpetual agony. *Our* pain was emotional.

I kept telling myself, forcing myself, to keep strong. I remembered the scripture, "All things are possible to him who believeth."

I heard a quadriplegic woman say, "I'm just thankful I didn't have a head injury. At least I still think the same way as before my accident." What an incredible statement to come from a young woman who would be paralyzed below the neck for the rest of her life. She was grateful for her unimpaired mind.

Dave was handicapped in both mind and body. And he struggled with the unfamiliar thoughts, strange feelings that were all different from the thoughts and feelings of the self he remembered. I struggled to accept this "new" person Dave had become, and I was distressed by the frustrations he also had to endure because of the changed person he had become.

The counselors who worked with Dave saw many disabled people in the workshops who were born with their disability. Many of them met the daily frustrations with a strength and determination, a determination to get out in society and find a place for themselves. They inspired their family and friends.

Dave was different. He hadn't been born with his handicap. He *had* been the kind of person he wanted to be. He *had* accomplished many things in his life, more things in thirty-three years than most people do in a lifetime. *He wanted to be the person he used to be.*

Many friends and relatives treated Dave differently after the accident. "Why do they think I don't remember them? I know who they are." Many people were surprised to find Dave did remember them. Rumors were rampant after the accident. People thought his head had been crushed, and that he no longer had a functioning brain. One man said, "I heard he was hit by a truck." I said, "No. He was hit by another car. He was a truck driver."

Dave didn't like being treated like a child. He didn't like being treated as if he were retarded. He wanted people to treat him as they did before the accident. Now he wanted the counselors to treat him the same way they would have if he had never been injured.

The more he disobeyed orders, however, the greater was the supervision from the counselors, and the more irritated Dave became.

Mr. Frank suggested another workshop. Perhaps Dave would fit in better at Goodwill Industries, he said. I was willing to try anything to help Dave. Mr. Frank said he would set up an appointment for us to be interviewed.

I thought of Dr. Emery. Dr. Emery dealt with head injuries all the time; surely he must know how to help us with Dave's rehabilitation. I felt so helpless, and life seemed so hopeless. I called Dr. Emery and left a message.

I heard someone say years ago that God never gives more than we have strength to endure. But wasn't this much more than I was able to endure? I had a job to cope with, three children to raise, and a husband who didn't fit anywhere. I felt as if I were raising Dave all over again, too.

Dr. Emery didn't return my call.

I continued going to work every day. Dave, between workshops, stayed home in front of the TV. When I arrived home in the evening, he was waiting and watching for my car to enter the driveway. His whole existence revolved around my going to work and coming home at night. In the time between those two events, he drifted with no desires or cares.

Friends would say, "Why don't you give him a hobby? He looks like he should be able to do *something*."

I had tried hobbies; I tried crafts. Dave was willing to accept any suggestions, but I ended up doing all the work for him. He would give up in frustration with his vision or problems with his hand coordination. A friend suggested, "Why don't you become an accountant, Dave?" Dave said that was a wonderful idea. Silently I wondered how Dave could handle other people's finances when he wasn't interested in ours in the least. Dave never mentioned the suggestion again. Fortunately the man never visited again.

With all the suggestions people handed me, I began feeling inept. Perhaps it was my fault, I thought. Although Dave had many problems to contend with no matter what he tried, he did cooperate with other people more than he did with me. Since I was his wife, he thought he didn't have to do anything I said.

Then I remembered the counselors at the workshop. After the first couple of days, they couldn't get Dave to cooperate, either. At the Adaptive P.E. class, the instructor couldn't get Dave to do all his exercises. I decided it wasn't all my fault. I knew I had to learn to ignore people who didn't understand the effects of Dave's brain injury.

Dave's skills in the kitchen didn't improve. He continued to slop together his lunch. Baked beans and mayonnaise were tracked across the kitchen floor onto the carpet. From outside he tracked in mud that was caked an inch thick on his boots. Nothing was safe from Dave.

I kept telling myself, "I have to be tolerant; I have to be patient!"

When I made Dave smoke outside, a friend told my mother that she thought it was cruel. "After all, a man should be able to smoke in his own house," she said. Soon Dave began working his way back into the house with his cigarettes. Nothing I said could persuade him to resume his smoking outdoors. Even the children argued with him, but to no avail. Steve saw a film in health class on the hazards of smoking. After school one afternoon he announced to Dave, "Do you know what your lungs look like?" Dave said nothing, but continued watching TV.

Now the ashtrays were filled to overflowing as Dave sat hour after hour, smoking cigarette after cigarette. After I vacuumed the carpet, Dave spilled the ashtray all over it. Burn holes were turning up once again in the sofa cushions, in Dave's shirts and pant legs, and in pillows. I wondered what kept the house from burning down around us.

A couple who had just joined our church called and asked if they could stop by and visit with us. They had only recently moved into the area. Mrs. Farrell said she was a housewife, and Mr. Farrell described himself as a non-practicing minister. I looked forward to their visit.

After Mr. and Mrs. Farrell sat down on the sofa, they began telling Dave and me about a tragedy in their own lives. Their daughter had been in a car accident, and although she had no lingering disabilities, she had experienced such great emotional problems, and her personality had changed so radically that Mr. and Mrs. Farrell finally had to place her in a mental institution. There was no sign of improvement, and they were living each day as it came.

I became quite uncomfortable as they began their story, and by the time they were ready to leave, I was terrified. *If a simple car accident can throw a minister's child into such an emotional state, what is stopping us?*

Every day I seemed to be dragging my feet a little more from exhaustion and fright.

This turned out to be another year when our Christmas tree was too large. This time it was too tall for the house. Dave was sitting in the family room watching TV as Steve and I struggled to bring the tree up to the front door. Just then our neighbor, Walt Townsend, stopped over. "Do you need some help?" he asked.

Steve and I stopped tugging on the tree. "Do we ever!" Walt examined the tree, looked inside the house as I pointed to where we wanted it positioned in front of the window. "I was beginning to wonder what we were going to do," I said. "I'm sure glad you stopped; God sent you over at just the right time."

Walt smiled and said, "I saw you drive in with it, and thought you might need some help." Steve brought Walt a saw. He sawed branches off, and then a hunk off the trunk. Then he brought over a five-gallon bucket filled with sand. He stuck the tree into the bucket, pushed the tree over to the window, and filled the bucket with water so the tree wouldn't dry out during the following days. Meanwhile Dave remained in the family room watching TV.

It was embarrassing for me to have my friend's husband help me with a problem while Dave sat engrossed in a TV program. But through out the previous year Walt and his wife, Elaine, had become good friends, and Walt understood the problem even though I couldn't exactly explain it to anyone. None of us completely understood what was wrong with Dave.

When I worked I knew I could depend on Elaine if Dave or the children needed anything. We soon had a path between the two houses as the Townsend children visited our house and our children visited theirs.

One morning I was vacuuming the living room carpet when I glanced out the window to see Dave driving by in our car. He had just backed out the driveway and was headed toward the main highway. I dropped the hose to the vacuum and ran out the front door. I ran up to the end of the driveway as Dave made a right turn in the direction of Boring. Frantic by now, I wasted no time getting over to Elaine's.

I pounded on her front door. When she opened it I pleaded, "Will you take me to Boring? Dave just took off in our car and I'm sure he's going into town." Elaine grabbed her baby daughter and we piled into her car.

As we approached the first little market in Boring, I saw our car sitting in the lot. Dave was just coming out the door of the store. Elaine pulled into the parking lot, and I jumped out of the car. I waved and yelled, "Thanks. See you back home."

By now Dave was nonchalantly getting into the driver's side. Without a word I jumped into the passenger's side. Dave started the engine as if I had been there all the time. He didn't seem surprised, nor angry. "What did you buy at the store?"

"Cigarettes," he answered naturally, as if I should have known.

Dave drove us back home. I remembered asking Dr. Emery one time, "How will I know when Dave is able to drive again?" Dave's driver's license expired the year of the accident.

Dr. Emery replied, "Just take him out and see how he does." I was surprised that it would be such a simple thing. I assumed he would need to be tested again since he had endured such a terrible brain injury.

Dave's truck-driving ability had stood him in good stead. He had limited use of his right leg, and none at all of his right arm, but he did quite well driving back to the house. A little swervy, but not too bad considering he hadn't driven in three years.

I decided to take Dave back to the ophthalmologist and have his vision re-tested. I didn't want Dave out on the road if he couldn't see. Before the appointment – which was a couple of weeks away – I did take Dave out for a few more sessions behind the wheel. Dr. Emery had said that was the way I could tell his driving ability, and I trusted him to know.

The first time I had taken Dave to the ophthalmologist was a year after the accident. The doctor said his vision tested to 20/40. Now he said it had improved to 20/30. "Good enough to drive," the doctor said. He handed me a note made out to the Motor Vehicle Department, informing them of Dave's present improved condition.

On our way home Dave and I stopped at the motor vehicle office to have Dave tested for a new driver's license. I parked the car and we waited in line for the driver's test. When Dave's turn came, I walked outside and watched as the examiner tested the car lights. Then he climbed into the passenger's side next to Dave.

The examiner closed the door. Then suddenly it flew open again, as the examiner jumped out of the car. He had just read the note from the doctor outlining Dave's condition. "I'm not going out with you until I call Salem." As I walked toward the car, the examiner said he would call the head office of the Department of Motor Vehicles in Salem, and they would be in touch with us soon.

A few days later I received a call from the DMV office. The man on the phone said, after checking all the information, "Your husband can be given a driver's license, but only for a two-mile radius around your home. He will not be able to drive on freeways, or at night." He added that Dave would not be authorized to drive in Sandy or Gresham, two of our nearest towns.

"But how can I be sure he will stay in that two-mile radius?" I thought the proposed restriction over carefully, and said, "I don't know. I don't think that's a good idea." So many of our friends lived outside that two-mile radius, and in fact the roads within the two-mile radius seemed more dangerous to me than the freeway. There were no shoulders, and children often rode their bicycles and horses on the narrow gravel strips. "In that case," I replied, "I don't want him to drive at all."

"But what about his ego?" the man asked.

"I'm afraid he will just have to learn to live with a bruised ego rather than risk causing an accident." I replied. I could never live with myself if I had willingly allowed Dave to drive a car and he had been responsible for an accident killing someone – or worse, leaving someone in the same condition he was in.

I couldn't understand these people. This man wanted Dave to have a license to keep from hurting his ego! Dr. Emery said it was okay to take him out for a drive, "just to see how he does." No one seemed to be interested in taking any responsibility.

My new place of employment was taking up more and more of my time and it was becoming necessary for the children to handle the chores around the house. When they arrived home from school they were to load the dishwasher, take out the garbage, run the vacuum through the house, or do whatever happened to be on the list for that day. Each child had a chore and the chores rotated daily so no one person was responsible for the same thing two days in a row. On weekends I took over the cleaning of the entire house.

"Why doesn't Dad do something? He sits around all day and never does anything," Steve complained. "We do all the work."

I tried to explain, "Dad can't, Steve. He isn't able to anymore." I was never sure if Steve could understand what I was trying to tell him since I didn't understand it myself. Even the experts were short-tempered with Dave and frustrated that he didn't cooperate. How could I expect a child to understand?

Conflict was growing between Dave and the children. On the days Lisa was scheduled to clean the kitchen she would greet me at the door wth her complaints. "Every morning when I clean the kitchen before I go to school, it's a mess when I get home. Dad won't pick up after himself. He leaves plates on the counter and he spills everything all over. Mom, can't you make Dad clean up after himself?"

I let out a sigh of frustration. I was tired from a day of work, but I told her I would try. Then I picked up a dish from the sink, and told Lisa to do something else. "I'll finish the dishes." Everyone was telling me to make Dave help; make him do something, they would say. Or, he looks like he should be able to help out. Why don't you make him?

At home the children were complaining daily. At work, I had to handle complaints from the bank's customers. And then there was Les, our attorney, calling every two months to tell me the trial had been postponed again.

The only time Dave spoke was to answer a question or yell at a child. Other than that there was no communication from him at all.

The pressure built up gradually. Oddly, my ear began to throb until the entire right side of my face ached. I couldn't comfortably open my mouth to eat. I managed to squeeze in food, but it took effort to open my jaws. I had some left-over ear drops from when Lisa had an earache, so I spent the next two months medicating myself. When three months had passed and my ear wasn't any better, I went to see Dr. Manning.

"Your ear looks okay," Dr. Manning said, asking me to open my mouth so he could look at my throat. The pain was excruciating. "It's probably coming from your teeth since there doesn't seem to be any inflammation in your throat either. Go to your dentist and have him check it out."

The dentist found the cause immediately. "You're really clamping down," said Dr. Norquist. "And it looks like your bite is off." He began drilling on my teeth. He drilled until he was satisfied with the result. "It isn't surprising, after all you've been through with Dave's accident. Stress causes it," he said.

After three weeks of relaxation exercise each night before I went to sleep, I no longer woke up with the pain in my ear.

Although I explained to the children that they were not to call me at work unless it was an emergency (a broken arm or death is an emergency, I said), they still called. With the other tellers' children calling, too, the receptionist said she could tell the moment school was out; the phone lines began to ring more frequently.

Sometimes the question would be from Lisa or Jan, "Can we go shopping this weekend?"

"We'll see," I'd answer. "We'll talk about it when I get home, I have to work now. Bye."

One afternoon Steve called. Aunt Peggy had given him a rabbit a few months before. He was tearful as he said, "Mom, the rabbit is shaking all over. I think he's really sick. Can you come home?"

"No, I can't come home," I replied. "I have a customer at my window right now, and I'm really busy. Why don't you call Aunt Peggy and ask her if she knows what's wrong?" I felt terrible, dropping the situation back into Steve's lap, but I hung up the phone and rushed back to my customer. In a moment I had forgotten about the trauma going on at my house.

A few moments later I was called back to the phone. Steve's somber voice came over the line. "The rabbit died."

"I'm sorry, Steve," I answered apologetically.

His voice brightened a little as he asked, "Can I keep the fur?"

"Sure, you can. Do you know how to skin it?"

"Yeah, I can do it," he replied.

"Don't forget to bury the rest of the rabbit really deep, so the dogs don't dig it back up."

That night by the time I got home Steve had buried the rabbit, saved the fur, and placed it under an upside-down picnic table to dry. He had sprinkled salt generously over the entire back side of the hide. He said he learned that at school.

The fur dried beautifully and Steve had a lovely white rabbit's fur as a trophy for what he was able to do when pressed with a problem. The sadness of the situation turned into a beautiful remembrance.

If only all of life's problems could be so easily disposed of! I was sinking further into despair every day.

I called Dr. Emery's office once again. I told the receptionist, "Would you ask Dr. Emery to give me a call. If I don't get some help, I'm going to go crazy."

"Oh, don't say that," she answered abruptly. I wondered if she thought I was joking. I certainly wasn't.

At least death brings an end eventually, but Dave's disability was slowly but inexorably sucking the life out of our family.

There were days when I knew I couldn't go on any longer. That was when I went into the bathroom again, turned on the water in the bathtub, and cried into my folded bath towel, cried and cried until I couldn't cry any more. I squeezed every tear out. Racked with exhaustion, I splashed cold water on my face, applied a little make-up, and walked out of the bathroom as if nothing had happened.

One day as Dave sat watching TV, I felt I had reached my limit as I scrubbed the sticky mess from the counter. "*Why* don't you do something? *Why* do you watch TV all day long? *Why* do I have to do everything?" I pounded the counter with my fist.

Dave looked away from the program he was watching. His face had a blank look as he watched me pound the counter, talking to myself. Then he turned back to the TV without saying a word. I wanted to scream, but instead I just gritted my teeth and threw the dishrag into the sink.

Dave's weight was dangerously high, and friends were telling me, "You *must* make him lose weight." Did they think I was forcing food down Dave's throat?

I took Dave to an internist who said, "Put a padlock on the refrigerator."

I protested, "But I have a teenage son who has to eat, too."

"Buy him his own refrigerator," he replied.

Everyone gave me such simplistic answers to every problem I had. If they only knew how difficult it was for me to influence Dave in any way. He resisted any advice or help I offered. At one point Dr. Emery said, "If he were a drinker, he would be an alcoholic." In one breath doctors told me to make him stop eating so much, and in the other they said he couldn't control himself.

Now Dave was beginning to show anger now and then. At first I was happy to see any sign of emotion. The first months it had been nothing but tears, then he added anger and irritation to his feelings. Now it seemed anything could make him explode in rage – a fall, difficulty accomplishing the slightest task, or just the presence of the children. Home had become a war zone.

Each night Steve greeted me at the door with the same pleading sentence, "Mom! Dad grounded me." The greeting only changed when he began adding "again" to the end.

"What for?" I asked in my usual exhausted sigh.

"He said I came home late, but I didn't. He told me to come home at six and I did – but he grounded me anyway."

"Okay. You're not grounded," I said, finishing the conversation.

Each evening Dave struggled to put together a dinner. He was getting better in his culinary skills, but I was getting tired of Hamburger Helper every night. There were many nights when I came home after dinner was over and the pot was waiting for me on the stove. Most nights I was too tired to eat, whether it was Hamburger Helper or anything else.

Lisa had volunteered to clean the kitchen for five dollars a week. After one week she quit. The money wasn't worth the work, she said. "Every day the kitchen is a mess when I get home from school," she announced. "Dad doesn't do anything around here but make messes!"

"Okay, okay," I said with deeper exhaustion. "I'll do the dishes. You do some of the other chores and I'll do the dishes when I get home from work."

Now I had another problem on my mind. I had to find out why Dave was grounding Steve every day. Steve had never been a problem and I couldn't understand why there was such a fuss all of a sudden.

On weekends I watched when Steve went to play with his friends. Dave would tell him to be home at six. While Steve was gone Dave would glance periodically at his watch. As I busied myself in the kitchen, I glanced periodically at Dave and then at the clock.

One evening Steve came home at 5:55. Dave looked quickly at his watch, pointed his finger at Steve and said, "You're grounded!"

Steve looked imploringly at me as I said, "What! He was five minutes early," and, in exasperation, "Steve, you're not grounded." Steve walked quietly to his room without saying a word.

I made an effort to leave work as soon as possible every evening, and each night I followed this ritual between Dave and Steve. If Steve came home at 6:05, he was grounded. If he came in at six on the button, he was grounded, too. This was too much. Every night Dave grounded Steve. Every night I ungrounded him.

I couldn't reason with Dave. As I tried to talk to him, his eyes were on the TV. When I thought I had gotten through to him one night, I came home the next night to find Steve grounded again. I wondered what Dave was trying to do to these children. He would never have done this to Steve before the accident. This was not like him at all. I no longer knew this man, and I was learning to dislike him.

One night I awoke from a frightening dream. I was standing in what appeared to be a junk yard and it was the middle of the night. Actually, I had a feeling of being up in the air and looking down over everything. I could see into a large machine that was more than double the size of a large automobile. Powerful flood lights lit up the entire area and it was then that I could see that the machine was a car crusher.

Out of nowhere a woman suddenly dropped helplessly into the machine. The moment she landed, it went into motion. Other people were standing by, but no one could stop the machine once it became activated. We were all standing there helpless to do anything.

The machine grabbed both of the woman's arms and began pulling furiously. Then with a sudden burst of energy, it pressed her violently against the back wall as if it were crushing an automobile. At that moment I awoke in fright.

I lay quietly for a moment thinking about the dream. It had seemed so real. What did it mean? Then I relaized that woman was me. Someday, after all the pulling and pushing, I was going to end up crushed like the woman in my dream.

XXI

It was the night before Thanksgiving, 1974. As I pulled into the driveway and parked the car in the garage, I glanced at the gas gauge. It was nearly full with only eleven miles on this tank. I had just filled up, for tomorrow was a holiday and there would be a long weekend ahead. Gas stations were still feeling the crunch of the oil shortage and stations were rarely open after seven at night or on weekends. Dave's sister had invited us over for Thanksgiving dinner.

I arose the next morning at eight and began making pies for dessert. Dave told me some tidbit of family gossip that he said his mother had told him. I wondered how he found out about it, but quickly pushed it out of my mind as I worked on my pies. Perhaps Dave talked to his mom on the phone, I thought.

We were all ready to leave by noon and I told the children to help take the pies to the car. I grabbed my coat and followed Dave and the children out of the house after making sure all the stove burners were off and the house was in order.

The children were seated in the back seat of the car and Dave struggled to get in the passenger's side. I sat down at the wheel and started to pull the seat forward. Then I wondered why it had been pulled out of its normal position. I said, "Hum, that's strange. I wonder why the seat's pushed back?" No one said a word. I considered the possibility that Dave had sat in the car to listen to the radio for a few minutes. Although I didn't know why he would do such a thing, I realized nothing he did now would surprise me.

As I turned on the ignition my eyes fell on the gas gauge. It was only three-quarters full. "Someone has siphoned gas out of my car!" I saw Steve out of the corner of my eye move forward in his seat. Still no one said anything. Dave gazed out the side window. Then my eyes fell on the speedometer. *It said 61 miles, fifty more miles than it had the night before when I drove into the garage.* "Someone has driven this car!"

I looked at Dave. He was still gazing out the window. Then suddenly I remembered Dave telling me something his mother had told him. "Dave! Did you drive this car?" He acted uninterested, as if he were entirely bored with this conversation. He continued staring out the window. "Well, did you?" He mumbled. "We're not leaving until you tell me!"

Angrily he jerked his head around. "Yes! Yes! Yes!" My heart was pounding, and my hands were clutching the steering wheel.

Slowly I began talking, "Do you realize you could have killed yourself? You *can't* see well enough to drive!" I explained to him that the Motor Vehicle Department would not allow him to have a driver's license unless he was limited to a two-mile radius. Dave had agreed with me at the time that it wasn't a good idea for him to have a license if he couldn't see any better than that. *And I thought he understood.*

177

Again I said, "Do you know you could kill yourself?"

"I don't care! I don't care! I don't care!" Everything he said was still in groups of three. Then he added, "Besides, what have I got to lose?"

At last I was beginning to understand his thinking. "Yes, you're right. You have nothing to lose. But the person you run in to has plenty to lose." I knew I couldn't give him the chance to hurt someone else the way he had been hurt. The way we all had been hurt. "Do you want to live with the responsibility that you might injure someone else the same way you were injured? They might not die; they might remain handicapped for the rest of their lives. I know I couldn't live with it; I couldn't live knowing I had *let* you do it."

Later that afternoon I learned Dave had driven out to his parent's home at five that morning – while it was still dark. He had a cup of coffee with his mother and father, then drove around. He drove out to Sandy, the small town the DMV official said he wouldn't be allowed to drive in, where his sister Sally lived. No one was awake there, so he just drove until he had driven a total of fifty miles.

From then on I knew I had to hide the car keys. Each night I put my purse in a new hiding place and hoped Dave wouldn't find it. I changed the secret spot so if he did come across it once, it wouldn't be there the next night. I knew, however, I couldn't go on like this forever.

I called our insurance company and the police department. I had to find out my liability in the event Dave had an accident. They said I probably wouldn't be held liable if I hadn't given him permission. I couldn't accept that information, however. Knowing that Dave was capable of driving, and knowing that he had already taken the car out twice – I had already convicted myself, I realized. Even if I wasn't legally responsible, I would never stop punishing myself.

This new fear just added to my already overburdened mind. I couldn't handle this alone. And it didn't seem fair that I should. Although Dr. Emery had not returned my last two calls, I decided to try one more time.

When Dr. Emery's secretary listened to the story, she said, "Call back tonight at 5:30 and I'll let you talk to him then." I wondered if she controlled all his calls, if she decided what was important enough for him to hear. She had said, "I'll *let* you talk to him." Perhaps he didn't even know I had called before.

Dr. Emery's voice sounded friendly as he said, "Well, now. What can I do for you?" I explained how impossible Dave had become, how he took the car whenever he decided to, and how I no longer had any control over him. "Why don't you take him over to the hospital and drop him off at the psychiatric ward."

"I can't do that! Besides, he would think I was deserting him. No, I won't do that." This was the first time I really stood up to Dr. Emery. In the past I wouldn't have considered refusing a doctor's orders, but now this answer to my problem seemed ridiculous. All I wanted was some help.

"Then why don't you get a divorce?" Dr. Emery was getting me more and more flustered. After all he did to save Dave after the accident, he can't be serious now, I thought.

"I can't escape this. If I try to run away, it will only follow me." Perhaps this suggestion might have been logical for another patient, but it wasn't for Dave and me. I couldn't divorce him.

Dr. Emery sounded irritated with me now, as if his suggestions were perfectly sound, and it was ignorant of me to ignore them. He said, "Well, then why don't you get a divorce, remarry, and adopt him?" I wondered if he was being sarcastic, or trying to make a joke. I wasn't amused, and I ignored the remark.

Finally Dr. Emery said, "There's a psychiatrist in my office. I'll have my secretary make an appointment for you and perhaps something can be worked out." I wondered why it had taken so long for him to suggest such a thing. An appointment with a psychiatrist wasn't exactly what I had hoped for, but it was near enough to it. If Dr. Emery didn't have better suggestions, then perhaps a psychiatrist would.

The rest of the week went by, but there were no calls from the doctor's secretary. Friday came and went and then the weekend had to be endured.

Dave continued to prowl the house at night and I still hid my purse hoping he wouldn't find the keys. He often got up at midnight and watched TV for a while. I slept fitfully and listened throughout the night for the car engine to start up.

By Monday morning my nerves were frazzled. I remembered when I was a volunteer at the hospital. I saw Dr. Emery doing rounds every day at ten o'clock. I decided to drive over to the hospital on my fifteen minute break and see if his car was in the parking lot.

As I drove into the lot I saw Dr. Emery's big white Lincoln Continental parked in the physician's parking section. I parked my car a few feet away in the visitor's lot and went inside. At north wing there was a nurse standing at the nurses' station when I aproached. "Is Dr. Emery here?" I asked. I knew this nurse from Dave's long hospitalization.

She smiled and said, "He's in surgery right now at west wing." I thanked her and went down the hall to west wing.

I approached the nurses' station at west wing and asked the nurse, "Is Dr. Emery here?" She was another familiar face. She greeted me with a smile, too. It was great to see all the nurses once again, but I didn't have much time.

"He's in surgery right now, but he should be almost through," the nurse said. "Just a moment and I'll check." She walked through the double doors to the surgical suite and peeked thorugh a window. She walked back out, "He'll be right out. He's just finishing up."

"I'm afraid I don't have time to wait," I said. "Do you have a piece of paper and a pencil?" The nurse picked up a pad from the counter and handed me a pen. I scribbled out a note, "I thought you understood this

179

was urgent. If you don't do something immediately to help me, I will no longer consider you Dave's doctor. I'm sure I can get Dr. Barrett to help me if necessary." I signed my name, ripped the paper from the pad, and asked the nurse to give it to Dr. Emery. I went back to the parking lot, and arrived at the bank a few minutes late.

I spent the rest of the afternoon on pins and needles. I had never done anything like that before, and I wondered what the doctor would do. Would he ignore my plea and expect me to call Dr. Barrett? I didn't think so. I was getting tired of being ignored. I had always tried to keep quiet and stay out of other people's way, but I had always heard the "squeaky wheel gets the oil." I didn't have to wonder long what Dr. Emery would do.

During my next fifteen minute break, I was sitting in the back room with my feet up and my eyes closed when I heard the phone ring. It had been ringing off and on all afternoon, but this time I had a strange feeling it was going to be Dr. Emery.

One of the tellers peeked in the door and said, "You're wanted on the phone." I jumped to my feet and took a deep breath. Without further hesitation, I walked to the phone.

After hearing my hello, Dr. Emery said, "I *do* have other patients, you know!" I could tell by the tension in his voice that he was angry. My knees were shaking.

My voice quivered, "I realize that. But this is very, very important. I have to have help immediately. I can't go on like this any longer."

Dr. Emery then said, "The reason you weren't called before this is because the psychiatrist is only in my office on Tuesdays." I thought, why didn't you tell me that before? He continued, "My secretary will arrange an appointement for you when he is in tomorrow, and then she will give you a call and tell you when it is."

I was still shaking when I hung up the receiver. If he had only told me it would take a week to see this psychiatrist, I wouldn't have been so impatient. At least, now he was taking me seriously. I would get help at last.

I began my first session wtih Dr. Jamison in the same way I did with Dr. Vale. "I'm not looking for a way out of my marriage, but help with it."

In the past all the doctors and therapists I had been in contact with wanted a complete run-down: Dave's injuries at the time of the accident, and everything about his mental recovery up to date. I began the dissertation. Each time I started I wished I had tape recorded it so I wouldn't be faced with telling it over and over so many times. Dr. Jamison cut in before the entire first sentence was out of my mouth, "You don't have to expain, I understand." By the end of the session I wondered if perhaps Dr. Emery had slipped into another body. It was as if Dr. Emery had become Dr. Jamison except in looks. Dr. Jamison had every piece of information possible about Dave's condition and his expected recovery. I relaxed completely, and soon found myself beginning to look forward to leaning on Dr. Jamison as I had Dave in the past.

Dr. Jamison suggested Dave be hospitalized for a four-week period of testing so he could evaluate exactly where he stood both emotionally and intellectually. He also agreed to help me prepare Dave instead of coldly dropping him off at the hospital as Dr. Emery had suggested. Dave would have to go willingly, I said, and Dr. Jamison agreed.

I remembered one of my sessions with Dr. Vale. I told her how Dave's intellect had not been impaired, and under direct questioning he could, for instance, explain the intricacies of flying a plane and determine air velocity. Our attorney, Les, was a private pilot, and to keep his license current he flew regularly. Les took Dave on one of his practice trips, and came back astonished at Dave's capabilities as a co-pilot. He said he thought Dave could fly again if he were physically able to, but unfortunately he wasn't.

Dr. Vale had listened to me, but she always appeared skeptical at my determination of Dave's abilities. One day she said, "He doesn't think the way you and I do." I wondered what she meant by this statement. I didn't ask because I had already made up my mind about her. I agreed he might not *feel* the same as she and I; perhaps he was even more sensitive. It was Dave who cried during the Sound of Music, and it was Dave who cried during emotional TV shows. Perhaps it was Dr. Vale who didn't understand Dave. If she couldn't help me, how in the world can she help Dave?

I carefully explained to Dr. Jamison how intelligent Dave was, how much I loved him, and how I had searched for someone to help me with his recovery. No one seemed to understand that Dave was not retarded, he was as intelligent as any of the doctors I had met so far. Dr. Jamison's understanding smile and soft blue eyes made me feel he was the one person who might be able to help us.

At the end of that first session Dr. Jamison said, "I think you need someone to talk to more than David does." I nodded as my feelings of desperation were beginning to melt. "If you're willing, I will set up weekly appointments for you alone, and then we will plan on David being hospitalized in a few weeks."

Each week for the next two weeks, I was to bring Dave with me when I attended my counseling session. Dr. Jamison talked to Dave for a few minutes, then Dave sat out in the waiting room while I had a complete session with the doctor. Dr. Jamison gradually brought up the suggestion of Dave's hospitalization – for testing only.

Dave showed no signs of hindering our plans, but trusted me implicitly. On the way home he said, "That doctor's a head shrinker." I laughed, and said, "Yes, I guess he is."

I looked forward every week to my visits with Dr. Jamison. He was the kindest, most understanding person I had ever known – not counting Dave. He didn't scribble on a notepad while we talked, nor did he give outlandish diagnoses for Dave's condition as Dr. Vale had. He just sat

181

and listened. He listened as if he cared, and he remembered everything I said. All of this without a pad and a pencil. I was impressed.

Dave got caught up in the whirlwind of the move to the hospital and the transition went smoothly. I was surprised that he accepted it all so easily, and relieved that he hadn't balked. Dr. Jamison told him how necessary it was for him to go into the hospital for testing, how important this would be. Apparently it was no different to Dave than the salesman who sold him the magazine subscriptions. Someone told him it was something he needed, and he agreed.

The first week Dr. Jamison said they only observed Dave to see how much he would do without being told. He did exactly what I had told Dr. Jamison he would do, nothing. He sat on the sofa every day and only got up when they told him it was mealtime.

The following week they added games and minor tests to his schedule. He cooperated as long as he was told what to do by a therapist. They monitored him closely throughout the four weeks, and added intelligence tests and group counseling sessions the last two weeks. At the end of the hospitalization, Dr. Jamison said Dave was operating at the level of a 12-year-old. It didn't sound good. Steve was thirteen, and Lisa was twelve. And sometimes, it seemed to me, Dave acted with less responsibility than Jan, who was ten.

The hospital was conveniently located behind Dr. Jamison's office. Whenever I had my therapy session, I stopped by to see Dave before left. Each day Dave would ask, "What am I doing here?"

"You're being tested," I responded.

"What for?" he asked.

"The doctors want to find out how much you can do. They're learning about your physical abilities, and it will benefit all of us when the four weeks is over." I felt as if I were talking in circles. I didn't want Dave to get alarmed, and I hoped he wouldn't become obstinate with the counselors. We had to get through this four week period in order to gain any help in the end. This was my only lifeline.

At my next visit Dave asked once more, "What am I here for?" We went through the conversation again as if he had never asked the question before. Every week for four weeks Dave greeted me with that question.

My life, however, took a sudden and drastic change with Dave in the hospital. I hadn't been this free of him in three years. I had felt him to be an albatross around my neck. I couldn't breathe when he was around; he was suffocating me. Now I went to work every day after the children left for school, and I was free of worry. I didn't wonder if Dave had fallen and become injured, I didn't fret about his accidently starting a fire in a sofa cushion. I didn't worry about his having seizures. He was being well cared for, and I knew I had four weeks to spend selfishly on the children and myself.

We could go to movies without checking first to see if there were any sad parts! We no longer were confined to comedies. Walking through a grocery store was unbelievable after three years of having Dave tag along. My grocery bills plummeted; Dave wasn't there to drop in escargot or boxes of TV dinners. Moreover, since I didn't have to walk slowly as Dave limped along behind with the grocery cart, I could whip through the store in record time.

Even doing nothing much was a pleasure. The children and I enjoyed our evenings sitting around watching TV. For the first time in three years, the children were watching their programs once again. They didn't have to worry about Dave changing the channel to the shows he wanted to watch.

When the children and I left the kitchen after the dishes were done, it stayed just as clean as when we walked out the door. Little things like not having sticky counters were a delight. And there were no more puddles around the toilet, no more mud tracked through the house. Apparently the children and I were a little neater than I realized. Only after Dave was gone did I fully appreciate this.

Steve could go out and play with his friends without the worry of being grounded when he arrived home. I didn't have the children pressing me for answers, "Why won't Dad help around here? Why don't you make him?" The quiet was invigorating and intoxicating. The freedom was wonderful! I realized this was my first vacation from Dave, the first time we had been separated except for the time he was in the hospital, and that didn't count since I spent so much time there with him. At last I could breathe again. The feeling of suffocation had disappeared.

But it wasn't going to last.

I told Dr. Jamison, "I'm locked into a situation with no way out."

"There's a way out," he responded.

"No, there isn't," I insisted.

"You have to think of yourself first," Dr. Jamison said. "You must put yourself first, your needs and your wants."

I told Dr. Jamison how wonderful Dave had been. He was the only man I ever loved. I never even looked at anyone else. He was everything I could have ever hoped for. I remembered a friend who married a man much older than herself. He wasn't everything she wanted in a husband, but she said, "A half a loaf is better than none." I told Dr. Jamison when he told me I could marry again, "I won't settle for half a loaf. I had a whole loaf at one time, and I couldn't live with less now." I couldn't imagine being married to anyone but Dave. He had been my whole life, my whole reason for existence.

As the weeks with Dave in the hospital passed, I realized how futile it all was. The children were happier. It was a vacation for us all to have Dave gone. Dave was impossible to live with, and the thought of taking him back home was almost more than I could endure. Life would go back to the way it was, and I couldn't face it again.

I remembered how much Dave loved the children. Before the accident he would have done anything for those three children. Now all he did was make their lives miserable. He wanted to assert his authority over them, to prove to them that he was the "boss." He was completely irresponsible, and didn't seem to care who he hurt as long as he got what he wanted.

Suddenly I realized something. If Dave were in his right mind, he would *want* me to put the children first. He would *want* me to protect them from him. I felt I owed it to Dave's memory, to the man he used to be; never mind the stranger living in his body.

My marriage vows were important, but there was something more at issue in this matter. There were no guidelines in the Bible for a situation like this. There was advice for the widows and orphans, but no advice for me. Doctors are saving people today who would have died years ago. If Dave and I lived fifty years ago, I would be a widow, for he would be dead.

I had to reason all this out carefully. I would be criticized for whatever choice I made. There were friends who refused to recognize divorce, saying it was a sin. But there were also friends who disagreed with the way I handled Dave's care. This group of critics included doctors, too. "He should be in an institution," some said. "He should be allowed to smoke in his own house," said others. And still others told me, "You shouldn't let him eat so much." And on and on . . .

I considered Dave, too. None of this was good for him either. Since the counselors, therapists and doctors thought I was too lenient with him, perhaps someone else could take over his care and have better luck with him. Perhaps because I was his wife, I wasn't getting the utmost out of him. Perhaps he would try harder to rehabilitate himself if he didn't have me to lean on.

A divorce seemed to be the answer for us all.

I had always tried to do things to make people like me. I hated criticism, and I worried about what people thought. Now I was going to go against God's laws by obtaining a divorce, and against the dictates of the society I moved in, too. Although divorce was common, it still wasn't approved of by many of my friends and relatives. And I was taking a step that I too considered to be tabu. Yet under the circumstances I didn't believe God would expect me to keep our marriage together.

I remembered the clash of personalities between my father and mother. Would life have been happier for us all if they had divorced and stepped out of an unsatisfactory relationship? I refused to stay together because of the children. The children could be destroyed in the process.

At my next session with Dr. Jamison, I explained my decision. He applauded my reasoning, and agreed that it was the only thing to do.

Dr. Jamison suggested putting Dave in a half-way house. There was a waiting list, however, and it would take a while to get Dave admitted. "No," I said. "I don't want Dave put in a half-way house. If that's the only solution, I guess I'll have to take him back home."

Dr. Jamison and I exlained to Dave that a divorce would be best for us all. Dave calmly accepted the news as if I had simply told him the sunshine outside was changing to showers. He acted as if life held no more meaning to him than having meals on time, and moving from one sofa to another.

When I explained to Dave's family about the divorce and the need for Dave to find a place to live, Dave's sister offered to let him move in with her. I jumped at the offer. She had always been devoted to Dave, and I knew he would receive excellent care from her. She would continue to give the attention I no longer had the strength to give. Everything was falling comfortably into place.

I stopped to see Dave after one of my sessions with Dr. Jamison and we went to the cafeteria for a cup of coffee. I told Dave the children were fine, although I wasn't certain he cared. At times, he seemed concerned about them, at other times not at all. He was definitely glad to see me whenever I came, but that did not surprise me, for it seemed that his only goal was to have me quit work and spend the rest of my life beside him on the sofa.

Then a counselor walked over to the table and sat down. Dave's face lit up, and he introduced me to Jerry. I continued my usual lighthearted conversation; I laugh and smile a lot no matter who I'm talking with. Especially with Dave I tried to focus on pleasant thoughts even though our lives were a disaster. This was my pattern.

Jerry surprised me when he said, "You're laughing too much, and confusing David. I don't want you to laugh any more when you talk to him." He then began a session of marriage counseling. He asked me to tell Dave exactly why I was divorcing him, and what I didn't like about him. Then he wanted Dave to respond and tell me what he felt.

Dr. Jamison had been holding sessions for both Dave and me since Dave entered the hospital, and I was immediately confused about what Jerry was doing. Certainly we weren't your average couple off the street who had just decided to get a divorce because of incompatibility. There was no way Jerry was going to force me to hurt Dave any more than he had already been hurt. What would be the use of making accusations or raking up all those old irritations now? For at least the past year I had occasionally lost my temper with Dave and told him exactly what made me angry, what he was doing that irritated me. He acted as if he didn't hear me. He wasn't the "normal" person that takes constructive criticism and then strives to improve himself. The brain injury had changed Dave and Dr. Jamison admitted, along with countless other medical experts, that Dave would never get any better. If I stayed with Dave, our lives would remain the same since Dave wasn't able to function normally in a family situation, as a father, and as a husband.

This counseling session of Jerry's began to seem humorous to me. The more he talked, the funnier it became. He looked at me. "I told you not to laugh," he said. "And don't smile either." I had all that I could do to keep from bursting out in hysterics. The more he told me not to laugh or smile, the greater the pressure built up in my chest. I couldn't help it. I covered my mouth with my hand, but Jerry wasn't fooled. "Would you please stop smiling?" he demanded again.

Suddenly, surprisingly, Dave cut in. "She's not confusing me. That's just the way Sharon is; she smiles a lot, but that doesn't confuse me." With all Dave had been through, he seemed truly to understand me. This counselor was only causing problems in a situation that was supposed to have been solved. Suddenly I couldn't take any more of his "marriage counseling."

"I have to go home," I said as I rose from the table. Jerry stood up, excused himself, and left the cafeteria. Dave struggled to his feet and walked me to the front door of the hospital. I waved good-bye and was on my way.

The next morning I called Dr. Jamison and told him about Jerry's counseling session. He said, "It won't happen again."

Laughter was a release that I needed even while Dave was hospitalized the first time. I thanked God for those wonderful friends who stopped by regularly and told me funny stories or related humorous incidents in their own lives. Laughter got me through many frightening episodes with Dave's therapy. I knew from experience that while crying was exhausting, laughter was exhilarating.

When Dave was discharged from the mental hospital, I drove him to his sister's home. This was the first time I informed him he wasn't coming home with me. We had only just arranged this living situation for him a few days before, and I couldn't bring myself to break the news to him until we were a few blocks away from his sister's home. I thought he would enjoy being with his sister, and closer to the rest of his family. However, I was mistaken. When I had finished unloading his clothes from the car, he glared at me as I backed out the kitchen door. He didn't say a word; but I thought, if looks could kill!

Dr. Jamison and I worked on goals to help me readjust to my new homelife, and I knew I had to put Dave out of my mind. I went to work every day, meeting new people at the bank, going out at night with the other tellers, and trying to establish myself as a single person.

I removed my wedding ring; I dated occasionally; and I struggled to bring forth my new identity.

Day after day I ran into problem after problem. Removing my wedding ring did not erase Dave from my thoughts. I saw Dave in nearly every situation. Steve looked like his father, his mannerisms were like Dave's. When I met other men, I was reminded how handsome Dave was, how intelligent he still was. Even in the condition he was in after the accident, he was in many ways more intelligent than many men I had met over the years.

Twice I went out to dinner with two girlfriends from work. Afterward we stopped at a nightclub. The second night as I looked around, I realized I was in a "dive." I had never felt so out of place anywhere in my life, and I couldn't wait to get home. If something came out of those two evenings, it was that I knew for certain I never wanted to go again. And I didn't.

I couldn't get Dave out of my mind, so Dr. Jamison told me to go to Parents Without Partners. He suggested I attend another singles group in the Portland area, too. I went to two meetings, and left disappointed. I don't know what I was expecting, but I felt out of place with these men and women. In a way I envied widows who no longer had to face the memory of their husbands in a walking human being. Dave seemed dead to me in many ways, but he *was* still alive. I even envied the divorced women. If all things worked out, they could resume their marriages; it had happened before – people re-marrying. As I looked around and saw the ratio of men to women in the meetings, I realized I could attend meetings at my own church and feel more comfortable. I've always been shy and the members of these groups seemed to be as shy as I or perhaps even more so. They weren't very friendly to newcomers.

I considered taking a class for widows at a neighborhood bank one night a week. It was given to teach widows how to take care of minor problems with their cars. But what would they do if they realized I was attending the class not as a widow, but as a divorcee? Even worse, what if the widows knew about Dave's accident and the fact that I was divorcing him because of it? I might get tarred and feathered, I thought.

I went back and told Dr. Jamison of my problem. "I'm disappointed."

"In yourself?" he asked.

"No, in the people I meet. There's no one like Dave and I don't know how I can ever forget him."

"Your marriage wasn't perfect," he said. I was devastated to hear Dr. Jamison say that. Of course, I knew my marriage wasn't perfect, and neither was I. Dave, too, wasn't perfect, but I thought I had been as close to perfection as I could get.

"If you lost your wife to an accident or a fatal illness," I asked Dr. Jamison, "would you go to Parents Without Partners?" He didn't answer, but slowly shook his head.

"Then *I'm* not going again either," I said with resolve.

The trial date was closing in on us again. I never knew until Friday, three days before the scheduled date, if it was postponed or if we were going ahead. This time Les called Friday afternoon and said, "Court convenes Monday morning at nine o'clock."

In the past few months I had given Les the final $5,000 that we would need for court expenses. My savings were almost gone. This was a one-shot deal, and I hoped we could win.

Not only had I spent all the insurance money on medical expenses and trial costs, but Les informed me he stopped keeping track of his hours when they exceeded $100,000. Whew! I ran my hand across my brow.

I had never realized a trial could cost that kind of money. When Les had told me it would cost about $7,000, I thought it was worth the risk for that amount. Now I had second thoughts. At this point second thoughts were useless, however. We were expected in court on Monday morning.

XXII

Les wanted to reconstruct the accident as closely as possible. This would be difficult since we didn't have the car that hit Dave. Les said we should buy a car that was similar. I promised to look through the classified ads every day for used cars.

One day I was sitting at the breakfast table drinking a cup of coffee, and skimming through the listings of the used car lots. My eyes fell on an ad for a 1967 Impala. This was the same year and model of the car that hit Dave. I called the car lot and asked for the engine model, which turned out to be the same, too. I was excited when I called Les and told him.

Les drove over to see the car that afternoon and he called me after he got home. He said the car was almost an exact duplicate right down to the white paint and snow tires. The car even had the same defect that we were suing for. It was almost too good to be true.

Les bought the car for a couple hundred dollars, and then put it through a series of tests to help prove his theory to the jury. He had to prove that the likelihood that this malfunction had caused the accident could be demonstrated by tests run on the car. We had to have a stronger case then the manufacturing company in order to win.

I took a leave of absence from the bank so I could attend every day of the trial. Every morning I picked Dave up and took him to the court-house with me.

The jury was selected Monday morning, and then court was dismissed for the rest of the day, while the jury visited the accident site. The car engine was sitting in the middle of the courtroom ready to be used as evidence.

The judge sat quietly at his bench through the succeeding days. He overruled most of Les's objections, but he sustained nearly all of the other attorney's objections. Throughout the entire presentation of evidence, he gazed at something on his desk, and seemed to be doodling on a piece of paper. And he smiled and smiled. He reminded me of a Cheshire Cat as he surveyed his court. Was he *amused* by it all?

We presented our witnesses and evidence, and then the doctors testified about Dave's medical condition and prognosis. Bill Folk and Larry Adams were character witnesses.

On Wednesday afternoon we were finished with our presentation. Then the other side began to present evidence to prove that the defect did not cause the accident. The men filed into the courtroom with their briefcases. Yvonne, who had come up from California for the trial, said they reminded her of the Mafia as they all marched in.

That evening Les called to tell me the judge was considering a mistrial. The judge felt he had been swaying the jury by his own remarks. "Please, don't let him do that," I said. "If there is any way to change his mind, please do. We can't afford not to finish this." Les said he would try to convince the judge to continue. I felt strongly that the jury would be with us when they heard the entire testimony of both sides. It was just a matter of allowing us to get through the trial with all of it.

The following morning the trial reconvened until lunch. Just after lunch when the judge was seated once again at his bench, I stepped out into the hall to call the bank and tell them I wouldn't be in for a few more days. As I crept back into the courtroom to take my seat at the plaintiff's table, the jury was filing out of the courtroom. I looked at Les. He was sitting at the table, holding his head in his hands. "What happened?" I asked as I glanced at Eric, Les's aide.

"Les didn't move as he said, "Tell her, Eric."

Eric explained that Les had used the word *fatal* as he questioned one of the expert witnesses, and then had mentioned another accident that was similar to ours. There had been a fatality in that car accident. The judge called a mistrial, Eric said. He had said he didn't want any other cases tried in this courtroom, and he considered this an inexcusable blunder.

I dropped Dave off at his sister's, and I literally folded. I went home that night, told the children not to disturb me, and I went to my bedroom and pulled the covers over my head. I slept throughout the night in a depression that didn't ease even with sunshine the following morning.

Dr. Jamison had given me a prescription for Valium, 100 tablets each refill. He suggested I take three a day, which I did. The Valium allowed me to make it through each day.

Hilda asked me to have lunch with her. We met in a restaurant next door to the bank. Hilda had never asked me out to lunch before and I was terrified of what this meant. Perhaps she wants me to relinquish the house to Dave, I thought. Many questions went through my mind, and I was surprised that what she did want was to have Dave moved out of his sister's house and into a half-way house. She said she didn't want her daughter giving up her life for Dave. It wasn't fair to her. I understood. I could remember what it was like, trying to cope with Dave. I agreed to call Dr. Jamison and have Dave's name put on the list. I didn't want to, but it was easier to do now than it would have been in the beginning.

Still, I hated moving Dave again. I felt guilty that it was because of me that he was getting bounced all over the city, and I think I felt as much pain moving him into the half-way house as he did. He wanted to come home, but I managed to convince him that this was the only way for us. He said he didn't understand why I wanted to get a divorce, and I was pressed into another explanation. "We can't continue on like we did. I can't go through any more. It's best for both of us." As usual, Dave accepted this calmly and in silence.

Dave had been admitted to the Goodwill sheltered workshop, and the mental hospital had him enrolled in outpatient therapy sessions. He

190

was making new friends, and I hoped he would find someone who could make him a good wife and fill the void in his life. This wasn't entirely unlikely; I had heard about another man who had been injured worse than Dave was; his wife divorced him, and he remarried. That would be a dream come true, I thought. But what strange thoughts for me to be having about Dave . . .

Dr. Jamison kept reminding me that I had to put myself first, but I couldn't help feeling selfish. I spent considerable time punishing myself for caving in, for not having enough strength to take care of Dave, for not being able to get him well.

There were increasing pressures at the bank. Perhaps it was growing pains. None of the tellers could understand why we were now having problems when none existed a few months before. The new manager would take each one of us out to lunch separately, and press us for information. He had always been friendly and kind from the first day he began at the bank, but now he was using "psychology" on us. None of us could put our finger on what was wrong. All we knew was that something terrible was happening, and none of us knew how to stop it.

The thing I said I would never do, I did: I placed Dave in a boarding home. The only thing I hadn't yet done was to forget him, as Dr. Vale had advised.

Problems developed with Steve. When I came home from work one night Lisa led me into her bedroom, where she pointed to a large hole in her wall that extended into the linen closet. "Steve did that because I wouldn't let him ride my bike. He punched the wall in the family room one time. Since he didn't make a hole, Jan and I covered it with the calendar." Ah, ha. That's why the calendar was moved! I wondered about that, but it wasn't important enough to do anything about it except just wonder. I asked Steve to patch the hole in Lisa's room.

Steve balked about going to school. He either had a stomachache or a headache when I woke him every morning. "Come on, Steve. You'll feel better after you eat some breakfast."

A problem had developed the previous year with a science teacher who was having great difficulties with his class. A group of parents insisted he be fired, but the administration refused to do anything about him. When Steve started science that year, I kept asking him, "How are things going in science this year?"

"Okay."

"Do you get along with your teacher?"

"Yeah. He's alright."

"You're sure there are no problems?"

"Yeah, I'm sure." Each time I asked Steve about it, our conversation was almost identical.

One morning when Steve didn't want to go to school, I called the counselor, Mr. Foster, and asked for advice. Steve said Mr. Foster was the only person he liked in the entire school. Perhaps he would know how to help Steve and me.

The result of the meeting was that Steve wanted Dave back home again. Mr. Foster and I explained to Steve that this wasn't possible, that it was beneficial to all of us that Dave not return. It was a situation that couldn't be changed. Steve seemed more relaxed and I hoped he could eventually understand why I made the decision I did about Dave. I was surprised that he wanted him back. After all, Steve and Dave were at each other's throats all the time when they were together. If Dave weren't so impossible, we could stay together.

One evening while I was doing the dinner dishes, the phone rang. The man on the other end identified himself as Steve's science teacher. "Steve has become a discipline problem in my class," he told me. "I cannot have him in my class any longer and I'm sending him before the school board."

"You're what?" I inquired. "You mean you're having him expelled?"

"That will be up to the board."

I stammered a bit, but my anger had been aroused, and I refused to be buffaloed by anyone. "I *refuse* to allow you to do that to him! I will *not* allow you to expel him after all he's been through!"

"What do you mean? What's he been through?" When I explained about Dave's accident, he responded, "Oh, you're the ones. Ahhh, just forget everything I just said. It was all just a mistake." I hung up the phone, but I wasn't about to forget anything he said. I could never get those words out of my mind. My personality was changing drastically. What I said to Steve's teacher I would never have said in the past, nor would I ever have used that tone of voice. Furthermore, I was not going to relax until I did something about all this. I called Mr. Foster.

Over the next few days I met with Mr. Foster, then with Mr. Foster and the superintendent and the principal. The superintendent listened to what I had to say, my description of what the science teacher said to me. "Why, he can't do that," the superintendent replied. "He can't send any child before the school board. Any problems he has must be sent to me first, and then I send them to the board if it is necessary. Up to now, I have never heard a word about Steve being a discipline problem."

Steve was quickly moved out of the science class after I demanded his removal. But I had to write a letter to the school, stating that the science teacher insisted Steve be removed, or there would have been a problem with other parents. For the parents of all the other students except two in this science class had also asked for their children to be removed.

The science teacher was fired at the end of the year.

Steve was having such a difficult time, just as difficult as I was; however, the transfer to another science class seemed to help him a little. And Mr. Foster took a special interest in Steve and filled in slightly as a substitute father when Steve was in school, telling Steve if there were any problems he should come directly to his office and they would work them out together.

I was trying to establish a credit rating in my own name. It turned out to be difficult to do. I was turned by J.C. Penney and Bank Americard. I didn't have a long enough work history, and social security was not enough to establish independence. Although Dave couldn't work and wasn't mentally fit to transact business, the credit rating we had built up would follow him; none of it would go to me. I was devastated, and concerned about the future for the children and myself.

Each night now I found myself coming home from work and getting through my evening chores as soon as possible. Then, after a hot bath, I changed into my bathrobe, turned out the lights in the living room, lay down on the sofa, and drowned my worries with music.

I felt so alone. Even being with customers every day at work, and associating with the other tellers, I couldn't escape from the loneliness.

Crying spells had been rare for me in the past, but now I found the tears near the surface every day, just ready to spill over at any moment. I asked to speak to the manager one morning when the pressure just became too much to bear, but I burst into tears before I could say a word. "Take the rest of the day off," he said. Just before I rushed out the door to get my purse and coat, I managed a tearful, "I'm sorry."

I went home, gave the children instructions as soon as they came home from school that I didn't want to be disturbed. I went to my room, and climbed into bed. Depression brought on intense sleepiness.

The children were used to my absence by now, since I spent most of my evenings in bed. As soon as I got home from work, I jumped into the tub, and then retreated to the bedroom. I had never felt such intense exhaustion in my life. It was causing me to withdraw from the world.

Until now I had been accepting my depression, although I hated the way I felt. I couldn't do anything about it. Dr. Jamison kept telling me it would end eventually. I just needed time, he said. But I felt worse now then I had when Dave was at home. And I was beginning to feel frightened. *What was happening to me?*

One evening I heard a tap on the bedroom door, and Lisa peered in. "Mr. Dyer is on the phone," she said. "He wants to talk to you." I turned on the lamp by my bed, and picked up the receiver. The moment I heard Les's voice, I began to cry again.

Les said, "I want you to go down and spend a week with Connie and Larry." I found my voice. "I can't do that. I can't afford it."

"You can't afford not to," he said. "Now hang up the phone so I can call them." I made a few more excuses, but Les insisted that I hang up.

Connie and Larry lived in Thousand Oaks, California. I had attended grade school and high school with both of them, and Connie had been Les's secretary after she got out of school. Dave and I renewed our friendship with them when Jan was about two years old, and Connie and Larry were expecting their first child, Paula Jeanne. Because Larry was a flight engineer for United Air Lines, they moved around quite a bit. In January, just before the accident, we had driven up to Seattle,

Washington, to spend the weekend with them. Dave, the children, and I had a wonderful time. Connie and I had kept in touch since then.

The phone rang agan. I picked up the receiver to hear both Connie and Larry. Connie was on one phone, and Larry said he was on the extension. They invited me down, and insisted I come the following day, which was Saturday. "I can't do that," I said. "I don't have anyone to stay with the children, and there are just too many things to do to get ready." They kept insisting until I finally said, "Oh, all right. I'll come down Sunday."

I talked to the children about staying with someone through the week. They didn't want to leave; they wanted to stay home. I didn't know anyone who could spend an entire week with the children – since we lived so far off the beaten path. We had limited bus service, and anyone without a car was stranded at the house. My mother could have stayed, but because she didn't drive I knew it would only worry her to be so far away from stores and conveniences she was used to. The only person I could think of was Dave. After all, he was excellent at disciplining the children before he moved out. And Steve was spending his evenings on the phone talking to Dave, anyway.

I still had Dave's bank charge card, so armed with that, I purchased a round-trip ticket to Los Angeles. I had flown a few times with Dave in a small plane, but never in a commercial aircraft. Flying had usually terrified me, but oddly enough, I boarded the plane as calm as could be.

As the plane made its way down the runway, I expected the familiar aura of fear to surround me. Instead I remained calm as the plane gathered speed and etched a path into the morning sky. I felt a sense of peace that I had never experienced before, perhaps strengthened by the sense of resignation that filled me these days.

Dr. Jamison kept telling me over and over that I needed to give myself time. I needed to get out socially and meet people. "But I meet people every day," I protested. Where better to meet people than at a bank, I thought. Dr. Jamison said that wasn't the same, and that I had to get out after work and meet people on a different basis. I didn't admit it to him, but I didn't really *want* to meet anyone.

I told Dr. Jamison that it was all too difficult. I'd been a comfortable wife and mother for eleven years, and then everything was brought to a brutal halt by that accident. From then on I went through constant change with Dave as he began to recover. Every day was change, not insignificant transitions from one day to another, but tough growing spells. I didn't have a choice, either. I couldn't sit down and rationalize decisions and sort out the best road to take. No one I knew had ever been down this road, and when I met a fork in the road I knew no one had the knowledge to tell me whether to go right or left. Facing problems before the accident, facing them with Dave by my side was frightening at times, but not like this. I felt as if I had been turned loose, like a top that has just been spun; no one knows where it will end up, controlled

194

and secure or topsy-turvy across the room.

After three years, friends and relatives assumed I should be over the grieving stages, especially since Dave had survived the accident and had spent those years recovering from an accident that might have killed him. Friends thought I should be happy. I felt as if people were saying, "Okay. Now it's all over. Get on with life and forget about it."

I nibbled on the sandwich that was on my lunch tray and looked out at the snow-covered mountain peaks across the Oregon and California border. It was all so beautiful from this altitude. It reminded me a little of the salt and flour mixture Lisa built for one of her school projects. She scooped out valleys and swirled mountaintops to build her miniature United States. When the pilot announced we were nearing Mt. Shasta, I realized how unreal everything looked. The whole world seemed unreal to me.

It seemed as if I were standing outside myself, watching and observing what I did, but not taking any responsibility for my own actions. I didn't have to worry about doing anything wrong since my automatic reflexes were constantly turned to "obey rules." I no longer felt like I was alive, but instead just existing as an invisible being, perhaps like a spirit.

I watched friends as they inter-related to one another, but I felt disassociated. It was as if they were in a circle and I was on the perimeter. I couldn't get into the circle to be a part of them any longer; I was different and alone.

I looked out the airplane window as it entered Los Angeles air space. The Pacific Ocean was directly below, the blue water stretched into the horizon. How easy it would be to slip right down into that water! All of the pain would end, and I would suffer no more. When I flew with Dave in the little plane, I never looked down. I was even terrified to look down when riding on a ferris wheel. Now, however, I gazed at the ocean and desired to be a a part of it. *Please, Dear God. If a plane has to crash, let it be this one. I'm sorry about all the innocent people on board, but I really can't take any more from this life.*

I was disappointed in the safe landing and the view of the airport terminal rapidly coming into view. As I entered the terminal, Connie was waiting.

I spent a wonderful week with Connie and Larry and their two children, Paula Jeanne and Jon. Larry asked, "What day do you want to go to Disneyland?"

"Oh, please," I answered. "I don't want to go to Disneyland at all."

Larry laughed, "You're the first guest we've had who didn't want to go to Disneyland the very first thing."

I craved peace and quiet. I needed to be away from people for a while, away from complaining customers and away from dissension among bank employees.

We talked about the trial, and about how I had to go on now and forget the mistrial. Connie and Larry shared my disappointment, but it was over and the money was spent. I couldn't change what had already been done.

195

We talked about Dave. That is, I talked about Dave, and they listened. I had so many wonderful memories, and I couldn't stop dwelling on them. I told about the times Dave would surprise me with a banana split; he picked them up on his way home from work. One for me and one for him sometimes, and other times just the one for me.

Then there was that memorable Mother's Day morning. When I entered the kitchen, there were streamers stretching across the kitchen ceiling, and balloons hanging in a bunch in the center, and the children were seated at the kitchen table, where the waffle iron was heating. "Happy Mother's Day!" they cried in unison.

The first few days at Connie and Larry's, Larry didn't have any flights which would take him away from home. One evening we had coffee with the neighbors, then Connie and I came back into the house while Larry stayed outside, finishing up some yard work before dark. As Connie and I sat in the family room talking, the children went to bed, and left us alone. I wondered why Larry was staying outside so long, and then I saw the kitchen door open and Larry entered, cautiously balancing three banana splits.

I ate my ice cream with tears in my eyes. It was delicious.

The week with Connie and Larry was great, but Sunday afternoon when my plane was approaching Portland airport, I knew I couldn't take any more frustration at work. I decided then and there to put in my two week's notice. The pressure had disappeared during the week in Thousand Oaks, but here it was, returning even before I could get back home!

I made arrangements to have coffee with the bank manager the following morning. I told him, "I can't go back. I'm giving my two weeks' notice right now."

"Why don't you start today?" Things were going well enough at the bank that my absence could be coped with, he said. I thanked him and we walked out of the restaurant. I went to my car with a lighter step. A tremendous load had lifted from my shoulders.

The following day one of my friends from work called, "Did John tell you something that made you quit?"

"No. I just realized I couldn't continue working there any longer. I put in my notice, and he said I didn't have to come back at all. Why?"

"Well, you'd never believe what's been happening down here. They transferred some of the tellers today, and everyone's at everyone else's throat. I thought John had warned you."

When we both said our good-byes and I had hung up the phone, I realized how badly I felt the previous week with just the normal chaos at work. If I had been there through this new transition, I'm not sure my mind could have stood the shock. Then I thought, *Perhaps someone did warn me. God, are you still up there?*

Dave went back to the halfway house when I got home. Mama called and said there had been some problems while I was gone; Dave had been grounding Steve again. Steve had called her and asked for the phone number where I was staying, but she wouldn't give it to him. Instead she tried to talk to Dave, to convince him that Steve was a good boy and didn't need to be grounded. But the children themselves didn't tell me about any problems they had while I was gone, and I didn't ask. I already knew what it was like to live with Dave.

I began looking for a new job. I couldn't stay unemployed for long; still, I realized that vacation with Connie and Larry had been all too short.

I found another office job immediately. Funny, how I could sell myself to employers, but I myself wasn't buying! I had a poor self-image at the time of Dave's accident, and when I had to give up Dave's care and put him into a halfway house, my self-confidence dropped to an all-time low. Starting a new job, moreover, forced me to take a $50 pay cut.

Dr. Jamison started me on an anti-depressant medication to be taken with the Valium, but I couldn't tolerate it. He wrote out another prescription for something else, and when I couldn't adapt to that one either he said, "Well, let's try another. Start this on Friday night so you can get it into your system by Monday."

The depression was so bad, I could hardly stand it until Friday night so I could renew myself with the new medication. I came home from work that evening in my usual state of jitters. I felt so shaky all the time I expected my teeth to chatter when I opened my mouth. Some nights in order to sleep I took 5 mgs. of Valium. But tonight Valium wasn't working as usual, and I considered taking another tablet. Then I had a terrifying thought, *What if I take another and I forget I have taken it? What if I wake up periodically and take more? What if I keep taking more until I'm dead?* I didn't want to live, but I didn't want to commit suicide either. What I wanted was just to stop existing.

I turned off the lights in the living room, turned on the stereo, and told the children I didn't want to be disturbed. I swallowed the anti-depressant medication and lay down on the sofa, waiting for it to take effect. Dr. Jamison said if the first one didn't work, to take one more in an hour, then take a tablet three times a day from then on. I waited. Nothing happened. I took another tablet, and then went to bed.

The following morning I woke with the worst bout of depression yet. I found I couldn't stop crying. I spent the first hour locked in the bathroom trying to get control of myself. *This is ridiculous,* I kept telling myself, *get control of yourself!* Why couldn't I just cry for a while and get it out of my system, as usual? But no, this time the tears wouldn't stop; they trickled down my cheeks as I sobbed and sobbed.

I managed to call Dr. Jamison. Calmly he said, "Go to the hospital and they'll give you a shot to bring you out of it."

"Are you kidding? I can't drive in this condition!" I cried.

"Then ask a neighbor to take you," he answered.

"I can't let anyone know about this! I'm *not* going to go to a neighbor."

Dr. Jamison paused a moment then asked, "Do you have any Valium?"

197

What a ridiculous question; he had just renewed my 100 tablet supply that very week.

"Of course I do. In fact, I have enough to blow my mind!" That was not a rational thing to say at a time like that, but I didn't feel rational at that moment.

"Sharon, give the bottle of Valium to Steve. Ask him to give you two tablets, and then tell him to keep control of the bottle. The two Valium tablets should bring you down." Then he added, "Now, give the bottle to Steve."

"Okay, I will," I answered as I hung up the phone. *Are you kidding, doctor? Do you really believe I would give the Valium to Steve to keep?* If I didn't want my neighbors to know about the mess I was in, I certainly didn't want to frighten my children. I took the bottle of Valium out of my purse, swallowed two tablets, and then dropped down on the bed to sleep.

I managed to sleep off the medication by Monday. Clearly, it wasn't the right thing for me to be taking, and I took no more. Monday morning I was back to my regular depression, not a drug-induced one.

I depended a lot on Dr. Jamison. He was someone strong, someone whom I could lean on once again. I missed Dave, the way he used to be, the control he had over everything. As for me, I couldn't even control myself, much less anything else.

One week as I was leaving Dr. Jamison's office, he said he wouldn't be there the following week. "Where are you going?" I asked, feeling stunned by the idea of his leaving, even for just one week.

"To Hawaii for a vacation," he replied. My head nearly went into a spin. *How can he go on vacation at a time like this, when I need him so much?* Then I thought of the money I had spent on psychiatric counseling. *All the money I have spent on therapy and he's taking it to use on a vacation in Hawaii!* Of course I understand that doctors need vacations, too, but at the time all I could think was *he's deserting me.*

Sometimes, too, I resented the amount of money I had to pay for therapy. But what *might* happen if I stopped? I had to keep going, and every week I looked forward to the following week when I could escape into the solitude of Dr. Jamison's office, away from the troubles of the world.

One evening a woman from church called. When Dave was still in the hospital, she had stopped to see me a few times, and then called occasionally after I brought him home. I knew there were people who didn't know Dave was in a halfway house, and I decided I would have to face up to admitting that I was getting a divorce. I explained to this woman that it was no longer possible for Dave and me to be together.

She said she understood, since she had been through a long illness with her husband. She knew what it was like, she said, and she knew the frustration that accompanied a lingering illness. "If I were young like you, I would probably have divorced my husband, too. It's important that you think of yourself first."

Dr. Jamison had been telling me to think of myself first. Now this woman, a deaconess of the church, was telling me the same thing. Then I wondered what difference it made how old I was. People sometimes implied that because I was young, I must consider the prospect of making a new life for myself. Since when does compassion and caring only fit into lives when we are old? Because I am young, I am to selfishly put aside everyone who might need me, people who would drain me and make life less enjoyable? That didn't seem right to me, but I trusted Dr. Jamison, and believed that I was the one who was confused, not the rest of the world. So far most of the doctors were telling me to make a new life for myself, to forget Dave even existed.

Forgetting Dave was the greatest challenge of all. I kept asking Dr. Jamison to tell me the secret to forgetting the past; how do I do it?

XXIII

"Have you ever considered suicide?" Dr. Jamison was sitting in an over-stuffed chair next to the sofa where I was sitting. A coffee table was separating us. Dr. Jamison never sat across from me at a desk. Our sessions were always casual, as if we were talking about world problems over a cup of coffee. He had a love for books that equaled mine, and he displayed several ancient medical books that he had rescued from a janitor that was just preparing to throw them out. Sometimes when he got called out of the office for a moment or two, I would gaze longingly at those leather-bound volumes, aching to flip through them but terrified of touching them because of their delicate-looking bindings.

I answered Dr. Jamison, "Yes, of course I have." Many times I thought Dr. Jamison must be reading my mind when he answered questions for me that were too difficult or painful to face. He always seemed to know what I was thinking. I continued, "But I couldn't leave my children behind." I knew what it was like to lose a parent, and losing two parents was almost unbearable to think about.

"You don't mean you'd take them with you, do you?"

"Well, I certainly wouldn't leave them alone in this world." From personal experience I knew the world wasn't the warm, loving environment that we all wish it were. Dr. Jamison rose from his chair, and I smiled at a new thought. "But I don't have enough Valium for us all."

"You could get it," he snapped back. I could? I thought. But I had enough trouble getting 100 tablets. Dr. Manning was tightfisted about any medication. I knew I couldn't get any more from him. I wondered who Dr. Jamison was thinking about; where could I get more? But I didn't ask.

Dr. Jamison walked over to his desk across the room, turned and said, "Sharon, you make my blood run cold." I shrugged. "Do you know I could lock you up right now?" The thought was almost inviting, as I viewed a new escape.

"Go right ahead," I snapped coldly. "Put me in the farthest corner and throw away the key!"

His attitude suddenly changed as he said, "Well, I don't want to do that." I realized the session was over as he handed me the paper to take to the receptionist who added this hour to my bill.

As I walked out the door Dr. Jamison called out, "Keep your chin up."

I turned, and looked at him for a moment.

"Please, don't ever say that to me again. I'm doing the best I can, and I don't need people to tell me to keep my chin up." He silently stood in the doorway as I walked away.

I wondered if Dr. Jamison would have allowed me to leave if he actually knew the thoughts that went through my mind. Perhaps if I had gone into greater detail, I would be cooling my heels in the far corner of the closed unit of the mental hospital just across the parking lot from Dr. Jamison's office. I handed the receptionist the necessary paper, and walked to the door.

I had heard it said that suicide is the ultimate cop-out, but I didn't stop to rationalize whether I was copping out or not. Feeling like I did, I didn't care who thought I was copping out, I only knew I couldn't continue on like this any longer. I just didn't know how to change it or get through it. I felt like a failure in everything. I had failed Dave, and now I couldn't even be a mother to my children.

I considered closing the damper on the fireplace, but I was afraid of that idea. I thought about stocking up enough Valium, but I discarded that idea, too. I didn't know how much to administer to each one of us. Any other means was too violent, and basically I was not a violent person. I couldn't stand the thought of hurting my children with physical force. The fireplace or the Valium was my only possibility.

Then I had a frightening thought, *What if it doesn't kill us all? What if one gets left behind? Steve is strong, he might be able to survive.* Then I thought an even worse thought, *What if I survive, and I am the only one left alive?* It was then that I realized I wasn't smart enough to tackle such an endeavor.

A few months later I talked to a young woman whose mother had committed suicide when the daughter was quite young. She only wished, she said, that her mother had taken her with her. At the time I thought how horrible that sounded coming from someone else, but how meaningful it would have been to me a few months earlier.

Every day was becoming harder and harder to endure. I managed to get to work every morning and satisfactorily handle my duties, but the exhaustion was getting worse. It took all my energy just to keep my head off the desk, I was so tired.

Dr. Jamison suggested hospitalization at the mental hosital for two weeks. "I'm sure you will be happy you did it. You'll feel much better when you get out." No, no, no. How could a hospital, a mental hospital at that, help me when Dr. Jamison couldn't? As I look back now, I realize two weeks on a desert isle might have been better, but my insurance company wouldn't pay for that kind of therapy.

But on a Friday afternoon in July, 1975, I realized I couldn't go on any longer. I quit my job, called Dr. Jamison and asked him to make preparations to have me admitted to the hospital as soon as possible. Steve went to stay with Dave's sister, Sally, and Lisa and Jan went to Springfield to stay with his other sister, Sue. I entered the hospital on Saturday morning. I parked my car in the parking lot just outside in the hospital parking lot, and I focused in on a two-week recovery. Dr. Jamison said I wouldn't be sorry; he was sure I would be much improved by the time I was discharged.

Immediately I was started on a heavy dose of medication and, it being a weekend, I was left alone to sleep. My roommate was gone for the night so I didn't meet her until the next day. She left a macrame hanger draped over the closet door. I dozed off and only left my room for meals and medication.

My speech became slurred and I had little control over my tongue. I felt drunk. Dr. Jamison said he would adjust my medication, and then suggested electroshock therapy as casually as if he were offering me a coke. Fortunately I had enough strength left to refuse. I'd read enough to know that I didn't need the extra problems that sometimes occur with shock treatments. I thought Dr. Jamison understood that I was only in the hospital for a rest. I assumed he had forgotten.

I made new friends among the patients who were hospitalized on the open ward. One young woman had tried to commit suicide by taking too many tranquilizers, and she now had a speech problem. "Are you German?" I asked. "No," she replied. "But you have a German accent." "I know," she answered. "I didn't talk like this before my suicide attempt."

I met Jerry, the one who had tried the marriage counseling with Dave and me. Now I found I like him. I realized he had been trying to help us in an off-beat sort of way. He was the first "expert" who gave Dave credit for being human. The rest of them thought that since he was brain injured, he no longer functioned normally in any capacity. I knew they were wrong, but I had run out of energy trying to fight them.

The first group I attended Monday morning was called the "Anger Group." Not all patients attended every group, so I had to assume Dr. Jamison arranged to have me enrolled in this group to get out any repressed anger I was harboring.

That first morning we could either participate or simply observe other patients who displayed their anger. Group therapy was a new experience for me, but not to the woman who volunteered to show us how it was done in the anger group. She sat down on the floor and beat the padded surface with her fists, shouting obscenities and declaring anger at her husband for taking her children away from her. I had never seen that kind of anger in anyone before. Perhaps, I thought, her children were better off with their father, but I couldn't help but feel sorry for someone who had so much rage inside her.

The next day as the therapists led my group to the Anger room, I noticed Barb, the therapy leader, carrying two batakas. This was the first time I had ever seen these padded clubs before; and I said, "Looks like a violent group today." Barb said, "Oh, not at all." There were about ten patients in the group, two therapists (Barb and John), and a visiting student therapist.

There weren't enough chairs for everyone, so I, along with a few others, sat on the floor. I sat with my back against a sofa and had my hands around my ankles with my knees drawn up. Barb asked me to tell the group about Dave's accident. I proceeded to do so, and I ended with a tearful description of Dave moving to the halfway house. I blotted the tears with the Kleenex I held in my hand.

Then suddenly Barb struck me with the bataka. She jumped to her feet and began dancing around me trying at the same time to get me to take the other bataka. I refused. She struck my ankles with the bataka she held in her right hand. Then she hit my legs, still urging me to take the other bataka, I presume to hit her back with.

I didn't understand what she was doing, but I couldn't hit her with anything, not even a padded bataka. I had withdrawn so much since Dave's accident, I didn't care whether I lived or died, and now I hoped she would just beat me to death and get it over with. I felt the blows against my legs. None of them hurt physically, but I couldn't understand why she kept hitting me. This just didn't seem right. I also kept my hair too perfect, she said as she struck me again.

Then I felt another patient behind me on the sofa. She tried to twist the tissue out of my right hand, to force me to open my hand and take the club. I clenched my fist tightly. She leaned over and spoke in my ear, "Blame God for what happened to your husband. Blame God." Suddenly I felt as if I were sitting in a witches' coven, completely surrounded by evil. I had never blamed God, and I wasn't about to start. I held tightly to my tissue, and steeled myself against the repeated blows. At this time in my life I would protect my children from any disaster, but I no longer felt I was worth saving. I didn't have the ability to protect myself from anything.

I felt a sharp pain on my right side as Barb struck me this time with the bataka, pinching me between the bataka and the sofa. By this time Barb was panting, as she slumped down into a chair. I learned later that this was a common form of therapy, but apparently I wasn't a "common" patient.

At that moment the student therapist jumped up from her seat, ran towards me, grabbed my hands, and pulled me to my feet. She pulled the other patients toward me and gathered them all in a circle around me. It was then that I began to sob.

I gathered my composure after a minute or two, and silently the class was dismissed.

When I was admitted to the hospital I was asked to rate myself on a scale from 1 to 100. I couldn't even list a number, except that it was in the minus category, and now I felt even farther down the scale. I wasn't sure how much farther I could go.

The Anger Group did nothing for my mental health. It only proved that there were always people out to inflict more punishment on me than I had already endured. A few days later I learned Barb had told all the patients in the group not to talk to me unless I talked to them first.

One woman who was not in the group found out about it from some patients who were talking about it after class. She slipped into my room and asked, "Would you like to talk to the chaplain?" I told her I would, and she hurried off. Someone had told me she was a doctor's wife. Her husband had admitted her to the hospital because he was having an affair with his nurse, and wanted his wife out of the way. I

204

couldn't have been more grateful for anyone's presence than I was for hers; she was a kindhearted woman.

A few minutes later the chaplain walked into my room. I was lying quietly on my bed trying to sort out my anguish and decide what I should do next. I was exhausted when I came into the hospital, and now I was racked with a deeper fatigue burrowing into my unhappiness. The chaplain asked, "Are you a Christian?"

"Yes, I am," I answered. "But I'm beginning to feel like Jesus when He was dying on the cross, when he said, 'My God, My God, Why Hast Thou Forsaken Me?' " I explained about the patient who told me to blame God. I told him about Barb, and the Anger group. "I felt like I was surrounded by a group of witches, telling me to "Blame God, blame God.' "

"God has not forsaken you," the chaplain answered. "He was with you in that room. He gave you strength to endure the therapy session." He let out a sigh, "I don't always approve of what goes on here." He sat with me for a few more minutes and then he left.

Some other friends came to see why I hadn't appeared at lunch. They weren't in my therapy group either, but had heard from the other patients what had happened. They sat with me for a while.

I stayed in my room for the rest of the day, and most of the night. About midnight I got up, went into the bathroom, stood up on the toilet seat, and looked in the mirror at my back. I had a bruise the size of a 50¢ coin. By now it was beginning to throb.

I remembered a therapist I had met the first night; he worked the late shift and we had a pleasant conversation. I went to the recreation room to see if he was there. Instead I found two other therapists playing a game of pool. They said Bob was not on duty; it was his night off. I sat down and watched the game for a few minutes and then returned to my room.

The next morning I went to get my medication at the nurses' station. I asked the nurse, "Would you tell Dr. Jamison I want to see him as soon as he gets here?" She said she would.

It was breakfast time and nearly 24 hours since I had eaten, but still I had no appetite. All I could think of now was talking to Dr. Jamison and getting out of this torture house. It was clear I wasn't going to get any better by being physically beaten.

The usual time for Dr. Jamison to do his rounds came and went. I waited for another half-hour, but still he didn't come. I decided to check again at the nurses' station; perhaps he was just late today. The therapist standing at the desk said, "Oh, he's already been here. Just a minute, he gave me a message to give to you." She went into the back room and came out with one of Dr. Jamison's cards with a message written on the back, presumably written by Dr. Jamison. It said he would see me after lunch.

I was furious! How could he do that, today of all days? "Anger Group" would be over by then, and I would be at the mercy of Barb's next form of therapy. I didn't say a word, but went directly to the telephone and called Dr. Jamison's office across the lot.

The receptionist who answered the phone apparently wasn't aware that I had been hospitalized. "But you have an appointment today to see Dr. Jamison," she answered when I asked her to have him call me.

"I'm in the hospital, and I'm scheduled for group therapy in a few minutes. And I am not attending any more therapy classes until I see Dr. Jamison!" I hung up the phone. Even before I could get back to my room, I heard Dr. Jamison's name paged over the intercom.

I'd made the bed earlier that morning so I laid down on top of the bedspread to wait for Dr. Jamison. Mary walked in and sat down on a chair. She was supposed to be my therapist for the two weeks, and I had been told, "If you have any problems or questions, bring them to Mary. She will help you." Mary had greeted me on Saturday afternoon, and said she would see me every day from then on, but it was now Wednesday and I hadn't seen Mary since I'd arrived.

Mary's voice was angry as she said, "You have no right to be spreading gossip about Barb."

"What gossip? I haven't spread any gossip."

"You've been telling stories about her to all the other patients," she said.

"Oh, no I haven't," I replied with irritation. "I wasn't the only one in that therapy group, and I have not left my room to tell anyone anything. Anything that's being spread around is being done so by other patients, and not me!" Just then Jerry walked into the room, and Mary got up and left. Jerry walked over and sat down on the floor beside the bed. I don't remember what we talked about, I just remember realizing how much I really liked him. Then Dr. Jamison entered the room. Jerry got up and left, as Dr. Jamison sat down in a chair by the door. He seemed a bit hesitant, so I started the conversation.

"I want out of here now!" Pause. "I'm not getting what I'm paying for. Mary is supposed to be my therapist, and I haven't seen her since Saturday." Pause. "I've heard rumors that I'm on the suicide list. Well, if I was planning to commit suicide, last night would have been the night. My roommate was gone for the night . . . I could have taken her macrame that's draped over the door, hung it up on the sprinkler and killed myself . . . if that was my intent." Still he didn't say anything. "Do you know I could sue you? I have a bruise on my back from therapy yesterday with Barb." He still didn't say anything. "Would you like to see it?"

"No," he replied.

"Well, I think you should." He stood up, took a pad from his pocket, and began writing on it as he walked toward me. As he finished writing what I assumed was my discharge papers, I turned my head into the pillow and said, "Oh, I'm so tired I could die." I meant that I was terribly tired, but I didn't actually mean I was planning to die, it was simply a figure of speech. However, Dr. Jamison put his pad back in his pocket.

"I'm sorry, Sharon. I can't let you go now." He walked out of the room. I sat up with a jerk. What did I just do? How could I have been so stupid? I looked at my watch. Anger Group was over, it was time for lunch. Suddenly I had an appetite again. Asserting myself had made me hungry. I also knew what I had said to Dr. Jamison was right, and he knew it. This was the first time in a long time I had stood up for myself. I'd spent so much of the last three years struggling for Dave and the children, that I had literally stopped existing, and therefore not worth fighting for.

First I stopped at the therapists' lunch room, and pulled up my shirt to show Barb the bruise on my back. I thought it was important that she know she could inflict injuries on people, and I felt a sense of satisfaction to see the surprise on her face. I sat down with all my new friends and joined them for lunch.

I learned there had been an impromtu meeting of doctors after the encounter I had with Barb the day before at the Anger Group. Now the group was renamed, Feelings Group. I never saw Barb again, and I heard she was fired, but that was a rumor that was never verified.

Mary became attentive, greeting me each morning to inquire how I was doing and if I needed anything. She was unusually friendly.

I didn't know that since I had signed myself in, I could have walked out of the mental hospital simply by signing myself out. I couldn't bring myself to walk out without the doctor giving me a little slip saying I was discharged. I assumed the police would come to my house, handcuff me, and haul me back. I was terrified of that.

The first week I stayed within the hosptal walls, but the second week I was allowed to leave whenever I wanted as long as I signed out and signed back in. I went home, picked up the mail, and wrote out checks for bills. Occasionally I took my new friends to the store, or just out for a spin in my car. I was the only one who had a car at the hospital. One college-age patient knew calligraphy so he started a class for those who wanted to learn. The second week turned out to be days of enjoyable group therapy and get-togethers with all the patients I had come to know.

One incident surprised me. I signed out for the afternoon, went home, and when I returned I looked at my watch. I was a half-hour late. I hurried to the nurses' station to sign myself back in, and worried all the way about how I was going to enter the correct time. This would be a blot on my record, I thought, if I entered the present time, and it was unthinkable for me to lie and write the time I *should* have been back.

After I finished my signature, I glanced at the box where the time was to be inserted. It was already filled in, not the present time, but the time I was *supposed* to have been back.

I never did find out who did it. My record was clear, and although the time was incorrect I refused to fret about it because I knew *I* hadn't written it.

Dave had a new Vocational Rehabilitation counselor, Marie. She replaced Mr. Frank. Since I was still married to Dave, Marie met with me while I was still at the hospital. She suggested I consider going back to school and learning new job skills. I had never thought about going back to school, but now I was eager to begin something new and start a fresh new challenge. Marie said the Vocational Rehabilitation would pay my tuition and books.

It would be two months before the fall term started, but I began to plan anyway. I also had to get another job to help pay these medical bills I had just spent two weeks building up.

I talked to Les and asked him to start divorce proceedings for Dave and me. "I wish you would reconsider," he said.

"No," I responded. "I have to follow through with this. I can't go back to the way things were. It just isn't possible."

Les suggested starting a new trial, and asked my opinion. "I don't see how we can win," I said. "It seems to me that we're fighting city hall when suing a major corporation. And the judge was awful. To me it's just a lark to think we can win."

"A lark," he replied. "I don't consider it a lark." Then he added, "Are you firing me?"

"No, of course, I'm not firing you, but we don't have any more money, and anything more you do now, you're doing on your own. We can't help you financially, and borrowing money is out of the question."

"Do you think I should borrow?"

"You certainly have a means to pay it back if we lose again." I presumed he could finance it with his current business income while I could barely keep my family fed. "For me it would be like buying a new car. I couldn't possibly think of taking out a loan for that, and I can't consider taking a loan for a new trial." Les said he would get a loan for $6,000 from the bank, and get things rolling again. "Dave and I are behind you, but financially and physically I can do no more. The mistrial upset me so much, I don't want to have any more to do with the case. I can't go through it again." Les said he understood, and by the time we both hung up the phone we were on the threshold of starting over.

During my hospital stay I still had one credit card application to be processed. I assumed since I hadn't heard from the department store, Meier and Frank, that it would be just like the others, a turn-down. Much to my surprise a card arrived during my second week of hospitalization. Meier and Frank department store had decided I was a good credit risk, good enough to handle a credit card. The thought was funny, since I was unemployed now. However, I was thrilled with the slight boost to my ego.

When I left the hospital, I had no way of knowing that I had a new transition to make, re-entering the world. Dr. Jamison told me how good I would feel for having been hospitalized, but I didn't really feel better. And he neglected to tell me about the withdrawal from the hospital environment.

I had hoped the memories of Dave would have been blotted from my mind, but that didn't happen. Perhaps electroshock therapy would have done it. Nothing else seemed to be successful.

XXIV

Coming out of the hospital was even more of a shock than going in. It seemed as if my nerves were exposed, as I struggled to get used to the sights and sounds of society going pell-mell. Although I was allowed to leave the hospital occasionally that second week, I still wasn't prepared for complete exposure to the rush of traffic on city streets and to the rapid pattern of conversation. Everyone in the hospital went in slow motion, especially the heavily-medicated patients. Even the therapists were calm, soft-spoken individuals, at least most of them. Some patients, too, were more emotional than others, but many were dazed from electroshock therapy, or, like me, were being given strong doses of tranquilizers. Now, even though my senses were still dulled by medication, I felt a sensitivity to noise, and to fast-paced movements. People around me no longer moved in slow motion.

I took the children to Sunday dinner at my mother's. Bonita, her husband Bill, and their three children were also there – just like old times. Mama scurried around the kitchen, preparing dinner and worrying whether she had cooked enough food. When dinner was ready, we all sat down at the table and began a friendly conversation. Mama was her usual self as she put bowls of food on the table, and when each one had made the full circle, she jumped up to take them off and put them back into the oven to keep warm.

Bill said something which I no longer recall, but I responded and joined in the conversation. Mama sat down quickly in her chair, said, "What did you say Bill?", but before he could answer, she said, "Dan, would you like more green beans?" My nerves snapped. No one seemed to care what anyone else had to say, I thought. Actually it was just Mama who was flitting around, but I had reached my limit of tolerance for this flurry of activity.

"Would you please sit down and be quiet?" I said. "You're driving me crazy!" Mama cautiously sat down in her chair, and *everyone* was quiet for the rest of the meal.

Ever since the accident I had begun to change. I would never have snapped at anyone like that before no matter how much they irritated me. I tried to be tolerant, but I couldn't take it any longer. This outburst was never mentioned again, and eventually my irritability decreased as I became used to the din around me. Mama shifted back to her old habits, and mealtime was just as animated every Sunday in the future as I had remembered it in the past.

My hospitalization was never spoken of. No one mentioned a word about where I had been or questioned me about my experiences. I occasionally spoke about them, but the person I was talking to rarely made a comment. Conversations about hospital happenings were met with silence. I accepted it because I knew it was difficult for people to understand why I was hospitalized. No one really knew, or seemed to be interested in finding out, why I decided to sign myself in. The subject made everyone uncomfortable, and therefore it was tabu. I learned to keep silent about my hospital experiences.

Contrary to Dr. Jamison's statment that I would feel better having been in the hospital, I felt worse. I had been stigmatized by going into a mental hospital, no matter what the cause or my reasons for going in. I had to deal with that new situation when I returned home.

The depression was still with me, and Dr. Jamison could argue that this was so because I didn't have the electroshock therapy he wanted to give me. I still didn't regret that decision, but I was terrified that I didn't feel as good as Dr. Jamison suggested I would.

I worried about having to go back to the hospital. I met patients at the hospital who had been there time and again. I met one woman who signed herself in whenever her job stresses became severe. She said the hospital was the only place where she could get a good rest. I thought about that desert isle and wondered if perhaps that wasn't the best idea yet, but I knew for certain the insurance company wouldn't agree.

Dr. Jamison continued changing my anti-depressant medications since I tolerated none of them well enough to stay on them.

I tried to be a good patient. I tried to do as my doctor told me, and I don't believe I was so very different from other women I knew. I thought doctors had all the answers, and when I didn't fit into the categories they tried to place me in, I assumed it was my fault.

When I asked my family doctor, "Are birth control pills really safe, should I be careful about taking them, and do they cause other illnesses?" He replied, "Oh, you women blame everything on the pill." Silently, I thought perhaps you're right, doctor.

A few years before Dave's accident I had begun having stress problems. My doctor told me to go home and get more rest. "After all, three children are bound to make anyone tired." I tried to get more rest, but my nervous problems increased. I started having symptoms of agoraphobia, a fear of public places, and a fear of crowds. What was my doctor's answer to this increasing phobia? – "I had another woman patient yesterday with the exact same problems; people like you should be drowned at birth." Yes, you're right, doctor, I thought.

For years I had menstrual pain so severe I ended up immobilized in bed for one or two days every month. The doctor said it was caused by tension, although the first doctor I went to as a teenager stated the cause was from a fibrous uterus. He admitted there was a physical cause. After I was married, and had three children, I asked my new doctor for some pain pills for cramps. He replied, "After having children, you shouldn't have cramps." Then he told me the pain was due to nervous tension. In other words, it's all in my mind.

After Dave's accident whenever I mentioned panic attacks and pelvic

210

pain, the doctors would say, "Of course, you're under a great deal of stress because of your husband's accident." But I'd had the same symptoms *before* the accident. The doctors were all telling me it was my imagination, and I believed they were right. I felt ignorant and worthless. If a doctor thought people like me should be drowned at birth, perhaps suicide wasn't such a far-out solution.

None of the doctors I had met had patience with Dave's recovery, nor did they want to deal with my problems.

I didn't know it then, but I was caught in a vicious circle. It was because of Dr. Jamison that I put Dave in the halfway house, and my depression became worse about that time – later I wondered if it precipitated the depression. Then as I became more depressed, it was the connection with Dr. Jamison that kept me hanging on, that gave me that last little thread of reality.

But since my hospitalization I felt different toward Dr. Jamison. I no longer had him as a comrade, I thought. I couldn't help but wonder if he was the one who actually set up my encounter with Barb – perhaps it was entirely his idea. He had been the only *real* friend I thought I had, and now it seemed I no longer had him.

I mentioned Barb at my next therapy session with Dr. Jamison. He said, "She's been severely dealt with," and changed the subject. I wondered, *If it was actually Dr. Jamison's idea, or his fault, it wasn't right to fire Barb.* But I remained my usual obedient self, and said nothing.

Then I told Dr. Jamison that I had a problem with severe pelvic pain, and that it was increasing in severity. "My doctor keeps telling me it's caused from tension, and it's worsening because of the stress from Dave's accident."

"That isn't my specialty. Perhaps you should see a gynecologist. But, stress *can* cause the pain." He saw the look on my face, as he continued, "Now don't get me wrong. The pain *is* there, but it's caused by nervous tension." It was that sentence that I realized I had lost Dr. Jamison for good – in my own mind. I knew the pain wasn't my imagination, and I knew it wasn't caused by tension. I had taken enough tranquilizers to know when I could control stress with them, and when I couldn't. I could ease the anxiety attacks and the phobic feelings with tranquilizers, but not the menstrual pain.

I continued my struggle to obey Dr. Jamison, however. I wanted to do what he told me, to bring about this great change in my life. I asked him why I couldn't get used to the change in my life, the accident, and Dave living in the halfway house.

"You haven't allowed yourself to mourn," he answered.

"How can I mourn someone who isn't dead?"

"It isn't easy, but in a sense David is dead, and you have to mourn the loss of that relationship." I still don't understand how that would help since it felt as if I had been in a period of mourning ever since I moved Dave to his sister's house. I spent countless hours in the bathroom crying into a bathtowel, but I couldn't seem to get myself into an acceptable state of mourning. Dr. Jamison kept telling me I wasn't doing it right, or I would feel better. You'll improve *when* you mourn in the proper way, he said. In other words, I thought, it's my fault again.

Dr. Jamison kept telling me I had to get out socially. Life would stay exactly the same unless I forced myself to meet new people and began dating again. "No one's going to break your door down," he said. That began the new phase of torment in my life.

I met a few eligible men that year, and the disappointment continued. I dated one man a few times. He took me to my first Trailblazer's basketball game, took the children and me to Snowbunny Lodge on Mount Hood, and had Sunday dinner at Mama's with my family. One day when I mentioned his ex-wife, he asked, "Which one?" This surprised me, "You have more than one?" I realized immediately he wasn't for me. He wanted me to get a divorce as soon as possible so we could get married, and I had only known him a few weeks. Marriage and good husband-wife relationships didn't seem to mean as much to him as it did to me.

I dated another man who reacted the same way; within two weeks he wanted to get married. "So you can make my breakfast every morning," he admitted. "But I hate to cook," I answered. "That's okay," he said, "we can work something out." Oh, no. I wasn't about to get married and turn into a slave for someone. I had had nearly a year of freedom, freedom from taking care of Dave, a year of having only the children to worry about. I wasn't about to marry someone who wanted to put me into the kitchen. I remembered how Dave liked to cook, how many times he took over in the kitchen, and how he accepted the fact that I hated fixing meals. He didn't care; he knew his way around the kitchen better than I did, anyway.

Another man came into my life for another two-week period. He called me on the phone the day after Steve Prefontaine, the Oregon track star, was killed in a car accident. I heard it on the TV news just as I was picking up the telephone receiver. When I announced my shock to this man, he asked, "Who's Steve Prefontaine?" I thought of Dave again. Even now, Dave wouldn't have to ask such a question. In many ways I considered Dave much more intelligent than some people I knew who had never suffered a head injury. Dave and I both kept up on current events. I couldn't relate to someone who didn't.

And what if I married one of these men, none of whom I could love as much as I had loved Dave, and then this new husband had a stroke or a heart attack which left *him* an invalid? I might end up with someone even more handicapped than Dave, and I would be expected to take care of him. Why try to build my life into something more convenient and happier, just to end up in the same situation all over again?

A friend stopped by the house one evening. He said his wife had suddenly decided she wanted a divorce and he was feeling quite troubled.

I asked him in for a cup of coffee, and we talked for a while. I didn't encourage him to come back, and he didn't. I had too many problems of my own to try and help someone else in sorting out theirs.

Another night another dejected husband stopped by my home. His wife, a relative of mine, had just announced her intention of getting a divorce which would also separate him from his baby daughter. Tears welled in his eyes as he sat on the sofa. "I feel like God is punishing me for not helping you after Dave's accident."

"Oh, no," I said. "God isn't punishing you. God doesn't do things like that." Deep inside, I wished that I believed God did. There were so many friends who made a point to stay away from us, who never called or stopped in to see us for the entire three years after the accident, including the following year while Dave lived at the halfway house. It was as if, to them, we no longer existed. It was inevitable that those people would eventually have their own problems whatever they might be, but I knew it wasn't punishment from God.

Throughout the summer Dave continued his outpatient counseling sessions. He had a high regard for Linda, his therapist. One evening a week a psychiatrist came to the halfway house to lead group therapy for the residents living there. Dave disliked this therapy group and often planned to be away from the house on that particular evening. Usually he and another resident hopped a bus and went to a movie.

Dave said the psychiatrist was hard on each person as he delved into their past experiences, and pried out painful thoughts. Each week a different person was exposed to the prying questions. One night the psychiatrist had chosen Dave. He asked Dave about the accident, and eventually got around to the divorce. Then he asked Dave the thing that seemed to interest most therapists and psychiatrists, "Why are you smiling? What do you have to smile about? You're handicapped, your wife is divorcing you, and your life is a mess; what do you have to be happy about?" That put a stop to Dave's efforts to communicate in group therapy. The next week he asked to visit with the children on therapy night.

Steve had taken to calling Dave often throughout the week, asking questions about problems I couldn't help him with. It was astounding that Dave could answer clearly nearly anything Steve asked, and he helped him with any mechanical problem he developed with his bike. Steve knew that when he had a problem, all he had to do was call Dad.

Dave's world was broadening. His therapists and psychiatrists, like mine, encouraged him to get out more, to visit the singles clubs in the area and to meet new people. Dave cooperated, as I did, and he came back with the same result: nothing.

As I look back it seems incredible how manipulated we both were. And it's a wonder we didn't run into one another on our evenings out at the various social clubs. Why couldn't the same amount of effort have been integrated into helping us keep our marriage together, instead of so much work going into showing us how to live apart?

It seemed the best way to erase Dave from my mind was to stay away from him as much as possible, but that was difficult. For one thing, I felt a certain sense of responsibility towards him and his recovery. At least once a month I drove to the halfway house to give him a check for the $200 room and board payment that was required. It hurt to see Dave living in that old three-story house in North Portland in a bedroom with two other people. Most of his housemates were drug addicts and misfits who couldn't make it in society. Dave might have been the most all-together person there.

I noticed another change in Dave. He no longer displayed anger at Steve, and he had learned to communicate. Instead of sitting silently through a conversation, he began to take part in the discussion. In the past throughout his rehabilitation, he had showed irritation whenever someone asked him a question, as if it was putting him out to answer it. Now he was willing and eager to give advice whenever anyone asked. His brain was like a filing cabinet with a wealth of information just waiting for the right person to push the right buttons. Steve seemed to sense this ability to share his past experiences and knowledge, or perhaps Steve was the one who helped Dave bring this ability back to the surface. Dave was beginning to act in ways resembling the man I remembered.

Dave continued in the Goodwill training program, trying to learn how to operate a cash register and getting on-the-job training as a night watchman. He had trouble with the cash register because, he complained, he couldn't see the numbers on the keys; his lack of motivation prevented him from trying to memorize them. And he couldn't handle the watchman position because he kept falling asleep on the job. After he burned his leg on a space heater, they fired him.

My self-image was still lodged at the bottom of the 1-100 scale, without an increase in sight. I had become a failure at something else: namely, I wasn't able to succeed at being single. There were single people all around me; wherever I looked I saw single men and women who appeared happy, people who could tolerate the ear-shattering music in singles bars and the other singles who frequented them. I hated the bars, and I couldn't make myself have a good time.

I felt separate from the women in churches who were married and had happy lives and wonderful husbands. I couldn't sit through their Bible studies and become a part of the world they lived in. Mine was entirely different, and it seemed as if we had absolutely nothing in common. There were those who admitted to me that they thought I hadn't prayed hard enough for Dave's healing, and I felt some blamed me because Dave was still crippled.

My mind was constantly on my children, and I worried about paying our regular monthly expenses plus Dave's room and board and a little cash for his spending money. The twenty dollars I could afford to give him each month often didn't stretch, so he took to selling his blood now and then at the Plasma Center. And each day I studied the classified ads for a new job – a part-time job, so I could attend college, too.

I still saw Dr. Jamison each week and he continued to switch my anti-depressant medication, trying in vain to find something I could take and still function in a normal fashion. One kind, I remember, made me feel as if I had been cut in half; my mind was in a whirl but my legs could barely move, as if I were mired in wet cement.

Dr. Jamison had moved with his associates into a new building in downtown Portland. At my first appointment just after I was discharged from the hospital, I was overwhelmed when I entered his office at the view of Mount Hood through the large picture window. Then my eyes fell on the wide sweep of freeways that twisted over and under seventeen stories below. Suddenly I felt dizzy. The building almost seemed to move. I closed my eyes, took a deep breath, and tried to get a grip on myself. *Is this good experience for therapy patients?* I wondered if Dr. Jamison ever had patients who were afraid of heights. Oh well, I guess this would be a good place to get over it, right here in the doctor's office.

After I sat down across from him, Dr. Jamison began listing all the many things I had accomplished since Dave's accident. I had managed Dave's therapy for three years, and I had done a good job, he said. I had taken care of the family responsibilities, raising the children, and hiring the construction of a new home. Normally I would have been embarrassed to hear someone saying so many good things about me, but I grew irritated at him instead. "Don't you see? I didn't do any of that." He looked at me, surprised, a question on his face.

"What do you mean? Of course you did," he said.

"No, I didn't. Dave did it all. I decided right after the accident, I would step into his shoes until he was well again, and that's exactly what I did."

"That's ridiculous," he responded. "You *did* those things! *You* did them!" He looked incredulous.

"No, I didn't!" I shouted right back. The conversation was ended. Dr. Jamison said nothing more, and the time was up – time for him to go on to another patient. I left his office thinking he was the most ignorant doctor I had ever known, if he couldn't see that I wasn't capable of doing all the things he listed. *Dave had to have done them, I knew I couldn't.*

One night I had another dream. There are only two dreams that have stuck with me my entire life; I have blotted out the memory of all the others. The first dream was the woman falling into the car crusher, and then that next autumn came another.

This time I was sitting in a classroom surrounded by empty desks. I was seated in the front row near the center of the room. There was a man standing directly in front of me at the blackboard with his back turned. He seemed to be wearing a black suit, typical of a teacher, perhaps.

He turned to face me. I don't remember his face, but just the words he said, "You will not get a divorce, but you will divorce yourself from your problems." The dream ended then and I sat up with a start.

I remembered those first days after Dave's accident when I felt so in tune with God, receptive to whatever He wanted me to do. I realized I had to get back to that receptive feeling again. I had spent the past few years praying and trying to live my life as I thought the Lord wanted, but I realized I hadn't felt that familiar sense of being receptive.

It was as if the Lord had stood slightly back and allowed me to make my own decisions, and live my own life, giving me the freedom to make the choices without obvious guidance from Him. Now and then He gave me a nudge, as in the dream, but He didn't do everything for me. I could actually say, I willingly made all the choices on my own while I, at the same time, considered the Lord's will. He was allowing me to be molded and tempered, but not by His direct guidance. It was completely up to me to make the decisions according to His will, and I was free to do the choosing without His interference.

We had two suits pending again, one against the manufacturer, and the other against the highway department for not erecting barricades at that dangerous section of highway. Many accidents had occurred at that location over the years, and nothing had been done to correct the obvious defect. That fall we lost our second trial. The judge declared we were not able to sue for maintaining a highway. We gained one thing, however. The barricades were being erected at the time we went to trial. An accident like Dave's would never happen again at that overpass.

I didn't take this trial loss as hard as the previous one. I was beginning to get used to losing.

And as the children started back to school after the long summer vacation, I found a new job as a typist in an insurance office, three days a week. Then, in the last part of September, I became a student at Mt. Hood Community College, where I enrolled in one course, Medical Terminology. School was about to bring forth a remarkable change in me. I began to study and memorize root-words, Latin and Greek abbreviations, which would give me the key to every medical word I would ever need to know.

I still didn't know what I was going to do with all this medical jargon, however.

XXV

Since it was nearing registration for the winter college term, I picked up a catalog listing of classes. On the bus the following morning on my way to work, I studied it carefully. There wasn't a single class I could take again this term except for Medical Terminology II, which was given as a night class, and a brush-up typing class which was also given at night. I was beginning to get discouraged. I called Marie, my DVR counselor.

"At the rate I'm going, it will take me ten years to get through this course – if I make it at all." I had decided to take the Medical Assistant program, but focusing mainly on medical transcription. It was a two-year course and I would receive an Associate degree when I graduated. Medical transcription was the most flexible work I could get into; working hours in most hospitals can be round-the-clock. I could pick my hours, and spend more time with my children.

Now, however, as I explained to Marie, I felt hopeless that I would even reach that goal. Most of the classes were split up throughout the weekdays. I worked Monday, Wednesday, and Thursday each week. I could register for the classes held on Tuesdays, but I couldn't attend the second half that was given on Thursdays.

"I have an idea," Marie said. "I'll call you right back."

A few minutes later Marie called to tell me that she had set up an appointment for me to meet with a counselor for the Comprehensive Employment and Training Act (CETA) at the Clackamas County office the next afternoon. "For every hour you attend class up to a total of thirty hours, you will receive minimum wage, and I know you are eligible." She also suggested signing up for food stamps.

The following afternoon I met Fay, who was to be my CETA counselor. I was enrolled, and at the beginning of the winter term, just after the Christmas holidays, I would be a full-time student.

I gave my resignation at work and worked for another two weeks. I didn't feel badly about quitting so soon after I had started because the job I was filling wasn't re-filled. They decided it was a position that wasn't needed. For the four months I worked there, I'd been thinking the same thing, but I didn't say anything to anyone. I thought they must know what they are doing. I always thought everyone else knew what they were doing, and I was the only one who didn't.

On one of my next visits to Dr. Jamison, I mentioned the severe pelvic pain that I was suffering from, the pain that was caused by stress. He handed me a refill prescription for my Valium and another for Darvon, a pain killer. The anti-depressants were doing no good so they were dropped.

The Darvon didn't seem to help the pain; instead, it made me feel lightheaded and more disassociated from the world than usual. Since the pain was supposed to be imagined, I dutifully took the pain medication in combination with Valium. I kept telling myself the pain would cease as soon as I relaxed enough, with the help of the muscle relaxant – Valium. However the pain continued, and I struggled through the following days. I had to. This was a chance I couldn't afford to let slip through my fingers – receiving a salary to go to school.

Looking back I know now that some of the doctors I had seen over the years came to an understandable conclusion: stop the stress and the pain will stop, too. However, a few doctors at the time were beginning to recognize that menstrual cramps are caused by a very real physical disorder. And since the early 70's doctors stopped pinning the condition strictly on stress or tension and began to medically treat the symptoms. Until my problem was correctly diagnosed I thought the doctors faulted me for imagining my own pain.

To receive food stamps I had to compile a list of receipts and expenses for the past few months, present it at the food stamp office, and get a booklet of stamps. I had thrown away my electric bill stub and all I had was the cancelled check for the previous month. The oil barrel was filled only in the wintertime so I took the cancelled checks for that also.

The food stamp lady motioned for me to take a seat across from her. I laid my stack of receipts in front of her and she began sorting through them. She picked up the check for the electricity, "How do I know if this is for only one month?" I hadn't given that a thought: one check could be for more than one month, I realized.

"I'm expecting another bill any day now, and when it comes I can prove that this is for just one month." I paused a moment. "I guess you'll just have to take my word for it today." It always took me by surprise, when people didn't trust me. I guess I thought "honesty" must be printed across my forehead.

The food stamp lady grabbed up the checks for the oil bill, "I can't tell anything by this." She sounded irritated.

"I'm sorry, but we only have oil delivered during the winter months, and I don't have anything more than that to prove how much I have purchased."

"What's their phone number," she snapped. I was surprised at this question. No one told me I would need phone numbers.

"I don't know. I'm sorry." I replied. "But, if you'll get me a phone book, I'll look it up." She ignored this and went on to the medical expenses, Dave's room and board at the halfway house, and my psychiatric bills. She sifted through the cancelled checks.

"I can't tell anything by this," she said in exasperation. "None of this proves anything!"

"My DVR counselor can verify everything. She's my husband's counselor, too." I felt the lump catch in my throat. *We will be in trouble if I don't receive these food stamps. Food was the only thing I could scrimp on, and I was doing a lot of scrimping. The children were also receiving free lunches at school because our income was below poverty level.*

"What's your counselor's phone number," she asked.

"I'm sorry," I replied again. "I don't have it . . . But if you will give me a phone book, I'll be glad to look it up." She ignored me again, and the stony look remained on her face.

Then the food stamp lady stood up. "I'll be right back." She walked out of the room. I was certain at this point that I had blown it. We weren't about to get stamps after this fiasco. I had never gone anywhere so ill-prepared, but it had happened so quickly that I didn't have a month in which to compile some of the receipts, and I certainly didn't know I would need those phone numbers.

Five or ten minutes passed while my heart pounded. This woman was the rudest person I had met in my life. I had never been in a position like this before. I had never had to ask for hand-outs. My mother never resorted to this even when I was young and my father was drinking so heavily. I didn't like it, and I didn't know if I could face up to doing it again.

Some people were against our lawsuits, but it seemed much more logical to make the person or corporation responsible for the accident pay instead of the taxpayers. I didn't want to pay for food with food stamps, and I didn't want to take away from society. Dave and I had been responsible people during the first decade of our marriage, and I never considered an accident throwing us into this kind of a situation. It was unthinkable. It only happens to other people, I thought.

The food stamp lady came back with a signed authorization for food stamps, and far more than I thought I'd get. But when I walked out of her office, she still had the sour look on her face. Apparently she took no pleasure in her job, and I wondered if she disliked the people who asked for stamps. I was certain she didn't like me.

The children and I ate better the next two months than we had in several years. But I was determined never to ask for food stamps again. Every year I would have to re-apply for them, and at the end of this year – only a couple of months away – I decided to do without. I couldn't bring myself to face that woman again.

Fay, my CETA counselor, was a complete opposite from the food stamp lady. Fay encouraged me throughout the following months of school, and slowly my self-image began to improve.

Even to me it became obvious that every A I got was as a result of my own efforts – not Dave's. I wasn't filling Dave's shoes, I was walking around in my own. I worked hard, and my grades showed it. I propped books at the kitchen sink while I did dishes. I read books while I soaked in the bathtub. I stopped watching TV and spent all my after-school hours memorizing body systems and building my medical vocabulary. These were all my very own accomplishments. That winter term I started out with a small collection of classes – 11 credit hours – for starters. I was nervous, but after all, I hadn't been in school for nearly fifteen years.

I was improving emotionally, but I wasn't free of problems. When we built our new house, the contractor insisted on putting carpeting in the master bathroom, even though I protested. To me, it seemed less hygienic than linoleum. "Oh, you'll be glad you let me put it in when you get up in the middle of the night and walk across the warm carpeting and not a cold, vinyl floor," he said. I gave in, and the carpet was installed.

A year later while vacuuming the bathroom, I pushed the vacuum across the floor in front of the shower. The machine scraped a large dent into the sheetrock. Surprised, I turned off the vacuum and pressed my fingernail into the wall. The wall was wet and soft to a height of four feet around the shower door. The next day a toadstool poked its head through the wall. I called the contractor.

The contractor promised to take a look at the problem in my shower, but he didn't show up. I called again. Still he didn't come.

I placed another call a few months and several toadstools later. The contractor's wife answered the phone. "I need someone to come look and see what's wrong with the sheetrock around the shower."

"Oh, yes," she replied. "We've just not had time to do it."

"Would you please remind your husband that the toadstools are difficult to live with. Something has to be done right away."

"Yes, I'll tell him. The problem with you is you just don't complain often enough. I think he's probably forgotten about you."

That seemed to be the story of my life, I realized as I hung up the phone. When I did complain I was treated as a nuisance, but when I didn't complain, I was told I hadn't received attention because I failed to make enough noise!

As far as I can calculate, every day for over three years water had managed to escape through the incorrectly grouted tiles and through the shower doorway; possibly the shower door was not hung correctly, either. The water dripped down onto the carpeting, soaked into the subflooring, and saturated the studs under the floor.

I was angry in great part at myself for not sticking with my choice of floor covering. If linoleum had been put on the floor in the beginning, I would have seen the water puddles on the floor.

The contractor also won out with the garbage disposal. I chose not to have one put in, but he insisted. I was afraid the septic tank would develop a problem, but the contractor continued to insist that I needed a disposal. I wanted to keep maintenance low since I knew I wouldn't have the money to hire a plumber to repair a problem.

A year and one month after the disposal was installed, it broke. I spent the next three years scooping food out of the drain every night after the dishes were done. It was impossible to keep food out of the sink, no matter how hard I tried.

When the contractor finally arrived to check the bathroom, he admitted I had a problem. He rolled the carpet back into the bedroom, opened the window, and brought in a large space heater to dry it out. This was in the spring of 1975, when I still worked at the bank, and after Dave had moved into the halfway house.

While at work one day, I noticed a man approach my window. His clothes were covered with a fine coating of white dust. "Do you hang sheetrock?"

"Yes," he replied.

"Once sheetrock has become wet, can it be dried out with a heater?"

"No," he answered. By this time the contractor had already finished "drying" out my bathroom, had replaced the carpeting, and had announced he was finished. Since he was a friend of a friend, I chose to take his word for it, that the sheetrock could be dried out.

The moldy smell still permeated the bedroom, and no amount of spray deodorant could dissipate the musty odor. The toadstools kept growing, blossoming out like flowers, and every now and then another – with larger petals than the previous ones – would pop out of the wall.

January and February of 1976 were difficult months. The pain was increasing in intensity, and the Darvon did nothing except make it more difficult to drive. I didn't know how much longer I could endure this agony, and I was certain by now that it wasn't my imagination. *It was real, and it always had been!* I made an appointment with a gynecologist. I had never been to a specialist before.

The doctor examined me and then discussed my condition with me. He said I had a uterine inflammation with endometriosis. It was necessary, in his opinion, that I have a hysterectomy as soon as I could arrange it. Since I was thirty-three and had three children, he said he assumed I was not planning to have any more children. I told him that was a correct assumption.

The doctor also said I had to stop taking birth control pills, since I had been taking them already for over ten years. They were now adding complications to my present condition.

I remembered when I asked Dr. Manning about them and he said, "Oh, you women blame everything on the pill." Perhaps, I thought, some things need to be blamed on the pill. At least in my case.

I told the specialist I wanted surgery scheduled as soon as *he* could set it up, preferably during spring vacation, around the 20th of March. He said he would.

As I left the doctor's office, I worked on my plan to keep myself in school. The doctor said I wouldn't be able to attend school that next spring quarter, but I had other ideas. I couldn't afford to waste any time, either financially or educationally. To receive my CETA grant, I had to be in class full time throughout both the spring and summer quarters. The fall term would begin my second year in college. Although I didn't tell the doctor, it was not my intention to stop my education because of an operation.

I told him that because I was the only driver in the family, and because we lived in the country, I *had* to drive as soon as possible. He said, "The incision will be as strong as it's ever going to get in three and a half weeks." I decided that would be my goal. Back to a full schedule in three and a half weeks.

This new attitude of mine was quite unlike me. I had always obeyed all doctors and authority figures in the past. Now I was beginning to take charge of my own life. The determination that got me through the first years of Dave's illness had resurfaced and I was not about to let anyone stand in the way of my goals. Not for any reason.

I approached my instructors, told them I had to have surgery during spring vacation, and asked if I could take final exams the week before spring break. They all agreed.

I enrolled for fifteen credit hours the following term. Visiting each instructor for those classes, I asked for assignments that would get me through the first three weeks. They all obliged. I then went to the book store and purchased all my books and supplies. I was all set – except for the children.

Because she didn't drive, I couldn't ask my mother to spend the week with the children, and the children were adamant about staying at home. They did not want to stay with anyone else the week I was gone. They had done enough of that during the months Dave was in the hospital, and they didn't want to do it any longer.

I thought of Dave.

Steve was spending more and more time in the evening calling Dave and asking for advice on various subjects. With Dave gone, there was an obvious gap in Steve's life that I could not fill, and although I wanted to eliminate Dave from my life as much as possible, I didn't discourage Steve from his calls.

It was painful to see Dave, to visit with him. I was constantly reminded of the person he used to be, the man I still wanted him to be. I ached to have him hold me as he used to and to feel the "bear-hug" he sometimes gave me. But when I was with him, I no longer had the feelings I once had. Dave needed a mother more than he did a wife. I had to forget him and meet someone else. The only problem was, every man I met I compared to Dave, I talked about Dave during the date, and I *couldn't* get him out of my mind.

A widow told me, "You're so lucky to have your husband."

I didn't feel so lucky. "You would want your husband back no matter what his condition was?" I asked.

"Oh, yes," she said, emphatically. I wondered if the grass is always greener across the fence, as we ponder someone else's life.

The first day after the accident, I had prayed that the Lord would take Dave if he couldn't be made whole once again. I didn't want Dave to live his life crippled, and never enjoying the pleasures he so loved. If I had asked for his healing no matter what his condition would be, I would have felt terribly guilty. Not only did I feel that attitude to be selfish, but I knew Dave didn't want it.

A friend's husband once said, "If that ever happens to me, I hope I don't live." When he did have a severe heart attack, and died, his son said he would have been tempted to kill his father if he had been left

222

an invalid.

At the halfway house Dave had been given responsibilties. He had to make his own breakfast, pack his own lunch for work, and wash his own clothes. He accepted these duties without complaint. Except for doing the wash, he was used to handling these chores. His responsibility level was changing, too, and his attitude towards Steve was like that of a buddy instead of a father.

Dave adored his two daughters and except for their frustrations in trying to clean up after him, there wasn't the antagonism between them as there had been with Dave and Steve.

Dave had learned to ride the bus and could travel all over Portland and the surrounding area with very few problems. Sometimes he missed a bus, but he calmly waited for another to drive up. His vision didn't improve much, but colors on TV and in movies no longer affected him. A movie in color remained that way from start to finish. Movies still affected him emotionally, but he went anyway, usually with friends from the halfway house.

Dave had finally become independent of me. Although I knew he still wanted to be a part of the family and come home, he was able to live without me. I kept thinking he would get over me just as I would get over him. After all, Dr. Jamison said we would. We just needed time, he said. We had been separated for a year and two months.

I called Dave and asked him to stay the week with the children while I had surgery. He was familiar with the bus service to the house and back into Gresham, so I knew he wouldn't be stranded without transportation.

Dave arrived the afternoon I left with Bonita for the hospital. Usually I spent a great deal of time worrying about the children when I had to leave them, but this time I didn't.

The morning before the surgery I was surprised by a visit from my cousin, Jody. She said she came to give me "happy" thoughts. Then a few minutes after her arrival, Dave walked in. I just assumed he had taken the bus into town.

Many months later Bonita told me the story. When Jody realized Dave had driven the car to the hospital, she tried to persuade him to leave the car at the hospital and allow her to drive him home. He declined the offer and said he could drive home okay. She then told him if he didn't allow her to drive him home, she would stand right there and scream at the top of her lungs. Dave decided it would be wise not to press his luck at this point. He gave her the keys, and Jody drove him back to the house. Later, Jody's husband Don drove the car home.

The reason I didn't think about Dave driving in was because he brought the children in a couple of days later on the bus. This was their first bus ride, and they made a point of having to hurry before the last bus left Gresham that evening.

Dave's intensive care nurses visited me. Even Dr. Emery and his office nurse who often accompanied him on hospital rounds stopped by my room.

I recovered quickly, was discharged a week later, and was left with less pain the day after surgery than I had the day I went into the hospital. The pain from an incision was much easier to handle than the severe pelvic pain I had endured for so long.

I had stopped seeing Dr. Jamison on a weekly basis after I started school. But since we were still working on another lawsuit, I had to meet with him occasionally to update him on my emotional status. And, too, as long as he was prescribing Valium for me, which I was still taking off and on, I needed to see him every few months as required by law. It was a relief to be off all the other medication, the Darvon for pain and the antidepressants.

Dr. Jamison's receptionist said, "I'm so glad that everything's going better for you. We all suffer from depression now and then, and it's good that you've finally realized that." I wondered if she knew about Dave and about our lifestyle over the previous four years, but I didn't ask. It was no longer important.

But I was equally surprised at Dr. Jamison. I sat down on the sofa, and began telling him how much better I was doing since I'd had surgery. I didn't even require pain medication except the day of my surgery, and that was small in comparison to the pain I had endured for so long. Dr. Jamison asked, "Why didn't you tell me you were in pain?" I looked at him for a moment and wondered if he could possibly be serious. He was looking at me as if he were. I remembered the countless prescriptions of Darvon and the discussion we had on stress-related pain. He had always remembered everything else I told him. How could he have forgotten something so vital to a patient's comfort?

This was another chip in his veneer. After spending a year of weekly sessions with Dr. Jamison, I realized how very little he really knew about me. And sometimes I wondered if he really cared. A few months before, I would have been crushed to think he wasn't really concerned about me, but now I realized I no longer cared whether he did or didn't.

I was finally climbing out of the pit. I no longer cared so deeply what others thought. After all, it was my life.

XXVI

Bonita picked me up at the hospital the day I was discharged. When she pulled the car into the driveway at my home, I saw the car positioned at a strange angle in the garage. Bonita said she had all she could do to keep from laughing when I said, "Look how I parked the car . . . I must have been sicker than I thought." I never did find out who parked the car that way or how many people drove it after Dave's drive to the hospital (which I learned about so many months later). I never mentioned the incident to Dave, and he never commented on it either.

As I carefully climbed out of Bonita's car, Dave came out the family room door. I tottered through the garage, passed the car, and slowly maneuvered the one step into the family room. Dave reached out protectively for me, took my arm, and steadied me across the floor to the sofa. We must have been quite a pair as we both limped through the family room.

Bonita went home after I was securely positioned on the sofa. Dave went into the bedroom to gather his things to take back to the halfway house. The children went outside to play with their friends. Suddenly I realized Duchess was laying alongside the sofa, and we were all alone in the family room. Then the phone rang.

I struggled to my feet. The phone rang a second time, and then a third. I shuffled across the family room toward the kitchen, where the phone was. The phone rang a fourth time. I felt like Dave looked during his rehabilitation, wobbling and limping and not getting anywhere very fast. As the phone rang the sixth time, I picked up the receiver only to hear a dial tone in my ear. The caller had hung up. Oh, how irritating, I thought as I shuffled my way back to the sofa.

I remembered Dave telling me why he stopped answering the phone, "By the time I get to it, they've already hung up." I understood the frustration, but for the first time I was actually feeling it.

Then, as if a light bulb went on in my brain, I had a startling thought. *What am I doing? I'm letting the doctors make all my decisions. I distinctly told Dr. Jamison I didn't want a divorce, and now I'm getting one. I don't believe this is happening!*

It was almost as if I had been asleep for a year, and had just awakened. I had become caught up in something I never wanted to happen. I didn't want Dave out of my life any more than I did any one of my children.

I thought, *How will you view yourself in twenty or thirty years? Will you be happy with the things you've done this past year? Can you say you've done your best?* The answer was an emphatic, No!

I knew I had to get a grip on things now before it was too late. Steve and Dave had made it through the entire week without any problems. They were a completely different pair than they had been a year ago; not only did Steve show respect to Dave, but Dave returned it in equal measure.

Dave seemed different in many ways now from the man he was when he entered the hospital just a year before. My surgery brought out in him some buried feelings. He showed compassion when I walked in the door that afternoon; he showed deep concern the morning of my surgery; he worried about me thoughout that entire week and even made the effort to bring the children in to see me. He showed them how to ride the bus system. He took care of them the entire week without any of them becoming angry over some minor incident.

Although none of the doctors observed the change that I saw, Dave had grown through the year, and if Dave could change that much in one year, I was certain his recovery was still continuing. Suddenly it seemed possible that we could become a family once again.

Although I regretted Dave's being in the halfway house and our separation that year, I realized it was important that we go through it. Dave had become independent; I knew he could exist without me when he needed to. As for me, I became separate from him for the first time in our married life. I had spent the previous six months building my self-esteem, and for once in my life I began taking credit for the things I did. I stopped worrying about making mistakes, and began to work on enjoying my family.

It didn't seem right that I was put on this earth to see how much I could grab for my own pleasure. Giving to someone else was as much important as looking out for my own needs. If I was going to be happy, I had to make others happy, too. Who better, I thought, than Dave and the children?

Although Dave and I didn't discuss the matter, I told him I thought it was time for him to come home to live. I asked him to think it over for a few days and make his decision as to whether or not he wanted to come back. He said he would, and he walked out the door to the bus stop.

I was an invalid that week. When the contractor tapped on the back door, I managed to bring myself to a sitting posision as he opened the door and peeked in. Duchess took a lunge at him and growled; I grabbed her collar. The contractor was terrified of her and always had been. "Are you holding her tight?" I assured him I was. "We're going to fix your bathroom," he announced.

I tried to relax on the sofa as I watched the workers hauling water-soaked studs and flooring through the house and out the front door. They ripped out the floor in front of the shower, and I now had a giant hole peeking at me from my bedroom. The bathroom carpet was rolled up against the side of the bed. Each night I had to maneuver across the rolled-up carpet to get to the bed, and every morning I struggled across it to get up. The bedroom reeked of mildew and rot. My bedding was damp and musty.

I don't know why the contractor chose this particular week to repair the bathroom, but I didn't ask. I was too eager to get the dangerous situation fixed. The floor was threatening to break through.

I came home from the hospital on Wednesday. Duchess had a litter of ten pups Sunday night. Although I was certain she was expecting, the vet kept telling me it was a false pregnancy. "I can't feel any pups in there," he said. The children and I watched as Duchess continued to balloon out.

We set up a "nursery" in Steve's closet, and all night long I helped Duchess with her new brood. Whenever a new puppy made its way into the world, I had to get out of bed after being awakened by its chirps and put it with the rest of the litter. For some unknown reason Duchess could only handle birthing them, cleaning them up, and then she immediately retreated to the wriggling mass of fur as they searched her for food. It took Duchess twenty-four hours to have her ten pups. I was amazed at what a false pregnancy could produce.

People were making mistakes all around me. The vet didn't detect the pregnancy, the contractor built a poorly-constructed bathroom, the psychiatrists and neurosurgeon considered Dave unable to live in the outside world. In contrast to these, any mistakes I might make seemed small indeed.

I called Les and told him to withdraw the divorce papers. He said he had never prepared them. "I hoped you would change your mind. All I did was take notes of the information you gave me, and I filed everything away in the hope they would never be needed."

Within a few days Dave had decided to come back home. I couldn't drive for three weeks, so I told him to bring the few things he needed on the bus, and in three weeks I would drive over to the halfway house and pick up the rest of his things. I was surprised to see him walk into the family room that very afternoon with an armload of clothes still hanging on hangers. He brought them on the bus, he said.

I remembered that Bonita's husband, Bill, worked in the vicinity of the halfway house. I called Bill and asked him to help Dave get the rest of his belongings. By that night Bill and Dave had successfully transported everything back home again.

I had no doubt in my mind that I had made the right decision. Remarriage for me was out of the question. Although I didn't realize it at first, I had spent at least a year doing the things I wanted to do. I was spoiled. I didn't want to marry someone who wanted me to prepare his breakfast every morning. Dave could cook his own and enjoyed slopping eggs into the skillet. He'd become quite proficient with that one hand even to successfully opening an egg.

I knew there would be problems, however, and I hoped to overcome them. I couldn't make Dave change so it was up to me to learn to tolerate those situations I couldn't do anything about.

One more time Steve asked, "Why doesn't Dad help around the house?"

"Steve," I replied, "Dad is in charge of the TV . . . to make sure it doesn't leave the room." Steve smiled as he considered this statement, and he never asked again. Somehow I finally reached him with a nonsensical reply.

The kitchen became messy again, and the complaints were inevitable, but I knew the children were programmed to leave home some day. It was I who had to make the choice of going through with the divorce or uniting us again. It would take a lot of effort from me to adjust and learn patience. I was willing to make the effort, and I wasn't about to change my mind.

As I spent the first week of my rehabilitation, I worried about what Fay would think. The doctors didn't know I was going back to school and Fay didn't know I had surgery. I couldn't attend classes until the third week of school, and I needed the money from my CETA grant. However, according to the CETA rules, I had to attend each class, have my card signed at the end of each week by all my instructors, and turn it in at the counseling office of the college. I couldn't do any of those things. *What will Fay do*, I wondered, *when I tell her I can't attend classes for three weeks? Will she be angry that I didn't inform her of my decision? Will she cut off my funding?* As I shivered from the fear of losing my weekly income, the phone rang. It was Fay.

Before Fay could ask any questions I said, "I have to tell you something . . . I had surgery last week, and I've just come home from the hospital. I won't be able to attend class until after the third week." Then I explained how I'd set up having my tests the last week of the previous term, how I'd obtained all my new assignments and my plan to return to school as a handicapped student for three weeks until my recovery from surgery.

Instead of blowing her stack, Fay said she was pleased with the way I'd handled it all. "If you need any books, I'll be glad to go to the college and pick them up for you," she said. I thanked her, and told her I had already purchased everything I needed. She said I was a very responsible student, the most responsible client she had, and my funding would continue. "I'm putting you on the honor system," she said. "I'll mail your cards out the first three weeks, you fill them in as usual, and mail them back to me. Until you're back in class full-time, I won't require an instructor's signature." Whew – the anxiety I had felt for so many days while I worried about Fay's reaction was all for naught.

I arranged for Bonita to take me to my medical office procedures class on Friday afternoon. I was a little weak and lightheaded, but I hoped by Monday to have enough strength to endure a full day of classes.

I began at the beginning of the fourth week. Parking in the handicapped parking lot helped keep the walking to a minimum, and by the sixth week I was back to parking in the regular lot, walking without difficulty, and feeling the best I had in years. I made the Dean's list that term.

By the end of the spring term, 1976, I was feeling intoxicated with good health. It had only been two and a half months since my surgery, but I decided to take my family on a vacation – to Thousand Oaks, California, to spend a week with Connie and Larry.

We piled our luggage and Duchess into the back of the Toyota station wagon I had purchased two years previously. I had the car serviced the day before we left, Steve and I practiced changing a tire, and I felt confident enough to make the trip, with our first night to be spent in Redding, California, at my sister Yvonne's home.

Steve wasn't old enough to drive, and Dave couldn't see well enough. That left all the driving to me. I was terrified of freeways, but within an hour I felt as if I had been driving freeways all my life. Dave was also learning to be helpful. He had an inborn quality of common sense which I learned to pry out as the need arose. He became my navigator, guiding me to the right roads.

We arrived at Connie and Larry's at nine o'clock on the second night. We spent a week soaking up the sun on Malibu Beach, and a day at Disneyland. Dave refused to be pampered and kept up with us all. We returned home just before my summer term started at the college.

Dave had so much information filed away in his mind. He taught me how to change a washer in the kitchen faucet. When I bought a stereo table that had to be put together, Dave taught me how to use the drill to make the screw holes bigger. He told me how, step-by-step, to replace a light fixture. Dave had the know-how, and I had the hands. We made a pretty good team.

We went back to see Dr. Jamison one last time. "Do you realize you have come full circle?" Did Dr. Jamison think we were failures, that we were right back where we began? But then he added, "Dr. Emery never expected David to recover the way he did." I realized none of the doctors did. Even I became discouraged along the way, and began taking advice from those who were sure that Dave would never recover.

I remembered when Dr. Jamison showed irritation at one of my sessions when I kept referring to my marriage. "Your marriage *wasn't* perfect," he said.

I realize now that *nothing* is perfect. Dave wasn't perfect, and neither was I. In fact, I was full of imperfections. But those imperfections helped me learn to understand the struggles of the handicapped, the patience we need to have for one another.

None of the professionals I came to meet were perfect either. Dr. Emery gave me the impression he didn't want to be bothered with rehabilitation, his specialty was surgery. Neither did he try to guide us to the experts for help.

The professionals eventually failed me because they could only think in terms of splitting up families. Our lifestyle may not be right for everyone, but couples should be helped to make the decision *correct for them* – and they should make it calmly and rationally, not in a fit of anger, hostility, or frustration.

I finished my summer term at the college, and before I entered my second year I found a job, training to become a medical transcriptionist. Dave held down the homefront, got the children off to school in the mornings, and had dinner ready and waiting when I came home from work. (I still got tired of Hamburger Helper, though!)

The following year I found a job working full time in the transcription department of a Portland hospital.

With a clear conscience I know I am prepared to come face to face with God and tell Him I did the best I could, and honestly feel that I am telling the truth. I was given a year to catch my breath by having Dave in the halfway house, but I have come back into his life and welcomed him back into mine and I do not regret that decision. I knew I couldn't run away, but it's because of my faith in God that I came back.

During one of my therapy classes while I was hospitalized in the mental hospital, I remember Jerry saying something peculiar about me. He described me as dependable, someone who would take care of others when times were tough. "Sharon is someone I'd like to have if I was injured."

I thought that a strange description of me, someone who I pictured as a great leaner. I leaned on others for security instead of giving it. At least that was what I thought. Jerry saw me differently, and at last I realized he was right. I could be depended on to take over; I could handle our family's affairs forever if I had to. I no longer needed or wanted to lean on anyone else.

XXVII

EPILOGUE
1984

After a second trial in 1977 the jury awarded us a settlement which was also upheld in the Court of Appeals in 1979. The long arduous years of legal battles were finally behind us. If I had known in the beginning that it was going to be so costly and difficult a procedure, I know I wouldn't have pushed it forward. It seems that it was best that I not know what the future would bring.

We have taken a few vacations which have brought about surges of growth that might not have occurred otherwise. Different locations are both physically and mentally stimulating to Dave, and require him to make an effort that he wouldn't ordinarily be forced to do. Travel also exposes him to situations that many handicapped people are prevented from experiencing. Dave "failed" all the training programs in the sheltered workshops, but he has become a seasoned traveler and quite capable in these endeavors.

Contrary to Dr. Vale's opinion, Dave did not hit a plateau and cease progressing. I do have to admit that he has hit plateaus, but he has always moved on from them and has not stopped growing and changing.

Although Dave has had setbacks, he is doing well now under a new doctor's care. He had a slight stroke, or perhaps just a threat of one, experiencing numbness of his thumb and index finger on his left hand and also one-half of his tongue. His blood pressure was found to be dangerously high, but is now under control with medication. He also was diagnosed as diabetic.

Living a normal life for a handicapped person can be difficult, but that doesn't mean they can't be useful citizens in the process. People like Dave have a place in society, not just in institutions.

Sometimes Dave and Steve can be found discussing a problem with Steve's pick-up; sometimes they – just the two of them – go out for a steak dinner; and occasionally they visit the tractor exhibits at the Pacific International building or go to the county fair in the summer.

On an icy morning, without mentioning a word to anyone, Dave has been known to clean the ice from the windshield of the car that will soon be driven to school. And he's the one who remembers all the necessary errands we have to do that day. *I* have a tendency to forget.

Oh yes, there is still sticky-goo on the counter every day! However, I can cope with that. I will never accept the accident that changed our lives – took away the father my children remembered, and the husband I will never see again – but we have adapted to the change in a positive way. I try to focus on the things Dave can do, not on the things he can't.

However even though I try to make light of minor situations, frustration is inevitable.

He still occasionally orders merchandise from telephone salespeople – items much like the magazine subscription years earlier. While I'm making the phone call to cancel the order, I remind myself that I have faults Dave may not like. He never voices any complaints about them, however, and rarely finds fault with anyone.

Although he still can't drive a car – and no longer tries – he does have a tractor with which he frequently putters around the yard and garden. Since he has difficulty walking, the tractor enables him to do things he wouldn't otherwise be able to do. And each year his garden gets a little bigger and more fruitful.

His limited vision causes countless problems for both of us. One afternoon he plowed under half of his tomato crop. Since none of the tomatoes had ripened, the green fruit blended into the bushy vines, and Dave thought they were weeds. Another time he plowed under a row of strawberries I had planted the previous day. He forgot they were there, too, and because the plants were so small he was unable to distinguish them from weeds too.

I just reminded myself of all the extra work strawberry plants would be – weeding and then picking the fruit when it was ripe. Perhaps I didn't want all that to do after all, I decided.

Dave and I developed a lifestyle that works for us. The acceptance that has entered our lives is in accepting the disability. It's an unfortunate reality that had to be faced, and we have made the adjustment.

Never for a moment have I regretted the reuniting of our family, I'm just sorry it took so long.

Perhaps I might have taken a little longer than the average person at adapting from the massive changes our lives took. With a play on words from II Cor. 4:8&9. I feel we were crushed, Dave physically and me emotionally. However, we were not destroyed in the aftermath and we all can joyfully admit to a true sense of happiness – of course not about the accident or Dave's injuries – but a happiness that came through eventually from a spiritual uplifting. Praise the Lord that although we *were* crushed, we *were not* destroyed.